Buddhism and Taoism
Face to Face

Buddhism and Taoism Face to Face

Scripture, Ritual, and Iconographic Exchange in Medieval China

Christine Mollier

University of Hawai'i Press

Honolulu

© 2008 University of Hawai'i Press

All rights reserved

Printed in the United States of America

13 12 11 10 09 08   6 5 4 3 2 1

Library of Congress Cataloging-in-Publication Data

Mollier, Christine.

   Buddhism and Taoism face to face : scripture, ritual, and iconographic exchange in medieval China / Christine Mollier.

     p. cm.

   Includes bibliographical references and index.

   ISBN 978-0-8248-3169-1 (hardcover : alk. paper)

   1. Buddhism—Relations—Taoism. 2. Taoism—Relations—Buddhism. 3. China—Religion. I. Title.

   BQ4610.T3M65 2008

   294.3'35—dc22

                                     2007042577

Designed by Paul Herr of the University of Hawai'i Press production staff

Printed by The Maple-Vail Book Manufacturing Group

Contents

Illustrations

Figures

Acknowledgments

The research presented here could have never been undertaken without the aid of my mentors and those who have given me their support. The passage of time has not diminished my gratitude to Kristofer Schipper, who, beginning with my studies as a graduate student, has greatly influenced my interest and direction in Taoist studies. The inspiration of two persons in particular stands in the background of this project. One is the late Michel Soymié, director and editor of the French Dunhuang project. It was under his guidance that I had the opportunity to work during the years 1989–1995 as a newly recruited researcher of the French National Center for Scientific Research (CNRS) in the redaction of the fifth volume of the *Catalogue des manuscrits chinois de Touen-houang: Fonds Pelliot de la Bibliothèque nationale,* thanks to which I was progressively initiated into the rigors of "Dunhuangology." It was Michel Soymié, too, who drew my attention to the *Sūtra of the Three Kitchens,* which is studied in the first chapter of this book. My interest in the field of Buddho-Taoism has also been stimulated by my participation in the collective readings of apocryphal sūtras that brought together a small team of historians of Chinese religions, organized by my friend and colleague Kuo Liying over the years 1998–2000.

My decision to undertake the present volume, however, was made during the spring semester in 2002 when I was invited to teach at the University of Chicago as Numata Visiting Professor of Buddhist Studies. The seminar I gave at the Divinity School and the Department of East Asian Languages and Civilizations, in collaboration with Donald Harper, provided me with the opportunity to deepen and synthesize my research on the canonical texts and Dunhuang materials that I had chosen to introduce to the participating students. The relevance of this research, not only for specialists of China but also for historians of religions in general, was brought home to me that same spring, when I presented a talk to the Divinity School under the title "Buddhism and Taoism Face to Face." That somewhat overambitious title has been retained as the work evolved into this book. I wish to warmly thank the dean of the Divinity School, Richard Rosengarten, who welcomed me at this world-renowned institution and generously expressed his enthusiasm regarding my research. I am also grateful to the Numata Foundation for its munificence in establishing the Numata Visiting Professorship. The students at Chicago were a pleasure to work with, patiently enduring my French accent while contributing much to the seminar.

The first chapter, in its original French version (first published in *Cahiers d'Extrême-Asie* in 2000), was improved by the critical comments of Michel Soymié and Jean-Pierre Drège. A presentation of this study was given in 2000 at the International Congress of Asian and North African Studies (ICANAS) in Montréal (Canada). I thank, too, Kuo Liying for her many helpful suggestions on the draft version of chapter 2, on sorcery. The third chapter, on the *Sūtra to Increase the Account,* was presented in its initial form in September 2001 at the European and North American Exchanges in East Asian Studies Conference ("De l'image à l'action: La dynamique des représentations visuelles dans la culture intellectuelle et religieuse de la Chine") held at the Collège de France in Paris. Jean-Pierre Drège has kindly permitted the English version of the text to be published here. My work on the cult of Great Dipper, the subject of chapter 4, was advanced by feedback received following my summary presentation at the International Association of Buddhist Studies (IABS) Conference in London, 2005. A first survey of the materials contained in chapter 5 was given in December 2002 at the IABS conference in Bangkok. The chapter was further enhanced by the suggestions of Poul Anderson. For their critical reading of the manuscript for the University of Hawai'i Press, I am grateful to him and to Gil Raz, whose numerous suggestions and corrections greatly aided the final revision of the work.

A number of institutions and individuals have been instrumental in making available to me many of the images reproduced here. At the British Library, I am grateful to Burkhard Quessel, curator of the Tibetan Collections, and Sam van Schaik, research project manager for the International Dunhuang Project, who generously provided me with illustrations from the Dunhuang manuscripts in the Aurel Stein Collection. I thank Nathalie Monnet, chief curator of Oriental books and manuscripts at the Bibliothèque nationale de France for her gracious help in locating the Dunhuang manuscripts from the Pelliot Collection that I required, and Georgette Ballez of the Bibliothèque's bureau of reproduction. Thanks also to Jacques Giès, chief curator of the Musée Guimet, for his permission to reproduce two images of the bodhisattva Guanyin belonging to the museum.

In China, I owe a debt of gratitude to the superior of the Wenshu yuan Buddhist monastery in Chengdu (Sichuan), who allowed me to photograph the monastery's series of paintings of Guanyin as Savior from Peril in 2001. The Bureau of Cultural Relics in Anyue County (Sichuan) lent generous assistance to facilitate my visit in the autumn of 2001 to many of its splendid archeological sites, and in particular to the remains of the Xuanmiao Taoist temple, a marvel despite the muddy conditions. Lei Yuhua, curator at the Chengdu City Museum, kindly offered me suggestions and recommended contacts during my visit to Buddho-Taoist archeological sites in Sichuan in fall 2004 and provided me with a photograph of the statue of the Heavenly Venerable Savior from Suffering located in Tongnan (Sichuan), reproduced here in chapter 5.

My special thanks go to Patricia Crosby, executive editor at the University of Hawai'i Press, and her expert staff, for their professionalism in publishing this work. I am especially grateful to Ann Ludeman, managing editor, and to freelancer Rosemary Wetherold, whose meticulous copyediting has improved the accuracy of the text throughout.

Above all, my heartfelt gratitude goes to my number one supporter, Matthew Kapstein, who has been involved in this project throughout, and certainly more than he ever expected to be. It is thanks to his unfailing, cheerful encouragements and his painstaking efforts at editing, correcting, reading, and rereading the text in its entirety that this project came to light.

Christine Mollier
Paris
November 2006

Introduction

The implantation of Buddhism in China, during the first centuries of the common era, was an unparalleled phenomenon in the history of religions. Unlike Christianity, which played a major cultural, social, and political role in the formation of early medieval Europe, Buddhism did not have such a pervasive effect in the Chinese world. Already five or six centuries old when it entered China, the Indian religion encountered there an ancient, highly advanced civilization. China had its own rich intellectual, philosophical, and religious traditions. It had also a strong sense of cultural and political identity, often expressed as a powerful ethnocentrism. Compared with the many other Asian nations in which Buddhism became a dominant vector of social and intellectual organization, the Celestial Empire seemingly had very little to envy with respect to India's great civilization. Erik Zürcher's masterpiece, *The Buddhist Conquest of China* (1959), which deals with the formative phase of this implantation, remains the first reference for anyone who wishes to understand the complex history of medieval Chinese Buddhism.

The remarkable establishment of the Indian religion in its Chinese setting has long been a subject of fascination for scholars of Buddhism and Sinologists, who have explored its various aspects: philosophy and doctrines, textual material, social and institutional organization, art, economy, and so on. Nevertheless, in considering the complex course of its sinicization, its manifold intellectual influences on Chinese culture, and the magnitude of its textual and artistic remains, one cannot be surprised that large areas have remained neglected. One of them, and not the least, is the interaction of Buddhism with the other major Chinese religion, Taoism, the indigenous tradition that, in spite of its long prehistory, began its development only in the second century of the common era. The encounter of these two great religions was particularly fruitful in medieval times, when they contributed to shaping one another in many ways. Their interrelationship only started to be regarded as a subject of fundamental interest in the late 1970s, however, when Zürcher opened the way in the field now usually referred to as "Buddho-Taoism."

Zürcher's interest in this large and tricky domain was, I believe, motivated by an ambitious project that had just started in Paris, namely, the detailed study of the Taoist Canon. This monumental effort was initiated and directed by the doyen of Taoist studies, Kristofer Schipper, who created a team of both senior and junior European Sinologists who would devote themselves to the analysis of the Taoist Canon's 1,500 scriptures. For those of us who joined this enterprise, the task seemed herculean not only in terms of the quantity of texts to examine but also in terms of their difficulty. Most of these Taoist scriptures were completely unknown and untouched, whether by Chinese, Japanese, or Western scholars. By and large undated, anonymous, and written in a hermetic, esoteric style, they had issued from different Taoist schools dating from the beginning of the common era down to the Ming dynasty, when the extant Canon was compiled in the fifteenth century. The topics found in the Taoist Canon (*Daozang* 道藏) were also extremely diverse, including philosophy, meditation techniques, exorcism, medicine, alchemy, hagiography, messianism, and, most importantly, liturgy. The scope of the task, therefore, among its other vicissitudes, explains why it took some thirty years of labor for it to be realized. This tentacular work was finally published in 2004 by the University of Chicago Press.[1] What is immediately pertinent here, however, is that, having already to deal with the difficult work of identifying and classifying such an enormous amount of material, the question of the possible Buddhist influence on some of these medieval Taoist works was not, in the first instance, viewed as a priority. It was shortly after the project had started that Erik Zürcher's visits to Paris somehow changed this state of affairs.

At the time, I was among Kristofer Schipper's students trying to find my way in the obscure new field of medieval Taoism and in this context had the opportunity to meet Zürcher a few times, as well as another great master and pioneer of the Buddho-Taoist field, the late Michel Strickmann.[2] I did not immediately realize, however, to what extent the Buddhist sūtras that Strickmann showed me as matter of comparison with the Taoist scriptures I was working on might prove relevant to my work. I already had too much on my hands just in trying to penetrate the Taoist arcana, and so did not feel any urgency to comprehend the interplay between the two great Chinese religions. My efforts were, for a few years, entirely dedicated to the study of an important

---

1. Schipper and Verellen (2004).
2. See esp. Strickmann (1982, 1990).

fifth-century Taoist work entitled the *Scripture of the Divine Incantations of the Abyssal Caverns* (*Dongyuan shenzhou jing* 洞淵神咒經), the chef d'oeuvre of medieval Chinese apocalyptical eschatology.[3]

While Buddho-Taoist comparison was already well established in Japanese scholarship, notably in the monumental work of Yoshioka Yoshitoyo 吉岡義豐,[4] in the West it only gradually began to be recognized as a field of some importance following the publication, by Zürcher, of two seminal articles in the early 1980s. One, entitled "Buddhist Influence on Early Taoism," illustrated the colonization of the imagination that Buddhism effected on Taoist soteriological and eschatological representations.[5] The second, "Prince Moonlight," dealt with Buddhist messianism and apocalyptism.[6] This last work was particularly interesting to me, for the Buddhist sūtras that Zürcher introduced there sounded like the perfect echo of the contemporaneous Taoist materials I was investigating. Both the Buddhist sūtras preached by the Buddha and the Taoist scriptures revealed by the supreme god Laozi were, with a similar tone of alarm, predicting the end of the world and the spread of billions of demons bringing disease and calamity all over the earth. Both were, in much the same terms, denouncing the moral and religious decadence of humanity, which would be responsible for the impending cosmic collapse. Messianism and more generally eschatology were definitely domains in which medieval Taoism and Buddhism influenced one another profoundly and enduringly, from a theological as well as an ideological point of view.

Following Zürcher's opening of the way in Buddho-Taoist comparison, further studies appeared in the 1990s that showed how the two Chinese religions affected one another in many domains. Stephen Bokenkamp, Kristofer Schipper, and Michel Strickmann, for example, produced key contributions in the field of liturgy and therapeutic exorcism.[7] At about the same time, Livia Kohn and Franciscus Verellen, dealing respectively with Buddhist and Taoist apologetic literature, shed light on some of the processes of assimilation and confrontation between the two traditions.[8]

My first steps in this field started also in the early 1990s, after I entered the research team run by the late Michel Soymié, a team that had been work-

---

3. Dz 335. (Dz = *Zhengtong daozang* 正統道藏, edited in 1445, reimpression in Shanghai in 1923–1926. Numbered here according to Schipper [1975].) On the *Dongyuan shenzhou jing*, see Mollier (1990).

4. Yoshioka (1959, 1970, 1976). See also Kamata (1986), which presents a selection of Taoist texts influenced by Buddhist scriptures.

5. Zürcher (1980).

6. Zürcher (1982).

7. Bokenkamp (1983, 1990); Schipper (1994); Strickmann (1993).

8. Kohn (1995); Verellen (1992).

ing for three decades on the descriptive catalogue of the Pelliot Collection of Dunhuang Chinese manuscripts kept in the Bibliothèque nationale in Paris. Three volumes had already been published covering some 2,000 manuscripts, the first of which was edited by Jacques Gernet and Wu Chi-yu in 1970.[9] The last catalogue, including a further 2,000 documents, was in preparation when I joined the project. It was published in 1995.

Walled up not long after 1000 C.E. in a chamber adjoining one of the famous Thousand Buddha Caves of Dunhuang, some 40,000 manuscripts and documents were discovered by Western explorers at the beginning of the twentieth century, English archeologist Aurel Stein and French Sinologist Paul Pelliot foremost among them. Mysteries still surround the raison d'être of this library cave at the Dunhuang Mogao site, which is known as cave 17. The most recent and plausible explanation is that it was mainly used as a temporary depository for one or more local monastic libraries while they were themselves being restored.[10] However that may be, the hoard of manuscript treasures discovered there date from the fourth century down to the beginning of the eleventh, when the grotto was sealed after the Xixia, or Tangut, invasion. Mostly written in Chinese and Tibetan, they also include documents in Khotanese, Uighur, Sogdian, Sanskrit, Hebrew, and other languages. Although the great majority of the scrolls, booklets, paintings, and other fragments found in cave 17 were of Buddhist origin, there were also manuscripts representing other religious traditions, Taoism, Nestorianism, and Manicheanism among them. In addition, the trove contained literary and philosophical collections, Confucian classics, pedagogical manuals, and encyclopedias, together with treatises on medicine, divination, and mathematics, and various documents such as calendars, local gazetteers, calligraphy exercises, administrative and accounting papers, letters, and so on. The sealing of the cave permitted the perfect conservation of this invaluable library for some nine hundred years. Since the beginning of the twentieth century, the Dunhuang collections have been a gold mine for scholars of medieval East and Central Asia, and for historians of religions in particular.

Among the Chinese Buddhist documents, which represent more than 80 percent of the entire collection, one finds a substantial proportion (perhaps 5 to 10 percent) of noncanonical scriptures. These sūtras, conventionally re-

---

9. *Catalogue des manuscrits chinois de Touen-houang, Fonds Pelliot de la Bibliothèque nationale,* vol. 1 (1970), ed. Gernet and Wu; and vols. 3 (1983), 4 (1991), and 5 (1995) under the direction of Soymié. (On the absence of volume 2, see the introduction to volume 3. A sixth volume concerning the Chinese fragments found among the Tibetan documents from the Pelliot Collection was edited by Françoise Wang-Toutain [2001].)

10. See Rong (2000).

ferred to as "Buddhist apocrypha," had, in many cases, completely disappeared after having been expunged from the canons. Some were of course edited in much later versions and therefore substantially modified or altered, so that the known redactions were less reliable than the ancient manuscript copies from Dunhuang that had luckily been preserved.[11]

Although the eminent scholar Paul Pelliot drew attention to the exceptional value of these apocryphal sūtras as early as 1911, it was only in the late twentieth century that Western specialists started to examine this long-disregarded facet of Buddhist literature. Michel Strickmann, Robert Buswell, Stephen Teiser, and Robert Sharf in the United States, Herbert Franke in Germany, as well as Antonino Forte and Kuo Liying in France were among those who began working in this area, following the traces of such great Japanese Buddhologists as Yabuki Keiki 矢吹慶輝 in the 1930s and, more recently, Makita Tairyō 牧田諦亮, who is now the doyen of the study of Chinese Buddhist apocrypha.[12] In the past few years, the rise of interest in Chinese Buddhist apocrypha has been given further encouragement thanks to an invaluable find, not in China, but in Japan. An entire medieval library was rediscovered in 1990 in a Buddhist monastery called Nanatsu-dera 七寺, in a suburb of Nagoya. About 5,000 scrolls, among which one finds many unpublished apocrypha, were stored there, for the most part dating to the twelfth century. The Nanatsu-dera collection is esteemed by Japanese scholars, such as Ochiai Toshinori 落合俊典, as the most significant find of ancient texts in East Asia since the discoveries at Dunhuang.[13]

Borrowed from biblical studies, the term "apocryphon" as it is used by contemporary historians of Chinese Buddhism refers to a complex notion relating to both bibliographic and doctrinal categories. For medieval Chinese Buddhist bibliographers, there mainly existed two types of sūtras: the "authentic," or "real" (*zhen* 真) sūtras; and the "false" (*wei* 偽) or "suspect" (*yi* 疑) ones. The first category was generally applied to sūtras that were translated from an Indian or Central Asian language into Chinese, that is, from "original" sources considered to be the transcriptions of the historical Buddha's preaching. Imported to China by adventurous monks and pilgrims, these prestigious and exotic scriptures were highly praised as the "genuine" canonical texts. The second category comprised the "indigenous" sūtras, that is, the "apocrypha" written directly in Chinese.[14]

---

11. See Makita (1976); Buswell (1990b); Franke (1990); Tokuno (1990); and Kuo (2000).
12. Yabuki (1930–1933); Makita (1976). For some examples of Western scholarship in this domain, see Forte (1976, 1990); Strickmann (1990); Kuo (1994b); Teiser (1994); Sharf (2002). Other pertinent works are cited in the following chapters.
13. See Ochiai (1991).
14. See Yü (2001): 95–102, who prefers the expression "indigenous Chinese scriptures" to "apocrypha."

These were scriptures whose earliest representatives were composed, for the most part, during the fifth and sixth centuries C.E., and then continued to be produced regularly, with a noticeable high peak between the sixth and eighth centuries.[15] Although they also claimed to be the words of the historical Buddha Śākyamuni and often adopted the structure of Indian texts, these "homemade" sūtras were, in many cases, stigmatized and rejected, assigned to the "erroneous" or "suspect" categories by Buddhist cataloguers. In reality, however, the problem of distinguishing between "orthodox" sūtras and "apocrypha" turned out to be much more complicated. The criteria of authentification varied considerably during the long history of Chinese Buddhism, mainly for political reasons. It is well known that the translations of the sūtras as well as the compilation of the canons were generally carried out under imperial sponsorship and control. They were consequently subject to more or less heavy ideological pressures.[16]

A new generation of researchers soon came to recognize, however, that these apocryphal sūtras cast light on little-known, unconventional aspects of sinicized Buddhism, a Buddhism mainly meant to appeal to the faith of the Chinese laity and to respond to their needs. As expressions of the intermingling of Buddhist beliefs and rituals with local cultural and religious specificities, they supply much matter for reflection on the part of historians of Chinese religions in general and Taoist scholars in particular. "They served," as Pelliot said in 1911, "as a kind of intermediary between the two religions."[17] Indeed, for the most part, the Buddhist apocrypha reframed indigenous Chinese rituals and texts.

If the extensive creation of Buddhist apocrypha was motivated to some degree by proselytic necessities, the Taoist superproduction of writings during the same period can undoubtedly be seen as a phenomenon of acculturation. When Mahāyāna Buddhism started to prosper in Chinese society around the fourth and fifth centuries, Taoism was still also in its formative phase. The first Taoist organization, known as the Way of the Heavenly Master (Tianshi dao 天師道), was originally a local, sectarian movement, confined to the western part of Sichuan Province. After a period of diaspora provoked by political pressures, it spread throughout China so that, by the beginning of the fourth century, Taoism had expanded beyond its sectarian confines to acquire the shape and status of a religion per se, whereupon new schools and new scriptures also emerged in South China. The combination of the ancient practices of the Way of the Heavenly Master with the southern esoteric traditions gave birth to one of the main currents of medieval Taoism: that of the

---

15. Kuo (2000): 684–686.

16. For more on this question, see Makita (1976); Buswell (1990b); Tokuno (1990); and Kuo (2000).

17. Pelliot (1911).

High Purity, or Shangqing 上清. Shangqing writings are divine instructions that were revealed to a visionary medium during the years 364–370. Soon after this first great wave of inspired literature, the scriptures of the Numinous Treasure (Lingbao 靈寶) appeared. The Lingbao movement, strongly influenced by Mahāyāna Buddhism, emphasized salvation through communal rituals into which were integrated Indian conceptions of hell, bodhisattvas, karma, retribution, and so forth.[18] During the following two centuries, other minor Taoist sectarian movements also created their own "bibles," like the aforementioned *Scripture of the Divine Incantations*.

Buddhism not only deeply affected traditional Chinese religious life and mentality, but it also operated as a trigger for the native religion. Taoism owes part of the formation of its identity, as a fully structured and organized religion, to its face-to-face encounter with Mahāyāna Buddhism. In response to the sophisticated eschatological and soteriological concepts imported by its foreign rival, Taoist theologians had to formulate and define their own ideas of the afterlife and human destiny, of moral precepts and ethical principles. To vie with itinerant and often zealous Buddhist preachers, skilled thaumaturgists, and miracle workers, Taoism had to organize its own clergy of physician-exorcists. Inspired by the already well-structured Buddhist canonical literature and impressed by the massive profusion of sūtras, whether "original" or "apocryphal," that were being diffused, Masters of the Dao also felt the urge to increase and classify their own literature. Most of the scriptures that came to light during this period were "revelations." In other words, they were considered as cosmic writs that were "translated" into profane language by their divine recipients in order to protect and save faithful Taoist adepts. During the fifth century, the first Taoist "canon" was thus created, and Taoism progressively acquired all the attributes of an institutionalized, nationwide religion.[19]

But other nativistic reactions also set in. In order to silence the omnipresent Buddhist rival, Taoists sought to reinforce the prestige of their own tradition. The polemical confrontations over the legend of the "conversion of the barbarians" (*huahu* 化胡), which lasted for about a thousand years, offer certainly the most famous, ferocious, and sustained examples of the attempts by the two parties to achieve predominance in the Chinese state. The *huahu* debates took shape in a critical historical and political context, at the beginning of the fourth century C.E., with the compilation of the *Sūtra of the Conversion of the Barbarians* (*Huahu jing*). Paul Pelliot was especially proud to have had put his hand on a late manuscript version of this text during his first selection of scrolls inside the li-

18. See Bokenkamp (1983).
19. On the history of the Taoist canons, see Schipper and Verellen (2004).

brary cave of Dunhuang. "This sūtra," he says, "lost since six centuries, is one of the texts that has played the most considerable role in the religious history of the Chinese world."[20] The legend on which this literature is based was probably first created with the sole goal of explaining the rise of the foreign but nonetheless familiar Buddhist religion in China. An early fifth-century Taoist text entitled the *Inner Explanations of the Three Heavens* (*Santian neijie jing* 三天內解經), found in the actual Taoist Canon, conveys a complementary vision. The text explains how the Taoist sage and divinity, Laozi, left China in the ninth century B.C.E. and, riding his blue ox, reached the frontier, where he met Yin Xi 尹喜 (the Guardian of the Pass). Laozi revealed to him the famous *Daode jing* 道德經 (*The Book of the Way and Its Power*). Then, with Yin Xi, he proceeded toward the West, where he converted the king of Kashmir and his people by transmitting holy scriptures he composed for them. Laozi and his companion then continued farther west to the kingdom of India, where the Taoist deity was reborn as the Buddha.[21] In other words, Śākyamuni and Buddhism are originally Taoist.

Soon, however, the legend was exploited by Taoist apologists in reaction against Buddhism. They pretended that Laozi undertook his western journey with the aim of converting the "barbarians" of Central Asia and the Indian subcontinent. If he transformed himself into Śākyamuni, it was to impose the strict rules of Buddhism, which could bring to heel the savage and immoral nature of the inhabitants of these regions. The newly composed versions of the *Huahu jing* were determined to prove the antecedence and the supremacy of the autochthonous tradition, while treating Buddhism as a by-product of Taoism. The Buddha's teaching was good only for taming and humanizing miscreant foreigners. During the following centuries, and above all under the Tang, the debates pro- and contra-*huahu* continued to nurse the quarrels between the two great religious traditions. The *Huahu jing* was often reworked and developed, with Buddhist and Taoist apocrypha striving to reduce, as the case may have been, Laozi or Buddha to decals of one another.[22] Taoists did not hesitate to provide their supreme god, Laozi, with all the qualities required of a divine missionary: miracles, inspired pedagogy, and all the other means needed for introducing the True Religion to foreign countries. To lead immoral people to adopt the right way, Laozi adapts his preaching to their inferior "Western" intelligence, and he advocates precepts and rigorism: the newly converted have to observe celibacy, to wear the robe with one naked shoulder, to shave their hair, to abstain from meat, to build monaster-

---

20. Pelliot (1911).

21. Dz 1205. 1/4a–4b. See Bokenkamp's translation (1997): 211–212.

22. See Zürcher (1959): 288–320; and Kohn (1995). See also Schipper (1994): 65n10, which provides a long bibliography on the subject.

ies, and to celebrate cults in his honor. The xenophobic flavor of such Taoist tales was, as has been noticed elsewhere, reinforced by the social context. The invasions of Northern China by foreign peoples during the Six Dynasties period contributed to the formation of a negative view of the alien religion.

First tolerated by the Buddhists, who regarded them as a means to introduce their doctrine as a sister of Taoism, these tales of Laozi, disguised as Śākyamuni Buddha, rapidly became the object of serious denunciation and rebuttal. The several anti-Taoist treatises produced by Buddhist literati in the context of court debates that took place at different times during the medieval period have been extensively studied by Zürcher and more recently by Livia Kohn.[23] Moreover, imperial officialdom took a jaundiced view of these *huahu* controversies and sometimes intervened in order to halt their escalation. The Tang emperor Zhong-zong 中宗 (705–710), for example, found himself obliged to promulgate an edict in 705, just a few months after his enthronement, prohibiting Taoist temples from exhibiting paintings of Laozi's conversion of the barbarians, declaring that anyone who attempted to circulate the *Laozi huahu jing* would be punished.[24]

Besides the canonical apologetic literature issuing from courtly Buddhism, which used mainly doctrinal weapons to dismiss its rival, one finds another type of Buddhist refutation of Taoism: the counter-*huahu* strategy expressed in certain apocryphal sūtras. There, in their turn, the Buddhists claimed that Laozi was nothing but the Buddha's disciple who came to China in order to convert people to Buddhism by preaching an alternative religion—that is, Taoism. One of the earliest examples of this Buddhist counteroffensive is found in an apocryphon rediscovered among the Nanatsu-dera manuscripts in Japan. In this sūtra, dating to the fifth or sixth century and entitled *Qingjing faxing jing* 清淨法行經, or the *Sūtra of the Pure Practice of the Dharma, Preached by the Buddha*,[25] we find Laozi described as a bodhisattva who—together with two other famous "bodhisattvas," Confucius and his cherished disciple Yan Hui 顏回—is sent by the Buddha to China to teach the Dharma. After accomplishing his mission, Laozi leaves for the West, which, in this case, means that he goes back to his Indian homeland.[26]

---

23. See Zürcher (1959): 288–320; and Kohn (1995).

24. Weinstein (1987): 47–48. The text of the edict entitled "Jin Huahu jing zhi" 禁化胡經敕, cited by Weinstein, is found in the *Quan Tang wen* 全唐文 17, Zhonghua shuju ed.: 202–203.

25. See Ochiai (1991): 26–29; Ishibashi Nariyasu, Naomi Gentestu, and Ochiai Toshinori, "The *Qingjing faxing jing*," in Makita and Ochiai (1996), vol. 2: 5–28. A French translation and analysis of the Sūtra realized collectively under the direction of Kuo Liying is forthcoming.

26. See Ochiai (1991): 26–29; and Kohn (1995): 16–17.

A New Approach to Buddho–Taoist Interaction

Far from these ideological polemics, the investigation that I propose in this volume adds a new dimension to the study of Buddho-Taoist relationships and turns on their concrete and practical aspects. For during mid- and late medieval times (from the end of the Six Dynasties through the Tang and Five Dynasties periods), religious life was far more confrontational than the considerable interpenetration of the two religions might at first have us suppose. An amazing competition was taking place between the two communities, a fight for hegemony in the domains of scripture and ritual.

In the past few years I have drawn attention to scriptures of various genres that occur in both Taoist and Buddhist guises. My exploration of these scriptural doppelgängers started when I was working for the French Dunhuang manuscript research team, mentioned above, and has been motivated by my formation as a historian of medieval Taoism, my direct contact with the medieval manuscripts, and my collaboration with Buddhologist colleagues.

Within the vast field of interaction between the two great Chinese traditions, some of the examples of apocryphal sūtras and Taoist "revealed" scriptures that I present in this book offer a previously unknown face of this complex process of interplay. What we find in these examples is not mere hybridization or passive borrowing, but a unique type of scriptural production, whereby the two traditions mirrored one another. One and the same body of material is set in both Buddhist and Taoist frames. Not only are some Buddhist sūtras strongly impregnated with Taoist elements, but indeed we find that they have precise Taoist counterparts. In such instances the sūtra follows, of course, the usual device used by authors of apocrypha, whereby it is said to have been preached by the Buddha to such and such a bodhisattva, while the Taoist parallel is held to have been revealed by Lord Lao (Laozi). The ascription of divine authorship to these texts provides them with the "appellation contrôlée," effectively guaranteeing, in the eyes of their practitioners, their authenticity and authority. Sealed with Śākyamuni or Laozi's hallowed name, such a sūtra could aspire to canonization.

The two most remarkable instances among the Buddho-Taoist doubles analyzed in this volume are the *Sūtra of the Three Kitchens* (*Sanchu jing* 三廚經) and the *Sūtra to Increase the Account* (*Yisuan jing* 益算經). Classified as "suspect" and as "human fabrications" by Buddhist catalogues since the mid-Tang period, these two sūtras prove to have been directly copied—in fact, calqued— on the basis of contemporaneous Taoist writings. It would be no exaggeration in these cases to speak of flagrant piracy.

The first of these two apocrypha, the *Sūtra of the Three Kitchens,* is the most fully documented case. It was already denounced as a Buddhist plagiarism in the tenth century by the renowned court Taoist Du Guangting 杜光庭 (850–933). Du accused a fraudulent Buddhist monk of stealing the well-established Taoist text entitled the *Scripture of the Five Kitchens,* changing its title to the *Sūtra of the Three Kitchens, Preached by the Buddha,* and adding a few Buddhist elements in order to create a credible sūtra. In spite of last-minute divine intervention, not all of the copies made by the arrogant monk could be destroyed, and several were said to have been diffused throughout the entire country. This is how, explained Du Guangting, the Buddhist forgery remained in circulation. In essence, Du Guangting's account was on target, for we indeed have today both a Buddhist *Sūtra of the Three Kitchens* and a Taoist *Scripture of the Five Kitchens.* The first, whose full title is *Sūtra of the Three Kitchens, Preached by the Buddha* (*Foshuo sanchu jing* 佛說三廚經), is an apocryphon dating from the end of the seventh or the beginning of the eighth century that was discovered in a dozen recensions at Dunhuang. It is also found in two manuscript copies of the eleventh and thirteenth centuries in the famous headquarters of the Shingon sect on Mount Kōya 高野 山 in Japan. The Taoist version, the *Scripture of the Five Kitchens, Revealed by Laozi* (*Laozi shuo wuchu jing* 老子說五廚經), which was edited in the Ming Taoist Canon with a Tang-period commentary by the Taoist Master Yin Yin 尹愔, seems also to date from the same period but was certainly derived from an older tradition. Both versions concern a method of meditation based on the recitation of a Taoist poem involving incantations of the Five Agents, which aims at salvation through complete abstinence from food. An examination of the two versions, as will be seen in chapter 1, lends support to Du Guangting's allegation that the Buddhist sūtra was indeed forged on the basis of a Taoist scripture.

A similar case is that of the talismans "to increase the account," dealt with in chapter 3 and found in the *Sūtra of the Divine Talismans of the Seven Thousand Buddhas to Increase the Account, Preached by the Buddha* (*Foshuo qiqian fo shenfu yisuan jing* 佛說七千佛神符益算經), of which several versions were also discovered among the Dunhuang manuscripts. The work has been labelled as a Buddhist apocryphon since the end of the seventh century, but in fact the *Sūtra to Increase the Account* should be more appropriately qualified as a Buddhist replica of a Taoist scripture. The latter, once more, may be found in the Taoist Canon. It bears the title *Marvelous Scripture for Prolonging Life and for Increasing the Account, Revealed by the Most High Lord Lao* (*Taishang Laojun shuo changsheng yisuan miaojing* 太上老君說長生益算妙經). The two texts, Buddhist and Taoist, are almost perfectly identical. Both versions are centered around the same incantations and the same two sets of talismans—one set of five prophylactic, astrological talismans and a second set of ten talismans for the exorcism of demons. The aim of these ritual implements is to guarantee full protection to the faithful so that they can achieve the optimal term of longevity, a span of 120 years.

How in reality were these scriptural "doubles" rendered possible? Were they strictly local occurrences involving only neighboring religious communities, or do they reflect widely ramified developments, due to the broad diffusion of manuscripts? Except for the *Sūtra of the Three Kitchens,* which is plausibly held to be a Taoist work pirated on the personal initiative of a Buddhist imposter, the circumstances informing these scriptural exchanges remain obscure. Through the juxtaposition and detailed comparison of the two sets of documents, we may come to understand somewhat better just how such sharing was effected and thus make evident the procedures utilized by the "forgers" to fabricate their duplicates. The "cut-and-paste" method seems to have proved its utility in more than one case of transformation of a Taoist text into a Buddhist sūtra, or vice versa. In general, the business was achieved just by a simple change of the narrative frame together with obvious terminological substitutions. As we shall see in chapter 3, the procedure was quite well described by Du Guangting, who deplores on several occasions its brazen use by his Buddhist rivals.

What Du fails to say, however, and for good reason, is that the Taoists employed the same subterfuge in order to appropriate certain Buddhist works. This was explicitly denounced by the *saṃgha,* which proclaimed loud and clear the superiority and integrity of Buddhism, while denigrating Taoism as a producer of heretical (*xie* 邪) texts and "false sūtras" (*weijing* 偽經). The first great Buddhist apologetic treatise, *Laughing at the Dao* (*Xiaodao lun* 笑道論), which was presented before the throne of the Northern Wei in 570 C.E. by Zhen Luan 甄鸞, does not mince words about this matter. In a section whose title is fully explicit, "Plagiarizing Buddhist Sūtras for Taoist Scriptures" (Gaifo wei dao 改佛為道), Zhen Luan denounces the counterfeits of the *Lotus Sūtra* forged by the Taoists and literally accuses them of stealing (*qie* 竊).[27] The monk Daoan 道安 raises the same charges in his *On the Two Teachings* (*Erjiao lun* 二教論) of 570, in a passage entitled "On Genuine and False Scriptures" (Mingdian zhenwei 明典真偽).[28] Taoist plagiarists would continue to arouse the indignation of the Buddhist authors of major polemical works, who tirelessly taxed the rival religion as fraudulent and incoherent. At the beginning of the sixth century, Falin 法琳, in a chapter of his celebrated *In Defense of What Is Right* (*Bianzheng lun* 辨正論) with the evocative title "Calling Out

---

27. Section 29, T. 2103, vol. 52: 150–151; refer to Kohn (1995): 130–132. The theme is taken up in section 8 of the great anti-Taoist polemic of the sixth century.

28. Section 10, T. 2103, vol. 52: 141.

Taoist Lies" (Chu dao weiniu 出道偽謬), manifests particular exasperation with regard to the borrowings from and misconceptions of Buddhism found in the Taoist Lingbao scriptures.[29]

In effect, the Taoists were not content just to react theoretically to the virulent attacks launched by their opponents. To calm criticism and to protect themselves, they took tangible steps as well. As Stephen Bokenkamp has shown, the writings contained in the Lingbao canon, indebted as they were to the Mahāyāna in terms of literary style, terminology, and liturgical outlook, were subjected, at the beginning of the Tang, to a veritable expurgation of the more obvious of the Buddhist elements they contained.[30] Nevertheless, parallel with this campaign for the "purification" of ancient canonical materials, we find a renovation of this same Lingbao tradition under the Sui and at the beginning of the Tang. More than ever, the many "Taoist sūtras" being produced are directly inspired by Buddhist works—indeed, literally copied from them. This phenomenon, however, was by no means unilateral, for the Buddhists, during the same period, also threw themselves into the fabrication of sūtras, the famous apocrypha that were presented as the genuine words of the Buddha. No more scrupulous than their rivals, the Buddhists showed no hesitation about trolling through Taoist collections and falsifying the writings they found there. For better or for worse, both parties thus attempted to conceal the origins of their pickings, in the interest of appropriating and integrating them on behalf of their respective literary patrimonies. The procedure was in any case identical: one changes, in a general manner, the introductory scene and, as required, attributes the text to the authorship of the Buddha or Laozi. The technical vocabulary that betrays the religious pedigree is erased and replaced by the terminology one judges appropriate. The titles of the works in question, however, are retained throughout the process, with only substitutions, as necessary, for the names of the Buddha or Laojun, for the designations of these scriptures are in effect labels of prestige, without which they would cease to be marketable.

Many of these texts are therefore readily identifiable in their double guises. We may cite, for example, the very popular *Sūtra on the Profound Kindness of Parents* (*Fumu enzhong jing* 父母恩重經), a seventh-century apocryphon of which numerous copies were found at Dunhuang, and which was also an object of pictorial representation. The sūtra lays claim to themes already treated five centuries earlier in a Buddhist work bearing an almost identical title and attributed to An Shigao 安世高 (ca. 148–170):[31] the pains and privations that parents endure

---

29. T. 2110, vol. 52: 8/542–544; dating to 626 C.E.
30. Bokenkamp (1983): 467–468, who quotes Ōfuchi (1978): 52.
31. See Makita (1976): 50–60; and Kamata (1986): 154.

to bring up their children, the hardships of the mother during her pregnancy and then while nursing her offspring, the promotion of filiality, and the central importance of repaying parental care.[32] Soon after its creation, the seventh-century Buddhist apocryphon was taken over by the Taoists, who, by means of a few additions and minor alterations, made it into the *Scripture on Repaying the Profound Kindness of Parents, Revealed by Lord Lao* (*Taishang Laojun shuo bao fumu enzhong jing* 太上老君說報父母恩重經).[33]

Two other examples also merit consideration in this series of Buddho-Taoist doubles. The *Sūtra for Pacifying Houses* (*Anzhai jing* 安宅經)[34] and the *Sūtra of Incantations of the Eight* Yang (*Bayang shenzhou jing* 八陽神咒經)[35] were both classed as "suspect," or apocryphal, by Fajing 法經 in his Buddhist catalogue of 594 C.E., the *Zhongjing mulu* 眾經目錄,[36] and both rediscovered at Dunhuang. They were "adapted" by Taoism, presumably during the Tang dynasty, and thus we find two Lingbao scriptures "revealed by Laojun," whose contents and titles are close to these Buddhist sūtras, edited in the Taoist Canon. Like their Buddhist counterparts, they were used for rituals intended to resolve the topomantic problems of dwellings, caused notably by the disturbance of earthly divinities.[37]

Also deserving of mention are the numerous commonalities linking the *Marvelous Scripture for Extending Longevity, Revealed by the Most High Heavenly Venerable of the Numinous Treasure* (*Taishang lingbao tianzun shuo yanshou miaojing* 太上靈寶天尊說延壽妙經, Dz 382), with the *Sūtra to Extend Destiny, Preached by the Buddha* (*Foshuo yan shouming jing* 佛說延壽命經), a Buddhist apocryphon mentioned in the bibliographical catalogues of the early seventh century and preserved too at Dunhuang.[38] The Taoist text was revealed in the course of a di-

---

32. See Cole (1998).

33. Dz 662. See Akizuki (1996). The *Daozang* also contains an abridged version of this sūtra entitled *Taishang zhenyi bao fumu enzhong jing* 太上真一報父母恩重經 (Dz 65).

34. *Foshuo anzhai shenzhou jing* 佛說安宅神咒經, T. 1394, vol. 21: 911–912. See, for example, Dunhuang manuscript P. 3915. Makita (1976): 346–347.

35. *Foshuo bayang shenzhou jing* 佛說八陽神咒經, T. 2897, vol. 85: 1422–1425. See P. 3915. A different version of the *Bayang shenzhou jing* (T. 428, vol. 14: 73–74) is allegedly Dharmarakṣa's translation (end of the third or beginning of the fourth century).

36. T. 2146, vol. 55: 136, 138.

37. Dz 634: *Scripture of the Eight Yang for Pacifying Houses, Revealed by the Most High Lord Lao* (*Taishang Laojun shuo anzhai bayang jing* 太上老君說安宅八陽經), and Dz 635: *Scripture of the Eight Yang for Amending, Revealed by the Most High Lord Lao* (*Taishang Laojun shuo buxie bayang jing* 太上老君說補謝八陽經). Hans-Hermann Schmidt, in Schipper and Verellen (2004), vol. 1: 563, mentions the proximity of these texts with a Buddhist work attributed to Yijing 義淨 (635–713), but he did not notice their relationship with the earlier apocrypha, mentioned above.

38. See Makita (1976): 80–83.

vine assembly beneath the tree of the "jewel forest" (Linglin shu 靈林樹),[39] while the Buddhist sūtra presents itself as the teaching of the Buddha delivered under twin Pāla trees (Poluo shuangshu 婆羅雙樹). The adepts of the Taoist work to obtain grace and an extension of life guaranteed by the "Heavenly Venerable of the Numinous Treasure Prolongation-of-Destiny" (Lingbao yanshou tianzun 靈寶延壽天尊), while the devotees of the Buddhist sūtra find that they are granted the same advantages by the bodhisattva Prolongation of Destiny (Yanshou pusa 延壽菩薩).[40] To be sure, many more examples of Buddho-Taoist doppelgängers could be added to the list, and some of them would merit the benefits of comparative treatment analogous to that which I have undertaken in the several cases analyzed in the following chapters.

The mid-Tang period (seventh–eighth centuries) seems to have been the golden age for this scriptural mix-and-match game that was played out between Buddhism and Taoism. Significantly, most of the apocrypha mentioned thus far were redacted during this period, as were the *Fumu enzhong jing* and the *Anzhai jing,* which inspired Taoist works, and as were also the *Sūtra of the Three Kitchens* and the *Sūtra to Increase the Account,* Buddhist plagiarisms of contemporary Taoist scriptures. The fickle policies of the Tang with respect to the two religious traditions certainly exacerbated their mutual desire to take advantage of imperial favor and may have incited the protagonists to engage in this literary duel and intensify their scriptural production. The Tang emperors appear to have opted for an unstable compromise between the maintenance of Buddhism, which was powerfully implanted and prospered at all levels of society, and the obligatory patronage extended to the "autochthonous" Taoist tradition in virtue of the legendary ancestral affiliation of the ruling house with Laozi. In the course of the numerous doctrinal debates orchestrated by the court between the representatives of the two religions, each side was eager to win imperial sponsorship and recognition. However, the bidding competition over scriptures in which Taoists and Buddhists were engaged cannot be reduced to an epiphenomenal outcome of this ongoing match. The aura of sacrality surrounding writing in Chinese culture was no doubt a weighty factor promoting their literary production, and to win by sheer numbers seems also to have been part of the strategy. The first true Taoist Canon edited at the order of the emperor Xuanzong 玄宗 (712–756) was monumental. It contained more than 3,400 scrolls (*juan* 卷), including not only the ancient canonical texts but also new, contemporary scriptures, among which were some virulent anti-Buddhist works. As a matter of comparison, the Taoist catalogues of

---

39. This forest is said to be located on Mount Golden Light (Jinguang shan 金光山) in the Southern Pole Heaven (Nanji tian 南極天).

40. On this apocryphon, see chapter 3, p. 105.

the preceding Sui dynasty (581–618) listed around 1,200 works in circulation.[41] Even more impressive, the Buddhist catalogue of Zhisheng 智昇 (668–740), the *Record of Śākyamuni's Teaching, Compiled during the Kaiyuan Era* (*Kaiyuan shijiao lu* 開元釋教錄), which was presented to the throne in 730 and served as a standard for the Tang Tripiṭaka as well as for later canons, listed no less than 5,048 *juan* of Buddhist works, among which we find some 400 "spurious," apocryphal sūtras.[42] No doubt this disposition of both religions to incorporate in their respective canons and bibliographies a maximum of works was prompted by a need to assert their proprietary prerogatives, to demonstrate the quantitative respectability of their libraries to the imperial authorities, and to ensure textual diffusion.

The Dunhuang collections and the monastic libraries of Japan are, in this regard, excellent indicators. Thus the number of copies of a given sūtra found in cave 17 sometimes reflects the extent of its distribution. Notably, most of the texts that enjoyed a double existence, Buddhist and Taoist, figure among the apocryphal sūtras of which more or less significant numbers of copies were retrieved at Dunhuang. Above and beyond this quantitative evaluation, the importation of these sūtras to Japan and their preservation in monastic collections such as that of Nanatsu-dera underscore the fame with which they were imbued in their land of origin, for this was surely a criterion to justify their export.

To some extent, the Dunhuang manuscripts indicate also how certain of these sūtras were transmitted. It is not rare to find booklets in which several are copied in series, presumably for cultic reasons. The term "chain sūtra" (*lianxie jing,* Jap. *rensha kyō* 連寫經) has been employed by Makita Tairyō to designate this sort of aggregate manuscript production.[43] It is of interest to note that several of the apocrypha that are thus "enchained" in the Dunhuang manuscripts show also some editorial contiguity in their Taoist versions. We find, for example, the apocryphal *Anzhai jing* and the *Bayang shenzhou jing,* successively calligraphed, together with other Buddhist sūtras, in a tenth-century *pothi* booklet of fifty numbered leaves discovered at Dunhuang (P. 3915), while the Taoist versions of these sūtras figure contiguously (fascicle 341) in the Ming *Daozang* as well. We may notice, too, that the *Sūtra for the Conjuration of Bewitchments* and the talismans of the *Sūtra to Increase the Account,* which will be examined in chapters 2 and 3, respectively, were copied "in chain" in a Dunhuang manuscript (S. 4524), while their Taoist counterparts, the *Scripture for Increasing the Account* and the *Scripture for Unbinding Curses,* were edited in the same fascicle 343 as part of the Dongshen 洞神 division of the Ming Taoist Canon.

---

41. See Chen Guofu (1963): 105–114. On the compilation of the Tang Taoist Canon, see also Barrett (1996): 60–61; Reiter (1998); and Schipper and Verellen (2004), vol. 1: 24–25.

42. See Tokuno (1990): 52–58.

43. See Makita (1976): 39; and Kuo (2000): 694–695.

One may of course argue that the juxtaposition of these texts, both in their Buddhist and in their Taoist environments, may not be so surprising, considering that they are dealing with the same topics. However, it is equally plausible that such bibliographical arrangements had liturgical justifications. Although sometimes dating to different periods, these scriptures might well have been transmitted together during the Tang dynasty as parts of ritual units by the Buddhist *saṃgha,* on one hand, and by contemporaneous Taoist communities on the other.[44] If, on the Buddhist side, many of the apocryphal sūtras that we are examining seem to have been transmitted in a Tantric context, for the Taoist texts they mostly belong to two main currents of the medieval period: the Zhengyi (Heavenly Master) and Lingbao organizations.

Although certain of these Buddho-Taoist textual exchanges involved veritable scriptural "cloning" and obvious forgery, others may be classed among more nuanced types of remodelling, more or less distant adaptation, or response. The Taoist anti-sorcery sūtra, taken up in chapter 2, seems to belong here. This *Scripture for Unbinding Curses, Revealed by the Most High Lord Lao (Taishang Laojun shuo jieshi zhouzu jing* 太上老君說解釋咒詛經), said to have been transmitted by Laozi to the Pass guardian Yin Xi in the kingdom of Khotan in Central Asia, offers a radical solution to the problem of witchcraft, deemed a major symptom of preapocalyptic times as well as a perversion derived from the West, that is, from the people of Southern and Central Asia. As in other "conversion of the barbarians" (*huahu* 化胡) accounts, when he delivers this sūtra, Laozi is on his way to India to propagate the True Doctrine. In this case, however, his apparently pragmatic concern to provide a shield against curses is in fact a pretext for a higher missionary program: to save the western populations from the eschatological torments of the end of the kalpa (*mofa* 末法) by converting them to Taoism. The text might well be a Tang response to the earlier Buddhist *Sūtra for the Conjuration of Bewitchments, Preached by the Buddha (Foshuo zhoumei jing* 佛說咒媚 經), an apocryphon dating from the end of the fifth or beginning of the sixth

---

44. Although there are no indications in the Dunhuang manuscripts that would allow us to determine clearly in which Buddhist milieu the transmission of the *Sūtra to Increase the Account* and the talismans of the *Sūtra for the Conjuration of Bewitchments* occurred, their Taoist counterparts, the *Scripture for Increasing the Account* and the *Scripture for Unbinding Curses,* belong to the Zhengyi (Heavenly Master) tradition, as we will see, and might have been part of a ritual corpus bestowed to its clergy during the Tang. Likewise, the Lingbao pedigree of the Taoist *Anzhai jing* and the *Bayang jing* seems clearly attested, but their Buddhist counterparts' context is more difficult to determine. The tenth-century Dunhuang *pothi* booklet (P. 3915) in which they are copied together with four other sūtras—among which are the famous twenty-fifth chapter of the *Lotus Sūtra,* entitled the "Universal Gateway of Guanshiyin," and two *dhāraṇī*-sūtras—would suggest a Tantric background. For this manuscript in particular, see the details in Soymié (1991), vol. 4: 403–404.

century. Several versions of the text were found among the Dunhuang manuscripts, and an eighth-century manuscript of the sūtra has also been preserved in the Nanatsu-dera monastic library. Like most of the Chinese Buddhist apocrypha, the *Sūtra for the Conjuration of Bewitchments* is allegedly taught by the Buddha Śākyamuni in the kingdom of Śrāvastī and aims to secure salvation for the faithful. In particular, the sūtra's priority is to free and protect them from the sufferings caused by witchcraft.

Besides their common calling in the battle against sorcery, internal evidence demonstrates the ritual and scriptural proximity of the two texts. Through the counteroffensive against sorcerers that they propose, they supply much unique data on medieval witchcraft, considered as a tangible, critical, and enduring problem for Chinese society in general, whether in relation to politics, social cohesion, or public health. The antidote to curses that the texts provide consists of a set of *dhāraṇīs* and invocations of deities that enables their practitioners to kill sorcerers and to protect and liberate their victims. This strategy conforms to the medieval Buddhist or Taoist exorcist's fundamental means to battle witchcraft, by making use of the same weapons as the sorcerers themselves: murderous formulae, incantations, talismans, and effigies. In the final part of chapter 2, several examples are provided that further demonstrate the ambivalence of such practices within Buddhist esoteric orthopraxis.

Another noteworthy example of the Buddhist appropriation of a Taoist ritual is the talismanic tradition of the Great Dipper examined in chapter 4. In this case, however, the process of adaptation went through different phases in the course of the Middle Ages and reached its culmination much later, during the Yuan dynasty, with the fabrication of a very influential work: the *Sūtra on Prolonging Life through Worship of the Seven Stars of the Northern Dipper, Preached by the Buddha* (*Foshuo beidou qixing yanming jing* 佛說北斗七星延命經). This Buddhist apocryphon, which is better-known under its abridged title as the *Great Dipper Sūtra* (*Beidou jing* 北斗經), has intrigued researchers for a century, including not only specialists of Chinese religion but also historians of Central Asia. The destiny of this modest work is indeed quite unusual, for besides the Chinese version, it exists in Tibetan, Mongolian, and Uighur recensions, as well as in a late Korean edition. If the Chinese version, which presents itself as an Indian sūtra transmitted under the Tang, was recognized to be a "suspect" work, it was nevertheless not until 1990, with the publication of an article devoted to it by Herbert Franke, that the true nature of the *Great Dipper Sūtra* was revealed. The work, according to Franke, is in effect a "pseudo-sūtra," a Buddhist apocryphon dating to the end of the thirteenth or the beginning of the fourteenth century that was redacted in China following a Taoist model composed some two or three centuries earlier, and it had a decisive role in the consolidation of Yuan imperial ideology.[45] Nonetheless, the "dossier" on the *Great Dipper Sūtra*, far from being closed, has continued to arouse the interest of new generations of Sinologists and specialists of Inner Asia who have explored other facets of its historical and international development. We shall see that the cult of the Great Dipper promoted in this Yuan-dynasty apocryphon can be assuredly traced back to a much earlier time. During the Tang period, it was current in both Taoism and esoteric Buddhism. It is attested, moreover, in Dunhuang materials of the ninth and tenth centuries. Antecedents of this cult can even be detected in Taoist sources dating to the Six Dynasties.

While the majority of the examples presented demonstrate how certain Taoist traditions came to be favored by Buddhism in medieval times, the last chapter of the book explores the opposite phenomenon: the creation of a "new" deity inspired by a Buddhist model long after it had been introduced into China. One of the most prestigious deities of the Taoist pantheon, the Heavenly Venerable Savior from Suffering (Jiuku tianzun 救苦天尊), was modeled on the figure of the bodhisattva Avalokiteśvara (Guanyin 觀音), drawing on his personality, function, titles, and image. Not just inspired by the charismatic persona of Guanyin, the Taoists went so far as to compose, at some point during the Tang dynasty, a kind of literary transposition of the celebrated twenty-fifth chapter of the *Lotus Sūtra*, the "Universal Gateway of Guanshiyin" (Guanshiyin pumen pin 觀世音普門品), in order to promote their deity to the great bodhisattva's level. As we shall see, the icon of this "Taoist Avalokiteśvara" played a central role in his cult and in the rites this involved.

THE QUEST, for both religions, was not only motivated so as to achieve scriptural hegemony. Buddhism and Taoism were also aspiring to strengthen their respective liturgical and evangelical monopolies. To integrate one another's favored rituals was undoubtedly viewed as the best means to consolidate the status of their clerical organizations and to attract or keep faithful followers by providing them with the most fashionable religious trends, even if this meant borrowing conspicuously from the opposing camp's heritage.

The sūtras and scriptures presented in this volume are all concerned with ritual procedures intended for the well-being of their practitioners. Their different fields of action embody fundamental preoccupations of medieval Chinese society: long life and immortality, salvation in this world and in the next,

---

45. See Franke (1990).

as well as prophylaxis against demons and diseases. Exorcism, meditation, and self-perfection figure prominently among the means deployed. Hence the historian of medieval Chinese religions will not be surprised to find that, in all of the cases studied in the following chapters, rituals in effect could easily be absorbed, without any substantial modification, into different scriptural environments. The rituals in question relied on the current liturgical technologies: talismans, incantations and, in some circumstances, effigies and icons.

Of all these implements, the most specifically Chinese were undoubtedly talismans (*fu* 符). Written on paper or fabric, or else engraved on wood or other materials, talismans have, from antiquity down to the present day, always been favored as the indispensable tools of parareligious practitioners as well as of ordained clerics who fabricate, consecrate, and administer them for the protection or curing of the faithful.[46] Privileged by the Taoists who produced them in plenty, the *fu* equally entered into the panoply of medieval Buddhists, above all among the Tantric masters, who adopted them for innumerable therapeutic and exorcistic ends.[47]

Composed of diagrams and characters in an archaic style to accentuate the metaphysical value regularly attributed to Chinese writing, talismans function as iconic writings incorporating the inherent forces of the entities they signify or represent. Submitted to the proper ritual methods, they are invested with coercive virtues acting upon the invisible world and permitting one to tap directly into it. According to need, they are the favorite weapon of exorcists in combat against deadly emanations, or, on the contrary, they serve as therapeutic cures that enhance the deficient vital energies of a patient, thereby effecting his or her recovery and protection. We will see that the talismans "to increase the account," as given in the *Yisuan jing*, and the talismans of the Northern Dipper found in the *Beidou jing* are perfectly suited to these prophylactic and apotropaic missions. In both of these cases, the iconic potency of the talisman is associated with the mantric power of the word.

Incantatory formulae (*zhou* 咒, *dhāraṇī*s and mantras) may complete and reinforce the thaumaturgical efficacy of the written sign or else act through an agency of their own. It is of course well known that incantations, *dhāraṇī*s, and mantras were extensively used in the framework of medieval exorcistic and therapeutic rituals. With the rise of Tantric Buddhism in the pre-Tang and Tang period this "*dhāraṇī* mania" reached its climax.[48] Indic and Chinese cultures share the idea that the compelling strength of the word permits,

---

46. See Mollier, "Talismans" (2003): 406–408.
47. On the problem surrounding the use of the term "Tantrism" in the context of medieval Chinese religion, see Strickmann (1996); Orzech (1998); and Sharf (2002).
48. See Strickmann (1996): 64–78.

through appropriate ritual protocols, direct communication with spirits and deities. Like ideographs, sounds are imbued with innate vitality. Words pronounced by the officiant disclose "breaths" or "pneumas" (*qi* 氣), which have the decisive potential to materialize and mobilize occult entities. Made tangible by the practitioner's voice, spirits are, according to the needs at hand, summoned for assistance or, on the contrary, banished.

Though all of the traditions studied here take stock in oral formulae, two of these traditions particularly emphasize their use. In chapter 1, I show how a particular incantational poem constitutes the basis of the Method of the Heavenly Kitchens in both its Taoist and Buddhist forms. The recitation of this poem of the Five Kitchens, addressed to the five directions, is the key to this meditation technique, which aims to achieve salvation through a total abstinence from nutrition. And in the aforementioned anti-sorcery sūtras, the weapons brandished by Buddhist and Taoist ecclesiastics alike in their fight against spells are also mainly *dhāraṇī*s.

Following analogous principles, the appropriation and manipulation of personal names allow similar actions to be performed upon a deity or a human being. In chapter 2, we shall see how the *Sūtra for the Conjuration of Bewitchments* denounces, among other things, the use by sorcerers of patronymics in order to curse and injure their victims. Nevertheless, the religious clerics who authored this sūtra adopted precisely the same strategy, advocating the pronunciation of the witches' names to wound, subjugate, and even kill them through dismemberment. The power of words finds here its most violent and radical expression. It is noteworthy that the same murderous formulae are advocated in the texts of both religions.

When used for inducing protection, the recitation of names can also be instantaneously effective. This principle is well illustrated by the private ritual advanced in the Heavenly Venerable Savior from Suffering's hagiography, which is discussed in chapter 5. It consists in calling the deity's name in order to obtain his immediate and unfailing assistance in the face of impending danger. As will be seen, this accessible and easy rite has a Buddhist origin that can be traced back to the *Lotus Sūtra*'s advocacy of the invocation of Guanyin's name to save persons from peril.

Another type of ritual paraphernalia is connected with the anthropomorphic representations that were actively used in medieval liturgies: effigies. Puppets, as will be seen in the second chapter, were among the favorite implements of Chinese sorcerers, who manipulated them to bewitch their victims. Analogous ephemeral icons were also fabricated by practitioners of esoteric Buddhism, who ritually mistreated and destroyed them in the course of exorcising their patients, as well as to injure persona non grata. By contrast, the liturgical function of icons is considered in chapter 5 with regard to the anthropomorphic image of the Jiuku tianzun. Like that of his homologue Guanyin, his representation was used in the context of both mortuary rituals and domestic worship.

Significantly, in all of these cases similar ritual methods, whether oral or written, form the core elements of specific traditions that were incorporated into either Buddhist or Taoist contexts. While the narrative garb of a scripture had necessarily to be modified so as to conform to the tone and style of its new religious frame, the ritual modules of the adopted tradition were in every instance kept precisely intact. Dhāraṇīs, incantations, and talismans, despite the repackaging procedure to which they were thus subjected, were maintained in their pristine, unaltered forms and, accompanied by identical prescriptions, fulfilled the same salutary purposes for both Buddhists and Taoists within their respective fields of action. Their transmission and modus operandi had to be rigorously observed and did not tolerate the slightest misstep, the smallest departure from the rules. Like the incantatory formulae, which depended upon the fidelity and legitimacy of their recitation to set in motion the intrinsic potency of sound, the divine virtues of the talismanic graphs became operational only if their rules of fabrication and utilization were punctiliously observed. This was the warrant for their efficacy and the condition sine qua non for maintaining their credibility. They had thus the capacity to transcend time and space, as well as to attract adherents among the different religious orders, and so eventually to find a place among the paraphernalia of "lay" technicians of divination and healing. We will see that the Dunhuang materials provide in this respect invaluable information, for some of the Buddho-Taoist traditions studied here were indeed removed from their original religious background to become part of the official "magico-scientific" patrimony of Dunhuang.[49]

The examples collected throughout this book illustrate just part of the history of ongoing exchange and active competition among Buddhists and Taoists in China. Whereas the great Taoist debt to Buddhism has been recognized now for a long time, some of the Buddhist sūtras here examined show clearly that the influence operated in the other direction as well, and that Buddhists on some occasions drank from the Taoist well. It is in this context of concrete exchange that the perennial question "Is it Buddhist or Taoist?" which often appears to be vacuous, becomes pertinent once again.

---

49. This is the domain commonly referred to as *shushu* 數術 (Number and Techniques); see Kalinowski (2003).

CHAPTER I

The Heavenly Kitchens

To eat plants is not as good as to sustain oneself with mushrooms and flowers.
To eat mushrooms and flowers is not as good as to feed oneself with minerals.
To eat minerals is not as good as to nourish oneself with primordial breath.
To nourish oneself with primordial breath is not as good as to not eat at all.
The one who [can do] without eating at all survives even to the collapse of
   heaven and earth.

The tradition of the Heavenly Kitchens concerns neither culinary art, nor, strictly speaking, Chinese food.[1] The recipes that it advocates aim at a total abstinence from food through meditational practices. Paradoxical as it might appear, the term "kitchens," *chu* 廚, as it is used here, is neither fortuitous nor provocative. In Chinese antiquity, it designated the banquets held by village communities, which were dedicated to the god of the soil. Taken over, codified, and perpetuated by medieval Taoism, unbeatable custodian of the Chinese ancestral patrimony, these collective repasts became vegetarian rituals in which only the consumption of alcohol recalled the sumptuous feasts of earlier times.

Over a period of several years, the late Rolf A. Stein devoted his seminar at the Collège de France to the study of the Kitchens.[2] As he remarked, these Kitchen assemblies (*chuhui* 廚會), traditionally performed as collective ritual banquets, became the object of constant criticism and even anathematization by institutional Taoism, which accused them of wasting large sums of money as

Epigraph: *Scripture of Food Interdictions and Prescriptions* [*for the* Daoshi] *Revealed by Laozi* (*Laozi shuo fashi jinjie jing* 老子說法食禁誡經), a Dunhuang manuscript from the Pelliot collection (P. 2447).
   1. The present chapter is a revised version of an article originally published in French as "Les Cuisines de Laozi et du Buddha," in *Cahiers d'Extrême-Asie* 11 (1999–2000): 45–90.
   2. Stein (1970, 1971, 1972).

well as of various moral excesses, among which animal sacrifices were the most violently condemned. The Taoists nonetheless preserved the celebrations of the Kitchens, as they did also many other ancient practices of the common religion, by incorporating them within their regular liturgy. The Taoist Kitchens, also called merit meals (*fushi* 福食), or sages' repasts (*fanxian* 飯賢), were organized in particular during the three great annual assemblies (*sanhui* 三會) of the Way of the Heavenly Master organization, on which occasions the adepts updated the Civil Records of their parishes.[3] The officiants of the Kitchens, chosen in precise numbers, initially had to undergo a purification by abstaining from sexual intercourse, from rich alimentation, and from plants with strong flavors (such as garlic and onion). A strict diet of vegetables and rice was also enjoined during the rituals, which lasted, according to their importance, one, three, or seven days.[4] The leftovers of the banquets were distributed to the faithful, who thereby communed with the gods. Performed also on exceptional occasions— for instance, in case of disease, moral pollution, or death—the Kitchen festivals had, in all events, an exorcistic and salvific function, bestowing "merits" or "happiness" (*fu* 福), upon the faithful. Under the draconian rules imposed by Taoist dogma, the convivial character of the ancient banquets largely gave way to the strictures of collective fasts. Wine, the sole festive element that had survived the radical metamorphosis of the imposing feasts of yore, was scrupulously restricted in order to prevent any dissoluteness.

Kitchens, fasts, and sacrifices were linked through their ritual relation to food. The purificatory repast (*zhai* 齋) consisted of a meager banquet, and the Kitchens included elements of sacrifice, since they were also offerings to the divinities. In fact, as Stein also noted, the fasts (*zhai*) and the sacrifices (*jiao* 醮) progressively supplanted the communal meals of the Kitchens. The relegation of the liturgical Kitchens to the background coincided with the arrival on the religious stage, at the beginning of the Tang dynasty, of an individual practice of the Kitchens that was shared by Taoist adepts of long-life techniques and by Buddhist salvation seekers. These Buddho-Taoist contemplative, or Heavenly, Kitchens form the subject of this first chapter.

In the Taoist context, the presence of these Heavenly Kitchens is not surprising, for they belong to an ancient and fundamental tradition of the psychophysi-

---

3. See the seventh-century *Penal Code of the Mysterious Metropolis* (*Xuandu lüwen* 玄都律文, Dz 188. 11b–14a), which is the most complete and precise work on the institution of the Kitchens in the Heavenly Master organization. See also *Laojun yinsong jiejing* 老君音訟誡經 (Dz 785. 13a–b) of the Six Dynasties period; Maspero (1971): 321–322; and Chen Guofu (1963): 325–326; and Kleeman (2005).

4. See the Tang-period *Yaoxiu keyi jielü chao* 要修科儀戒律鈔 (Dz 463. 12), which mentions gatherings of as many as a hundred participants.

cal arts of longevity or immortality. Their performance as either collective festivals or individual disciplines is in no way contradictory. Liturgy and meditation often represent two complementary facets of a specific tradition, relying upon common spatiotemporal concepts and the same pantheon, and having usually similar apotropaic, restorative, or therapeutic goals. The Kitchens are no exception to this general principle. Heavenly or mundane, consumed individually or collectively, the foodstuffs that they sublimate are subjected to analogous ritual procedures.

Described as a way of immortality in the words of Laozi, this technique of self-perfection was equally hailed as a path to enlightenment by the adherents of the Three Jewels, who claimed to have derived this secret from the Buddha's teachings, as set forth in the *Sūtra of the Three Kitchens, Preached by the Buddha* (*Foshuo sanchu jing* 佛說三廚經). This text, which was discovered among the Dunhuang manuscripts, has been qualified as apocryphal by the canonical bibliographies since the eighth century, but it might be more accurately labelled a forgery. A Taoist *Scripture of the Five Kitchens,* as well as additional Taoist sources explicitly denouncing its Buddhist misappropriation, lead us to conclude that, more than just a Taoist text rewrapped in Buddhist packaging, we have here an unmistakable case of Buddhist plagiarism.

In all events, the double emergence, Buddhist and Taoist, of the scriptures of the Kitchens, together with the diffusion of the apocryphal *Sūtra of the Three Kitchens* at Dunhuang and its exportation to Japan toward the end of the eighth century, amply demonstrates the popularity attained by the Method of the Heavenly Kitchens during the Tang dynasty.[5]

A Case of Buddhist Forgery?

The history of the Heavenly Kitchens may be best introduced through the tale of its Buddhist appropriation as related by the Taoist savant Du Guangting 杜光庭 (850–933) at the beginning of the tenth century. In his *Record of Miracles in Support of Taoism* (*Daojiao lingyan ji* 道教靈驗記), Du recounts the details in a story entitled "Miracle of the Disfigurement of the *Scripture of the Five Kitchens* by the Buddhist Monk Xingduan" (Seng Xingduan gai wuchu jing yan 僧行端改五廚經驗).[6] The affair runs like a news item: a shameful Buddhist fraud ends with a divine and fatal punishment. It can be summarized as follows.

---

5. See Makita (1976): 348–351, according to whom the first mention of the sūtras of the Kitchens, in Japan, goes back to the end of the eighth century. Two manuscripts dating from the eleventh and thirteenth centuries relative to the Kitchens have been kept at Mount Kōya 高野山 (see below).

6. Dz 590. 12/2b–3b; also edited in *Yunji qiqian* 雲笈七籤 (Dz 1032. 119/24a–25a).

The Buddhist monk Xingduan 行端, who, according to Du Guangting, was known for his arrogant and deceitful character, falsified the *Scripture of the Five Kitchens*, a Taoist work composed of five rhymed incantations (*zhouji* 咒偈). He changed its title to *Sūtra of the Three Interrupted Kitchens, Preached by the Buddha* (*Foshuo santingchu jing* 佛說三停廚經), redescribed its five incantations as revelations of the Tathāgata, and added a hymn at the end of the text. He went so far as to amplify the commentaries of the Taoists Yin Yin 尹愔 and Zhao Xianfu 趙仙甫 with his own. Xingduan completed his forgery and had already distributed five or six copies of the work, when, sitting under a window copying manuscripts, he suddenly saw in front of him a divinity eight to nine feet tall who threatened him with his sword and said: "This genuine scripture of the Most High has been venerated by one generation after another. How dare you treat it lightly and stupidly decide to change it?" The fraudulent monk attempted to ward off the divinity's blow and thus lost several fingers. Terrified, two other monks who witnessed the scene begged for mercy. Xingduan was spared and, with his companions, tried to recover the copies of his forgery, but they were able to find only half of them. Monks had already sent the rest off beyond the frontiers. Xingduan then prepared ten copies of the original Taoist work, offered them incense, repented for his misdeeds, and consigned the counterfeits to the flames. However, the forger's repentance was insufficient. The divinity returned and told him that he would not be able to escape capital punishment. Xingduan fell in prostration and died on the spot. Thus, concludes Du Guangting, the forged work has continued to remain in circulation.

In this way, Du maintains, there arose a Buddhist forgery of a well-established Taoist text. We will see in chapter 3 that the *Sūtra of the Three Kitchens* is hardly an isolated case. In the same *Record of Miracles,* Du also deplores the fraudulent creation of many other Buddhist works.

The Apocryphal Sūtras of the Kitchens

Du Guangting was, in fact, even closer to the mark than he might have imagined. The forgery perpetrated by the fraudulent monk (if he ever existed) could well be the very *Sūtra of the Three Kitchens* that has come down to us in different versions in China and Japan. Three recensions are found among the Pelliot and Stein collections of the Dunhuang manuscripts, one of which served as the basis for the edition of the text in the *Taishō shinshū daizōkyō*.[7] Another version—of

---

7. T. 2894, vol. 85: 1413b–1414c. This edition is based on Dunhuang S. 2673 followed by S. 2680.

which there are two manuscripts, dating respectively from the eleventh and thirteenth centuries—was preserved at Mount Kōya 高野山 in Japan.[8]

These four versions form a homogeneous corpus. But for one character, they bear an identical title. A first Dunhuang recension (S. 2673 and S. 2680), the one used for the *Taishō shinshū daizōkyō* edition (T. 2894), is entitled *Sūtra of the Three Kitchens, Preached by the Buddha* (*Foshuo sanchu jing* 佛說三廚經). A second Dunhuang version (P. 3032) bears the same title and presents some small variations and a slightly different organization of the contents.[9] A third Dunhuang recension, represented by two manuscripts (P. 2637 and P. 2703 R°) and much shorter and quite different from the other versions, is included in a Buddhist pharmaceutical manual under the title *Sūtra of the Interrupted Kitchens, Preached by the Buddha* (*Foshuo tingchu jing* 佛說停廚經).[10] These various Dunhuang texts seem to complement one another. The Kōyasan recension, entitled *Sūtra of the Three Interrupted Kitchens, Preached by the Buddha* (*Foshuo santingchu jing* 佛說三停廚經), is close to these Dunhuang editions but adds further prescriptions and rites. It perhaps issues from a later phase of the tradition, or even from a mixture of the "original" apocryphon with commentaries that were elaborated during the five centuries or so of its practice in Sino-Japanese circles.

Virtually one and the same, the Method of the Kitchens exposed in these sources consists of fasting, meditation, and invocations. The progression and the goal of the asceticism they teach are also identical: the adept obtains visions of the Heavenly Kitchens and perceives their exquisite aromas, which so satisfy him that he has no further need of mundane food. The main variations involve minor ritual procedures and some additions of *dhāraṇīs* and *gāthās*, without affecting the homogeneity of the overall content. Stylistically speaking, the major difference lies in the fact that the *Sanchu jing* does not include the introductory scenario (*nidāna*), while the *Tingchu jing* and the Kōyasan manuscripts provide a similar narration of the circumstances in which the text was preached: during the final age of the Dharma (*mofa* 末法), under the twin *sāl* trees of the capital

---

8. The most ancient of these two manuscripts, dated 1099, was housed at the Chimyō in 持明院 monastery. The other, dated 1270, was found at the Kongō sanmai in 金剛三昧院 monastery. See Makita (1976): 357–360.

9. S. 2673 + S. 2680 is incomplete (the end is amputated). Some repetitions appear, most likely due to the copyist's negligence. The text also presents an additional rite, a "supplement" that seems to be issued from a different Buddhist context and bears a Tantric flavor. The text of P. 3032 includes a final passage that does not appear in the preceding version.

10. I follow here Paul Demiéville's translation of this title: "Sūtra, prononcé par le Buddha, sur la cuisine interrompue" ("Byō" 病 [Disease], *Hōbōgirin*, vol. 3 [1974a]: 260; trans. Mark Tatz as *Buddhism and Healing: Demiéville's Article "Byō" from Hōbōgirin*. For an edition of this version of the sūtra, see Ma (1998): 695–698.

city Kuśinagara (Jushina, 俱[拘]尸那),[11] the Buddha teaches the Method to an assembly of buddhas and bodhisattvas before entering *nirvāna*. In the *Tingchu jing*, he deplores crimes committed by human beings who indulge in mundane food, kill and wound living beings, practice cannibalism, and so fall into the evil ways of rebirth (*edao* 惡道). The Buddha first reveals this saving sūtra to Ānanda,[12] while, according to the Kōyasan text, we owe the transmission of the Kitchens to the patriarch Bodhidharma. Thanks to this teaching, the masses in distress will never suffer from hunger or thirst, from heat or cold. They will be rejuvenated, win longevity, and enter *nirvāna*.

The *Tingchu jing* gives no indication of its presumed translator, while the *Sanchu jing* includes an introductory paragraph in which it presents itself as a sūtra preached by the Buddha and "reverently taught and translated by the Brahmans of the western country (*xiguo poluomen* 西國婆羅門僧) Damo-duoluo 達摩多羅, Shenajueduo 闍那崛多 et al.," that is to say the Indians Dharmatrāta and Jñānagupta.[13]

Though its claimed Indian origin is of course fictitious, there is no doubt that the *Sūtra of the Kitchens* was in circulation at the end of the seventh century or the beginning of the eighth, for it is mentioned by Zhisheng 智昇 (668–740) in his *Record of Śākyamuni's Teaching, Compiled during the Kaiyuan Era* (*Kaiyuan shijiao lu* 開元釋教錄), dated 730, where it is classified as "suspect" *yi* (疑), that is, as an apocryphon.[14] It is not at all improbable that the sūtra said to have been falsified by Xingduan under the title *Foshuo santingchu jing* (the exact title of the Kōyasan version), to which Du Guangting refers, is none other than this *Sūtra of the Three Kitchens* that has come down to us in slightly different forms.

The *Sūtra of the Three Kitchens, Preached by the Buddha*

The translation of the *Sanchu jing* presented here is based on the Dunhuang manuscripts S. 2673 and S. 2680 (T. 2894), which constitute the most ancient

---

11. This is where the Buddha entered his final *nirvāna*. It is identified as the city of Kasia, northwest of Patna.

12. P. 3032 also mentions the revelation of the Method of the Three Kitchens to Ānanda.

13. Jñānagupta (523–600), originating from Gandhāra, arrived in Chang'an in 560. The identity of Dharmatrāta (Daduoluo or Damoduoluo) is uncertain. Three figures of the second, fourth, and early fifth centuries, respectively, are known under this name; see Demiéville et al. (1978): 252, 258.

14. T. 2154, 18/672a 4–7. Zhisheng also mentions the *Sanchu jing* in one *juan* as a "human compilation." If one practices it in conformity to the rules, he specifies, one obtains all kinds of benefits. The sūtra is also mentioned in other Buddhist catalogues. See Makita (1976): 347–349.

and the most detailed of the extant versions. Major variations found in other recensions, notably in P. 3032 and the Kōyasan manuscripts, are noted as required.

The work, following the title and the names of the alleged Indian translators, gives a list of the Three Kitchens: "1. the spontaneous Kitchen of compassion and consciousness of the self; 2. the Kitchen of the four steps towards the enlightenment of a *pratyekabuddha* (a 'self-realized buddha') and the non-conceptualization of the auditors (*śrāvaka*); and 3. the spontaneous Kitchen of being, non-being, and non-divine."[15] Then the *Sūtra of the Three Kitchens* expounds the Method:

> Reciting this Method of the Three Kitchens allows [one] to be free from hunger, [to attain] clarity and limpidity [of the mind], and [to acquire] longevity.[16]
>
> At the outset, one should believe devotedly in the Three Jewels,[17] respect them, and permanently honor and revere them morning and evening, and without fail contemplate them assiduously. One must [also] piously care for the masters, the monks, one's parents, and relatives, close and distant. It is recommended [besides] that one observe the Six Perfections (*ṣatpāramitā, liu poluomi* 六波羅蜜)[18] and practice self-abnegation.
>
> One is thus fit for the conduct of this Method of the Three Kitchens: the Spontaneous Kitchen of all the buddhas and bodhisattvas of the three aeons, and the Kitchen of immutability, of quietude, of non-movement, of the successive kalpas, and of compassion.[19]
>
> This Method of the Three Kitchens was preached by the Buddha at the moment he attained *nirvāṇa,* during an assembly of the eight categories of beings,[20] in front of all the buddhas and bodhisattvas of the ten directions, to all the buddhas of the three periods, past, present and future. He recited the following *gāthās*:
>
> (*There follows an esoteric poem in five strophes corresponding to the five directions and the five agents. I do not offer here a translation of these cryptic verses, which also constitute the text of the Taoist work on the Five Kitchens [see below], but only the accompanying instructions.*)
>
> The *gāthā* of the wood, to the east:

---

15. The same list of Three Kitchens is found, with small variations, in the Kōyasan version.

16. P. 3032 and the Kōyasan edition add that it permits "white hair to become black and new teeth to grow."

17. *Triratna*: the Buddha, the Dharma, and the religious community (*saṃgha*).

18. They are 1. *dāna*, charity; 2. *śīlā*, moral behavior; 3. *kṣānti*, patience; 4. *vīrya*, energetic application; 5. *dhyāna*, contemplation; and 6. *prajñā*, wisdom.

19. The third Kitchen is not listed here. This enumeration is different from the one given at the beginning of the text.

20. The eight categories of supernatural creatures are listed as *deva, nāga, yakṣa, gandharva, asura, garuḍa, kinnara,* and *mahoraga.*

. . . Here is the *gāthā* of the wood for long life. To be repeated 90 times.

The *gāthā* of fire, to the south:

. . . Here is the *gāthā* of fire, [which allows one] not [to suffer] from heat. To be repeated 30 times.

The *gāthā* of the earth, in the center:

. . . Here is the *gāthā* of the earth, [which allows one] not to [experience] hunger. To be repeated 120 times.

The *gāthā* of metal, to the west:

. . . Here is the *gāthā* of metal, [which allows one] not [to suffer] from cold. To be repeated 70 times.

The *gāthā* of water, to the north:

. . . Here is the *gāthā* of water, [which allows one] not to be thirsty. To be repeated 50 times.

(*The text, certainly corrupt, now continues with the discussion of the preaching of the Buddha that preceded the poem:*)

Whoever is receptive to the words of these Heavenly Kitchens and recites them every day will know neither hunger nor thirst. Reciting them while keeping still, without moving and without thought, just like the buddha Amitābha of the land of Limitless Longevity (Wuliang shou guo 無量壽國, Sukhāvatī), one will have no [need] of nourishment for a period of one hundred days, for ten years or a hundred years consecutively, or for a thousand years, ten thousands years, or [even] for a small kalpa.

The Buddha informs the great assembly: It suffices that one who practices this Method be entirely predisposed to place faith in the Three Jewels and to adore them. Whoever wishes to make a retreat in the depths of the mountains to study the Way may begin by practicing and propagating this Method. Should someone manifest doubts and lack of conviction [or even formulate] criticism with respect to it, one must not in any case transmit it to him, for there is reason to fear that the blasphemer will fall into [one of the Three] Evil Ways [of rebirth].[21] This is why, in this world, one must take care not to diffuse it carelessly.

The recitation of [the poem] from the ninety repetitions to the eastern direction to the fifty repetitions to the north, constitutes a complete practice [of the Method]. If [after doing this] one still does not become satiated, one begins the recitation once more. Two recitations assuredly suffice [to put a stop to sensations] of hunger and thirst.

One must always begin the recitation of the *gāthā* during the *yin* 寅 hour (i.e., between three and five a.m.). Four moments [during the day] will be chosen by the adept for the recitation, whose number must conform to that which is indicated above. Prior to this silent recitation, one prepares oneself by means of movements of

---

21. These Three Evil Ways (*durgati*) are rebirth in hell, as a hungry demon, or as an animal.

the mouth and rotations of the tongue. When saliva forms, one swallows it. At the outset, [one practices] for one to three days. If it so happens that the urine becomes reddish, one should not be disturbed. By the end of the third day of recitation, one's physical forces will dwindle considerably, [but,] following this period of time, at the end of the seventh day, one steadily regains energy.[22] After a hundred days, mundane dishes of great refinement appear in each dream, and one finds oneself fully satisfied. Celestial perfumes become manifest. [At the end of a practice] of altogether three hundred days, one's forces attain a perfect plenitude. One may eat if one so wishes, [but] one will no longer [experience] hunger or thirst.[23]

The words of the Heavenly Kitchens have their origin in the *Gāthā of the Five Agents* (*Wuxing jie* 五行偈). These are the words of the Heavenly Kitchens. This Method was transmitted orally to Master Gupta (Jñānagupta), [who came] from the south. The One [of the first poem] corresponds to the earth, the Three [of the second poem] to fire, the Five [of the third poem] to water, the Seven [of the fourth poem] to metal, the Nine [of the fifth] to wood.

(*The text then returns to the preceding enumeration, referring to the directions and agents corresponding to the number of recitations—90, 30, 120, 70, and 50—but without the* gāthā. *It repeats almost word for word the modes of recitation explained above, adding simply that one must begin the practice of recitation on a* ren 壬 *day*).

All those persons who have a natural disposition for the energetic [practices] of Yin and Yang for the perfection of the self [can] henceforth add to them the breath [practice] of the Heavenly Kitchens and derive physical benefits from it.

(*The text again takes up the aforementioned indications regarding the stages of practice and the sensations that they entail, in particular dreams of celestial flavors and aromas, and the attainment of merits and of awakening,* daoguo 道果.)

One thus wishes solely to progress and to eliminate the Three Poisons, *sandu* 三毒.[24]

Compassionate beings who respectfully take refuge in the Three Jewels and who permanently concentrate upon Amitābha come to see him within a year, [if] their determination is flawless.

The Master of the Law of the Tripiṭaka (*Sanzang fashi* 三藏法師) says: "One who seeks ultimate awakening (*wushang pudi* 無上菩提, *anuttarabodhi*) and devotes his whole heart and his determination to it, but endures hunger and hardship, runs up against obstacles to his mediation, and cannot attain *bodhi*, [must] straightaway turn to the *Sūtra*

---

22. The sentence that follows is hardly comprehensible: 法成不宜誦之 "If one thus achieves the Method, one should not [continue] the recitations."

23. This passage is followed by the title of the sūtra: *Foshuo sanchu jing* in one *juan*.

24. The Three Poisons are hatred (motivating murder, curses, and malevolence), desire (motivating lust, greed, and theft), and error (responsible for perverse views). See Demiéville et al. (1929): 19–22: "Aku" 惡 (Evil).

of Divination (*Zhancha jing* 占察經), which says: "Once one has performed penance and has repented of his faults, he must [retire] to a mountain, a forest, or a peaceful valley, [or even] to the meditation room (*jingshi* 靜室) of a closed dwelling." One begins by sitting cross-legged, the left hand placed on the right,[25] with the eyes closed, the upper and lower teeth [lightly] joined, and one meditates until one becomes calmed—thus, four times each day, between five and seven o'clock and eleven and one, morning and evening. One turns toward the different directions, pacifying one's heart and [practicing] mental recitations [of the Method] as if they took place in the lower belly.[26] One must not [turn one's attention] to illusory perceptions (*panyuan* 攀緣) or to external phenomena. If, [on doing this,] one is not yet satisfied, a second series [of recitations] will suffice in order to reach satiation.

(*Following are the same indications given earlier, with only small variants concerning the movements of the tongue, swallowing, and the cycle of seven days of practice.*)

Those who are able to feed themselves entirely with the Three Kitchens during seven days will not know any limit nor obstacle to their progress: they will gain merits and be sin-free; they will enter *samādhi* (*chanding* 禪定) and obtain *bodhi*. By reciting the *gāthā* 360 times, one will be hungry no more.

The World-honored (Shizun 世尊, the Buddha) utters then the following incantation (*here follows a formula in pseudo-Sanskrit*).[27]

To receive the Method mentioned above requires that one first change into clean clothes. In the meditation room, one then burns all sorts of high-quality incense and worships all the saints and sages, following which one recites the Method twenty-one times. Throughout one's life, it is necessary to adhere to it regularly and seriously. For a period of seven days, one must not speak with anyone. It is absolutely indispensable to act with great care. One must not have contact with women or animals.[28] If one is thirsty, he may drink cow's milk and eat jujubes or broth. For those who desire to know the names of the divinities of the Kitchens, I reveal them:

Shi-jie-qie-mo-si-po 十偈伽末四婆, Mo-qie-mo-zhi-na 末伽摩志那, and Zhi-bo-luo-ti-si支缽羅涕死.[29]

---

25. Contrary to the usual Buddhist practice, where the right hand is placed on the left one.

26. I have preferred to read *qixia* 臍下, "under the navel," instead of *qixia* 齊下, which seems meaningless in this context.

27. This incantation, which begins with the characters *nazhi* 那致, is called the Nazhi incantation (*nazhi zhou*) in the Kōyasan version, which specifies that if one recites it 108 times after washing one's hands and face with cold water, it guarantees the protection of the body. The Kōyasan version also recommends the same incantation for a rite of water consecration (see below).

28. P. 3032 gives the list of the animals: chickens, dogs, cats, and the six domestic animals.

29. The *Tingchu jing* (P. 2637 and P. 2703 R°) gives a list of three divinities with similar names. The list of the manuscript P. 3032 bears eight names identical to the one presented in the Kōyasan version: Shi-ye-qie-mo-sa 十謁伽末薩, Duo-qie-mo-po-na 多伽摩波那, Jiu-si-luo-di-xin 救思羅諦信, and Duo-luo-a-ti-qie 多羅阿提伽, then Ye-qie-mo-si-sha 謁伽末四

At dawn, one turns in the *chen* 辰 direction (southeast, toward the sun). Gong of the earth, drum of the sky![30] After fourteen days, one is nourished by the broth of jade (*yujiang* 玉漿, saliva). All good male and female disciples who want to practice this Method of the Three Kitchens must first succeed in controlling and purifying their hearts; they must burn the finest incense and secretly recite the names of the aforementioned divinities, perform rites of contrition, and pray to obtain protection and support. These rites of the Kitchens should be repeated forty-nine times. When one has thus attained a perfect mastery of the form and names of these divinities, one utters the *gāthā*. If one recites them without halt for one hundred days, one will not be hungry. If one seeks to escape from one's karmic condition and to rapidly traverse the Four Stages to awakening (*siguo* 四果),[31] one must receive the names of the divinities of the Kitchens. The illiterate men of this world can orally obtain the names of these divinities. [But] the disrespectful who neglectfully [try] to elevate [themselves] to the Method, will not arrive at any result.[32]

Four *wu* 戊, four *ji* 己, the entrails are firm and cold.[33]
Four *rengui* 壬癸, there is no longer any need to eat.[34]
Six *jia* 甲, six *ding* 丁 (*erroneous for* yi 己), the great granary is full.[35]
Five *geng* 庚, five *xin* 辛, the five viscera are pure.[36]

(*Here ends the manuscript S. 2673. The continuation of the text is found in manuscript S. 2680:*)

The immortals and the Jade Maidens are at the service of my mind,
The Mobile Kitchens (*xingchu* 行廚)[37] of the celestial officials make offerings
to my body,

沙, Mo-qie-mo-si-na 末伽摩四那, Jiao-ba-luo-mo-si 交跋羅末四, and Tan-luo-he-wei-he 檀羅訶尾呵. These names appear to be pseudo-Sanskrit.

30. *Diwu tiangu* 地鳴天鼓. This term refers to a well-known Taoist practice that consists of twisting the tongue in one's mouth and clacking the teeth. The Kōyasan version more simply says: "One rolls the celestial drum twenty-four times, then one eats the jade broth (*yujiang* 玉漿, saliva)."

31. The four *phala*, or fruits of the stream-winner, once-returner, non-returner, and arhat.

32. In the Kōyasan version, the poem that follows is preceded by the well-known Taoist formula for invoking the four heraldic animals: "To the left the green dragon, to the right the white tiger. To the front the red bird, to the rear the dark warrior."

33. In Chinese traditional medicine, an excess of Yang (heat), in the entrails is considered pathological.

34. For these two verses, I have followed P. 3032, which gives the number four instead of six.

35. In Taoist psychophysiological techniques, the "great granary" (*taicang* 太倉) designates the stomach.

36. The cyclical signs *wu* and *ji* correspond to the center, *rengui* to the north, *jia* and *yi* correspond to the east, and *gengxin* to the west. The invocation is then addressed to the five directions. However, the numbers given do not seem to conform to the usual system of correspondences of the five agents.

37. On the Mobile Kitchens, see below.

Until I seem permanently satisfied and happy,

[And my] longevity increases by tens of thousands of years.

The Buddha reveals a "*dhāraṇī* to invite the three meals of the Kitchens" (*qing chu sanshi tuoluoni shenzhou* 請廚三食陀羅尼神咒): (*Here follows a* dhāraṇī *in pseudo-Sanskrit.*)

This *dhāraṇī* is a supplement to the Method. To practice it, one must retire to an isolated place. At daybreak, one washes an almsbowl with pure water and a willow sprig to brush its interior. One places a sheaf of purified plants on the bowl, above which one spreads a strip of cloth, [equally] pure. One sits cross-legged, turning to the east. With eyes closed, the tip of the tongue glued to the palate, one silently recites the incantations 108 times. One reopens the eyes to look at the food that has arrived (in the almsbowl). One may eat it if one so desires. If some remains, one recites the incantation seven times with eyes closed and in a state of concentration. The remainders of the food then return to whence they have come.[38]

(*There follows once more the title of the sūtra.*)

To aid the Three Kitchens, the Method of the Gu 谷 Family.[39]

The method that follows is an annex transmitted by a Brahman (or Indian, *poluomen* 波羅門) in order to make the Three Kitchens more efficient.

Guanyin 觀音 transmits the Method to me.

The immortals offer me victuals,[40]

Which, conforming to the colors of the five directions—

Green, black, red, white, yellow—

Unify in harmony to create food,[41]

[And] all the medicines [that spontaneously] protect me.[42]

The incantation says: (*Here follows another formula of invocation of the Buddha, the Law* [Dharma], *the religious community* [saṃgha], *i.e., the Three Jewels, as well as the* polisha 婆利莎 [? perhaps Skt. *pariṣad,* the assembly of the faithful]).

This incantation, if one fears that malefic demon-kings are coming to afflict men and make problems for them . . . [is to be recited fifty times].

(*The close of the text is missing.*)

---

38. The Kōyasan version includes an analogous ritual (see below). Here, the reading of the text is uncertain, due to missing characters (see the edition as given by Makita [1976]: 359).

39. *Gu jia fa* 谷家法. This Gu family is not mentioned in other versions (see below).

40. I have preferred to interpret the character *liang* 糧 as "food," instead of "grains" or "cereal," which seem here inappropriate. The question of abstaining from cereal is considered below.

41. *Hehe de ? er* 和合得口餌. The missing character of S. 2680 is *tong* 同 "together" in P. 3032 (col. 32). *Er* (food) also means "wheat flour cake."

42. Here I have followed the P. 3032 version. S. 2680 gives the character *chen* 塵 (dust, stain) instead of *yi* 醫 (medicine). The meaning of the verse would then be "[and] spontaneously protect [against] all stains."

Recitations of incantations, invocations to deities, and meditation to harmonize the physical and the mental are the main components of the Method of the *Sūtra of the Three Kitchens*. It is advertised as a practice of immortality particularly suitable for persons who have a special disposition for the energetic practices of Yin and Yang, and it leads the adept to complete satiation, longevity, clarity of mind, and eternal youth. The effort of the sūtra's author(s) to insert this technique of obvious Taoist flavor into a Buddhist frame is perceptible in its terminology and some of its specific stipulations. As is usually the case for Chinese Buddhist apocrypha, the sūtra emphasizes its Buddhist origin by claiming to represent the Buddha's words. It mentions the bodhisattvas, *pratyekabuddha*s, and *bhikṣu*s (particularly Ānanda), all adepts of its Method, and insists on the conditions of its transmission, expressly submitted to Buddhist regulations. In order to receive this teaching, one must initially take refuge in the Three Jewels and imperatively study the Six Perfections while abandoning the Three Attachments (the Three Poisons). In other words, the transmission of the Method of the Three Kitchens is permitted only after adopting Buddhism, and it demands that its followers wholeheartedly guarantee their sincerity and the firmness of their faith. The adept who achieves its teaching is compared to Amitābha, of whom he will surely attain the vision, says the sūtra, after one year of unfailing training. Moreover, the Method permits him to gain merits, to enter *samādhi*, and, when totally mastered, to escape from his karmic condition, leading him even to realize enlightenment, or *bodhi*. The references to Guanyin and other deities, the inlay of pseudo-Sanskrit *dhāraṇī*s, and a quotation from the *Sūtra of Divination* relative to penance and purificatory retreat contribute to lending the Method of the Three Kitchens a perfect Buddhist coloration.[43]

The other versions of the *Sūtra of the Three Kitchens* present the Method in almost identical terms. The Dunhuang *Tingchu jing*, however, sets it in a different context: the sūtra as given here belongs to a collection of Buddhist pharmaceutical recipes, "recipes larded with culinary Sanskrit," as Paul Demiéville ironically puts it.[44] The *Tingchu jing* mainly lists precisely measured doses of vegetal and

---

43. This work is certainly none other than the *Zhancha shan'e yebao jing* 占察善惡業報經, the *Sūtra of Divination to Examine the Karmic Retribution of Good and Evil Actions* (T. 839, vol. 17: 901–910), an apocryphon that likely dates from the second half of the sixth century. See Lai (1990); Kuo (1994b); and Wang-Toutain (1998): 72–77. The quotation given in the *Sūtra of the Three Kitchens* does not, however, correspond to any passage in the extant edition of T. 839.

44. Demiéville (1974a): 260. Besides the *Tingchu jing* (P. 2637), the texts that compose this compendium are the following: "Book of Medicinal Recipes" (Yaofang shu 藥方書), "Recipes of the Spouting Spring" (Yongquan fang 湧泉方), "Recipes for Herbal Eating" (Chicao fang 吃草方), "Recipes for Expelling Poisons [Caused by] Curses" (Chu chongdu fang 出蟲毒方), and "Method of the Bodhisattva Guanyin's Excellent, Marvelous Perfumed Pill" (Guanyin pusa zuisheng miaoxiang wan fa 觀音菩薩最勝妙香丸法). Cong et al. (1994)

mineral drugs, which, accompanied with ritual prescriptions and invocations of buddhas, are said to confer supernatural powers and to stop hunger. Although, with the exception of cow's milk, jujubes, and broth,[45] none of the other Buddhist versions of the Kitchens advocates the use of materia medica, the therapeutic background of the Method is undeniable. The Buddha's Kitchens as well as the rival method revealed by Laozi must be situated, like many other Taoist traditions, at the crossroads of religion and medicine, of practices of "nourishing life" and alchemy.

The *Scripture of the Five Kitchens*

What about the Taoist scripture of the Kitchens that Du Guangting claims was plagiarized by the Buddhists? In his "Miracle of the Disfigurement of the *Scripture of the Five Kitchens* by the Buddhist Monk Xingduan," Du writes:

> The *Scripture of the Five Kitchens* belongs to the Taiqing 太清 section (of the Taoist Canon). It bears a commentary by Yin Yin, imperial remonstrator (*jianyi dafu* 諫議大夫) and superior of the Suming monastery 蕭明寺 during the reign of Emperor Xuanzong, in which it says: "[When one recites] the secret formulae of the five divinities one hundred times in order to [nourish] the genuine breath of the Five Viscera, the Five Breaths are spontaneously harmonized. One may then abstain from taking food."[46]
>
> During the Kaiyuan 開元 era (713–742), the Heavenly Master Zhao Xianfu wrote a commentary on the scripture, which commentary is entirely dedicated to the breathing practice and spiritual harmonization.[47]

It is well known that Du Guangting composed his *Record of Miracles,* wherein he reports this story, to defend the prestige of Taoism, the autochthonous religion, against the alien and rival tradition, Buddhism. Du's work, which received a preface by the emperor Zhenzong 真宗 (r. 997–1022) at the beginning of the eleventh century, is therefore considered an important witness to the polemical

---

have classified these texts under the rubric of "Buddhist Recipes for Abstinence from Cereals" (Dunhuang zhong yiyao quanshu, 687–694), which classification I find too imprecise.

45. In China, milk was considered to be highly nutritious and was part of the diet of high-class Tang society. See Schafer, in Chang (1977): 105–107. Jujubes seem to have been also known for their nutritious and thirst-quenching virtues by Chinese dietetics. See Needham (1986), vol. 6, part 1: 540–541.

46. This follows a quotation of the five first verses of the *Laozi shuo wuchu jingzhu,* which constitute the "first incantation of the scripture."

47. Dz 590. 12/2b; also edited in *Yunji qiqian,* Dz 1032. 119/24a–b.

tensions between the two religions under the Tang and the Five Dynasties.[48] The story of Xingduan's trickery goes beyond the character of a mere miracle anecdote. By openly accusing a monk, it casts doubt upon the honesty of Buddhists in general. What is more, Xingduan's case is not unique. In the same chapter of his *Record of Miracles,* Du Guangting denounces, with the same indignation, the swindle perpetrated by another (equally unknown) monk named Facheng 法成. Feigning a Taoist vocation, Facheng succeeded in settling himself in a temple, where he managed to appropriate no less than 160 Taoist scrolls, which he forged into Buddhist sūtras by altering their titles and terminology. We will see in chapter 3 that, like Xingduan and in spite of a similar repentance, Facheng died of divine punishment.[49]

The solid reputation of Du Guangting among literati lends full credibility to the bibliographical information he provides in the "Miracle of the Disfigurement of the *Scripture of the Five Kitchens.*" The scripture, he asserts, is a Taoist work dating back to the eighth century or earlier, belonging to the Taiqing section of the *Daozang* (a section that includes mainly alchemical manuals), and has been the subject of commentaries by the Heavenly Master Zhao Xianfu and by Yin Yin.

As matters stand, this *Scripture of the Five Kitchens,* whose profanation Du Guangting deplored, has also come down to us. Anonymous, it is included in the Ming Taoist Canon under the title *Scripture, with Commentary, of the Five Kitchens Revealed by Laozi (Laozi shuo wuchu jingzhu* 老子說五廚經註, Dz 763). Although no commentary by the early eighth-century Heavenly Master Zhao Xianfu, to whom Du Guangting alludes, appears in the text,[50] there is indeed a commentary by Yin Yin, alias Master Sizhen 思貞子, who was a well-known Taoist as well as an official who served under Emperor Xuanzong (r. 712–756) and held the position of abbot of the Suming monastery in the capital, Chang'an.[51] The work's preface is also signed by him and dated to the twelfth month of the twenty-third year of the Kaiyuan era, that is, 735. Another ver-

48. See Verellen (1992).

49. Ibid., 248–249.

50. A court Taoist during the Kaiyuan era under Emperor Xuanzong's reign, Zhao Xianfu contributed to the edition of the imperial commentary of the *Daode jing.* Cf. Verellen (1992): 250–251.

51. Yin Yin's biography figures in the *Xin Tang shu* 新唐書 (chap. 200, Zhonghua shuju: 5703) among Confucian figures. A literatus originating from Qinzhou 秦州, in the district of Tianshui (modern Gansu Province), he died at age forty. He would therefore have composed the preface of the *Wuchu jing qifa* 氣法 at the age of thirty-four. See also Verellen (1989): 163, who quotes the *Lishi zhenxian tidao tongjian* 歷世真仙體道通鑑 (Dz 296. 40/11a–13a). During the Kaiyuan era, Yin Yin occupied a position at the Bureau of Remonstration (*jiansheng* 諫省). On the Suming monastery, see *Chang'an zhi* 長安志, chap. 8. 5b, in Hiraoka (1960), vol. 6: 106.

sion of the *Scripture of the Five Kitchens* (with small variations) is found in the grand Taoist anthology of the Song dynasty, the *Yunji qiqian* 雲笈七籤, under the title "Method of the Pneuma of the Scripture of the Five Kitchens" (Wuchu jing qifa 五廚經氣法).[52] Finally, we shall see that the Method of the Five Kitchens is also expounded in the *Fundamental Treatise for the Absorption of Pneuma* (*Fuqi jingyi lun* 服氣精義論), a Taoist work attributed to Sima Chengzhen 司馬承禎 (647–735), which is also edited in the *Yunji qiqian* in a section entirely dedicated to the arts of absorption and circulation of the *qi,* entitled "Pneuma Techniques of Different Schools" (Zhujia qifa 諸家其氣法).[53]

The *Scripture of the Five Kitchens Revealed by Laozi* is composed of twenty verse lines of five characters each, concerning the circulation of the cosmic pneuma within the five viscera, whereby it becomes possible to abstain from eating. The text is deliberately esoteric (and so I will not risk a translation). Yin Yin's commentaries, which follow each verse and rely on quotations from the *Laozi* and the *Zhuangzi,* do not really clarify the meaning of the abstract terminology employed here. Instead, Yin Yin just specifies some small technical aspects of the meditation accompanying the recitation of the poem. The goal here is to harmonize (*he* 和), while in a state of concentration, the primordial or original pneuma (*yiqi* 一氣 or *yuanqi* 元氣)—the cosmic part with which every human being is endowed at conception—with the Supreme Harmony (*taihe* 泰和). One thereby attains to the One (or Dao). The practice is also called the Method of Supreme Harmony (Taihe zhi fa 泰和之法). As in all Taoist techniques for perfecting the self, one nourishes one's essence (*jing* 精) and the mind (*shen* 神), so as to achieve constant heart (*changxin* 常心) and fusion with the Origin (*ben* 本). In his short preamble to the poem, Yin Yin elucidates the use of the term "Five Kitchens" and the relationship of this with food:

> This scripture, like a kitchen that supplies nourishment, is the place where the five viscera are provisioned. This is why it is called the Five Kitchens.[54]

The sole additional indication that can justify the scripture's appellation is given in Yin Yin's comment on the seventeenth verse of the poem, where he explains that when harmony is achieved, the adept's mouth enjoys flavors and the five viscera are satisfied. With these two exceptions, no other manifest analogy between the method and the nourishment it provides can be found.

---

52. *Yunji qiqian,* 61/5b–10b.
53. Dz 1032. 57/10a–11b. *Fuqi jingyi lun* (Dz 830. 9b–10a). On the authenticity of the *Fuqi jingyi lun,* see Engelhardt (1989).
54. Dz 763. 1a; also edited in *Yunji qiqian,* 61/6a.

The Origin of the Heavenly Kitchens

Considering all the elements we find in the Taoist documents, it seems that the *Scripture of the Five Kitchens* cannot be dated prior to the end of the seventh century or the beginning of the eighth. The Taoist version of the Kitchens as commented upon by Yin Yin and its Buddhist "forgery" would consequently be contemporaneous. It is nonetheless highly probable that the *Scripture of the Five Kitchens* existed long before Yin Yin assured its fame by affixing his seal to it. Ge Hong 葛洪 (283–343), in the bibliographical section of his *Inner Chapters of the Master Who Embraces Simplicity* (*Baopuzi neipian* 抱朴子內篇), mentions a *Scripture of the Traveling Kitchens* (*Xingchu jing* 行廚經), as well as a *Scripture of the Kitchen Food of the Sun and the Moon* (*Riyue chushi jing* 日月廚食 經).[55] It is imaginable that one or the other of these works stood at the origin of our *Scripture of the Five Kitchens,* for, as we know, the rewriting of sacred texts was an established mode of scriptural production in medieval Taoism. Offered as the ne plus ultra among divine revelations, these reinscriptions or apocrypha were often more praised than the originals that inspired them.[56]

The practice of the Kitchens is also elsewhere attested in Ge Hong's work. He refers several times to the Traveling, or Mobile, Kitchens (*xingchu* 行廚), specifying them to be among the supreme arts of immortality and as techniques for the absorption of various substances and drugs in particular.[57] In Ge's other famous work, the hagiographic collection entitled *Traditions of Divine Transcendents* (*Shenxian zhuan* 神仙傳), one reads that recourse to the Traveling Kitchens was favored by such legendary practitioners of immortality as Li Gen 李根, who

> could sit down and cause the Traveling Kitchens to arrive, and with them could serve twenty guests. All the dishes were finely prepared, and all of them contained strange and marvelous foods from the four directions, not things that were locally available.[58]

Ge Hong also describes the sumptuous Kitchens that the "Hemp girl" (Magu 麻姑), another mythological celebrity, shared with her guest, the diviner (*fangshi* 方士) Wang Yuan 王遠:

---

55. *Baopuzi neipian,* chap. 19, Wang Ming, ed.: 334.

56. Consider, for example, the question of the rewriting of texts in early Shangqing Taoism, on which see Robinet (1984), vol. 2: 7.

57. *Baopuzi neipian,* chap. 11, Wang Ming, ed., 196, 203, 205. Just as he can produce clouds and fire, the saint, says Ge Hong, can also cause the Mobile Kitchens to arrive (*zhi* 致) while sitting in meditation or by "kneading some black elixir (*heidan* 黑丹) and water with his left hand" (ibid., chaps. 19 and 4, Wang Ming, ed.: 337, 78).

58. Refer to Campany's translation (2002): 219.

When they were both seated, they called for the Traveling Kitchens. The servings were piled up on gold platters and in jade cups without limit. There were rare delicacies, many of them made from flowers and fruits, and their fragrance permeated the air inside and out.[59]

The power to "cause the Mobile Kitchens to arrive while [one is] sitting [in meditation]" (*zuo zhi xingchu* 坐致行廚) continued to be one of the spiritual goals of the Taoist adepts of the early Shangqing 上清 movement. Accessible to those who mastered the techniques of visualization of divinities residing in cosmic space as well as in the human body, the summoning of the Kitchens permitted them to control these spirits and to accomplish wonders: to become invisible, release thunder, and produce rain.[60] Highly esoteric, the practice necessitated an initiation whereby the adepts were duly endowed with the talismans of the Six *jia* 六甲. We shall see in chapter 3 how these talismans played a major role in Taoist rituals, in particular in Heavenly Master Taoism, where the Six *jia* were viewed as potent military deities ranked as "Generals."

Here, however, we should insist on a particular aspect of the close relationship existing between the Kitchens and the Six *jia*. The *Scripture of the Most High Luminous Mirror of the Six* Ren *Tallying with* Yin (*Taishang liuren mingjian fuyin jing* 太上六壬明鑑符陰經)—a presumably post-Tang Taoist work, but one that is certainly based on much earlier materials—gives an interesting account of their background.[61] The introduction of the text relates that the *Heavenly Kitchens of the Six* Jia (*Liujia tianchu yijuan* 六甲天廚一卷) were transmitted together with the *Heavenly Kitchens of the Six* Ding (*Liuding tianchu yijuan* 六丁天廚一卷) to the famous strategist of the Warring States period, Sun Bin 孫臏, a descendant of the even more renowned military expert, Sunzi 孫子.[62] Sun Bin, says the text, was pursuing his training in the martial arts with his master, "Sir Phantom Valley" (Guigu xiansheng 鬼谷先生), in a grove, when one night a white monkey (*baiyuan* 白猿) appeared suddenly to steal fruit. After threatening the animal with his weapon, Sun discovered that it was in fact a transcendent being charged with secret writs to transmit to him. The monkey transformed itself into white light and vanished, only to return the following day, as agreed, to deliver the two scrolls of the Heavenly Kitchens. Sun, not knowing their titles,

---

59. Refer to ibid., 262.

60. See Robinet (1984), vol. 1: 24–25.

61. Dz 861. This scripture is related to the Dz 858, the *Marvelous and Mysterious Veritable Scripture of the White Monkey of the Dongshen* [Canon] (*Taishang dongshen xuanmiao baiyuan zhenjing* 太上洞神玄妙白猿真經), which is placed under the patronage of the "white monkey."

62. Sun Bin would have been the author of the *Sun Bin bingfa* 孫臏兵法, lost since the end of the Han, but recovered in a version written on bamboo strips found in a tomb in Shandong in 1972; see Lau and Ames (1996).

called them the "writs of the white monkey." Significantly, the *Scripture of the Most High Luminous Mirror of the Six* Ren *Tallying with Yin* also stipulates that these methods of the Heavenly Kitchens permit one, after a period of purification, to abstain from nourishment and to become invisible to spirits and demons for a period of a hundred days.

We may speculate that the mysterious Method of the Gu Family (Gujia fa 谷家法), mentioned in the final *dhāraṇī* of the *Sūtra of the Three Kitchens* (S. 2680), refers to Guigu zi, "Sir Phantom Valley," who was Sun Bin's master. The same *dhāraṇī*, moreover, contains an invocation of the cyclical signs, notably the Six *jia* and Six *ding*. All of this coheres well with what we know otherwise of the link holding between the techniques of hemerological divination, in particular the system of the so-called hidden periods (*dun jia* 遁甲), and Chinese military strategy. We shall have the occasion to return to this too in chapter 3.

Communal banqueting in ritual celebrations and communion with divinities, post houses and food for journeys (which explains the term "mobile"), storehouses (*zang* 藏, also meaning "viscera"), visualization of the spirits inhabiting the organs, and abstinence from cereals all figure among the elements, already noted by R. A. Stein, that form the semantic fabric of the tradition of the Kitchens.[63] Though uncertain in the corpus of the revealed Shangqing scriptures, the relationship between the Mobile Kitchens and the Heavenly Kitchens becomes manifest in a Tang Taoist scripture, the *Discussion of the Works of Taoism* (*Daodian lun* 道典論). A passage dedicated to the "Absorption of the Yellow Pneuma" (Fu huangqi 服黃氣) explains that the adept, in ingesting various mineral and vegetal substances and by feeding himself with the yellow pneuma secreted by his own spleen, will be satiated thanks to the Mobile Kitchens that he thus "summons."[64] The substances concerned are well known to healers and to Taoist adepts seeking immortality: cinnabar, mushrooms, and medicinal plants. As at Magu's banquet, the Mobile Kitchens are served by divinities on plates made of gold, the transmuted, incorruptible material supposed to confer long life to the one who employs it.

Miraculous foodstuffs and immortality are inalterably correlated. Like the expression "spontaneously [produced] clothing and food" (*yishi ziran* 衣食自然), the term "heavenly food" tends to become a cliché in Taoist literature, describing paradisiacal lands, whether those of the postmortem world or utopian societies. The "Heavenly Kitchen," as a designation for the imperial kitchen in secular life, becomes in Taoist usage nearly synonymous with the

63. Stein (1972).
64. Dz 1130. 4/10b–11b. Mentioned by Stein (1972): 491–492, who insists that the tradition on which this text is based goes back to the Han dynasty.

"celestial palace" (*tiantang* 天堂), the place from which the essential products miraculously arrive.[65]

Taken together, these data allow us to discern the conceptual framework of the Mobile Kitchens, namely, Taoist alchemy, wherein empirical science entails a merger of religious metaphor, laboratory experiment, and psychophysical practice. Seen in this light, it requires no great leap to suppose that the Tang *Scripture of the Five Kitchens* was derived directly from this milieu and emerged as a reworked version of the texts that Ge Hong had mentioned some four centuries earlier.

Are we therefore justified in accepting the anecdote of Du Guangting as approximating the literal truth of the matter? Are the Heavenly Kitchens essentially a Taoist work that was appropriated by the Buddhists? If the question of tracing the "original" Central or South Asian antecedents of indigenous Chinese Buddhist materials is now often considered as vain or superfluous, our present investigation may be of particular relevance.

Buddhism has of course extolled the virtues of fasting: "Not to eat is a property of *nirvāṇa,* for *nirvāṇa* is a shelter from the torments of birth and death, of cold and heat, of hunger and thirst," explains, for instance, the monk Sengzhao 僧肇 (374–414).[66] Abstaining from food is seen as an ascetic discipline aimed at the elimination of attachment to objective materiality; it is a form of transcendence.[67] The eulogization of anorexia, however, though entirely grounded in Buddhist soteriological values, is not at all the standpoint of our *Sūtra of the Three Kitchens,* wherein extreme asceticism is conditioned by the pragmatic need to do without material nutriment, rather than by doctrinal considerations.

Nevertheless, the expression "Heavenly Kitchens" (*tianchu*) is indeed attested in early Buddhist literature—for instance in the *Zhongben qijing* 中本起經, an *avadāna* translated into Chinese in 207, where it is used broadly to refer to food of superior quality.[68] Also worthy of mention is the *Dalou tan jing* 大樓炭經, trans-

---

65. See the *Taishang dongxuan lingbao yebao yinyuan jing* 太上洞玄靈寶業報因緣經 (Dz 336. 1/2a): 天廚天供味羅列, "the heavenly kitchens [where] multiflavored celestial offerings are displayed." See also an ancient Lingbao canonical text, the *Taishang dongxuan lingbao benxing yinyuan jing* 太上洞玄靈寶本行因緣經 (Dz 1115. 5a), which says: 死逕昇天堂衣食天廚 "the deceased ascend directly to paradise, [where] clothing and food [come from] the Heavenly Kitchens."

66. *Zhu Weimojie jing* 注維摩詰經, T. 1775. 2/348; quoted by Lamotte (1962): 152n21.

67. The observance of long periods of fasting such as the three-month fasts (Three Fasts, *sanzhai* 三齋) was commonly respected in popular Buddhism as early as the Northern Wei dynasty. It becomes generalized under the Sui and the Tang through the impulsion of imperial edicts. These so-called three-month fasts were in fact periods of fifteen days of abstinence observed during the first, fifth, and ninth months of the year. They were considered as meritorious actions allowing one to advance spiritually and morally. See Forte and May (1979).

68. In section 13, entitled *Fo shi mamai* 佛食馬麥. T. 196, vol. 4: 3/163, trans. Kang Mengxiang 康孟詳 et al. (end of the second–beginning of the third century). Another version

lated by the monk Fali 法立 (265–316), which speaks of the celestial nourishment reserved for the inhabitants of the Four Heavens, the *deva*s. Should they wish to eat, states the text, they instantly find containers made of precious substances before them, filled with a broth of sweet nectar. For the *deva*s whose merits are poor, this broth is dark green, while it is red for those of middling merit and white for those who have acquired superior merits. How delicious and voluptuous is this divine nutrition! The *deva*s' enjoyment of the chromatic feast is not even troubled by the effort to chew: it melts in their mouth, says the *sūtra*, dissolving like volatile sesame oil thrown into the flames. But just how, asks the *Dalou tan jing,* is such food produced? It is by the force of their concentration (*yinian* 意念) that the *deva*s cause this nourishment to appear spontaneously.[69]

Clearly, there is an analogy between the *deva*s' miraculous meals and the "spontaneous kitchens" (*ziran chu* 自然廚) that fill the purified bowls of the practitioners of the Three Kitchens who recite the *dhāraṇī*s given in the appendix of the Buddhist apocryphon. Except for the quality of the chosen vessel—luxurious platters for one, a simple almsbowl for the other— we find here a common conceptual background. In both instances, foodstuffs are ritually sublimated, visualized, or mentally realized, whether in the succulent dishes of the adepts' dream-visions or in the monochrome alimentation of the *deva*s in their celestial paradises.

One should also consider the food "impregnated with all aromas" and served up in a fragrant vase, the subject of a long passage in the *Teaching of Vimalakīrti* (*Vimalakīrtinirdeśa, Weimojie suoshuo jing* 維摩詰所說經), translated into Chinese during the fifth century by Kumārajīva.[70] The feast, which is provided by the Tathāgata to an emanational bodhisattva sent by Vimalakīrti in order to sustain innumerable bodhisattvas, stupefies both men and gods, for it is as sublime as it is limitless:

> Even if all beings throughout innumerable great chiliocosms, during a kalpa or a hundred kalpas, were to swallow these foods, while making their mouths as vast as Sumeru, these foods would not be thereby diminished. Why so? Because they emerge from the inexhaustible elements of morality, concentration, wisdom, libera-

---

of this section appears in the *Foshuo xingqi xing jing* 佛說興起行經 (T. 197, vol. 4), also translated by Kang Mengxiang, but without any mention of the Heavenly Kitchens.

69. T. 23, vol. 1: 4/297. Later translations of this work present the same passage with minor variations. See the *Qishi yinben jing* 起世因本經 (T. 24, vol. 1: 7/346), trans. Jñānagupta (652–710), and the *Qishi yinben jing* (T. 25, vol. 1: 7/401), trans. Dharmagupta (?–619).

70. T. 475, vol. 14: 9, "The amassing of nourishment by a fictive bodhisattva." See Lamotte (1962): 317–334.

tion, and the knowledge and vision of liberation, the leftovers of the Tathāgata's food contained in this bowl are inexhaustible.[71]

As a product of moral virtues, this nutriment can be assimilated exclusively by virtuous beings: "You must not give rise to any mean sentiment, for otherwise you will not be able to digest it."[72] It confers unequalled happiness on those who eat it and consequently "produce from all the pores of their skin a perfume resembling that of the growing trees of the universe Sarvagandhasugandhā."[73]

The notion of food produced miraculously by mental ascesis in response to the desire of celestial beings, as expressed in the *Dalou tan jing,* and the Heavenly Kitchens of our Tang apocrypha may be seen as belonging to a common continuum of religious representations. It must be stressed, however, that the specific term "Heavenly Kitchens" occurs neither in the *Teaching of Vimalakīrti* nor in the *Dalou tan jing.* It does not turn up until centuries later in certain Chan Buddhist sources, and then with the same sense of nourishment emanating from celestial realms, provided by masters secluded in the mountains.[74]

If the idea of transcendental and spontaneous nutrition is by no means the exclusive preserve of Taoism, it is nevertheless unwarranted to infer that the different versions of the *Sūtra of the Three Kitchens* are the fruit of an adaptation of the Indian Buddhist conception of "heavenly nutriment" to the Chinese tradition of the Kitchens. More than the Taoist terminology that peppers the Buddhist sūtra—I am thinking, for example, of the terms "mobile kitchen," "great granary," and "jade maidens"—or its stylistic awkwardness due to its numerous repetitions and added passages, it is its very structure that betrays the editorial mismanagement of its author(s) and pleads in favor of Du Guangting's allegations.

The Taoists and Buddhists agree on a fundamental point: the poem in five strophes, or "*gāthā* of the Five Agents," is the foundation of the ritual method of the Kitchens. The twenty verses that form this poem are indeed exactly the same in both traditions. The poem is said by the Buddhists to be the heart of their *Sūtra of the Three Kitchens,* and its practice constitutes the totality of the *Scripture of the Five Kitchens* commented upon by the Taoist Yin Yin.[75] What ap-

---

71. Ibid., 328. On the miraculous powers and the symbolism of the Buddha's bowl, see also Wang-Toutain (1994).

72. Ibid., 327–328.

73. Ibid., 329.

74. See the work of the Japanese master Dōgen 道元 (1200–1253): *Shōbōgenzō* 正法眼藏, chap. 1 (*Gyōji* 行持); T. 2582, vol. 82: 129.

75. The five stanzas of the text are also quoted in a section of the *Fuqi jingyi lun* (Dz 830. 9b–10a; also edited in *Yunji qiqian,* 57.10a–11b), related to the "absorption of the breaths [allowing one to] abstain from cereal."

pears to be perfectly logical on the Taoist side, where we find a Method of the Five Kitchens based on a poem of five stanzas, reveals itself to be quite problematic in the Buddhist sūtra, where the same *gāthā* of the *five* agents constitutes a method of *three* Kitchens. Possibly the desire to define the Three Kitchens in relation to the Three Jewels, the basic adherence of Buddhism (condition sine qua non for receiving the Method), explains this conspicuous semantic slip. The *Sūtra of the Three Kitchens* is no doubt the product of an attempt to inscribe a popular Taoist practice within a Buddhist framework.

The Kōyasan edition has also preserved, almost verbatim, the list of the Three Kitchens together with the Taoist poem in five strophes. It is only in the version of the *Tingchu jing* edited in a Buddhist pharmaceutical treatise discovered at Dunhuang (P. 2637 and P. 2703 R°) that one notices a striking variation. The poem has been replaced with a formula for the invocation of the Tathāgatas of the five directions: Akṣobhya (Budong rulai 不動如來), the Buddha of the eastern heaven; Ratnasambhava (Baosheng rulai 寶生如來) in the south; Amitābha (Wuliang shoufo 無量壽佛) in the west; Vimalaghoṣa (Weimiao sheng rulai 微妙聲如來) in the north; and Vairocana-samantamukha (? Pubian rulai 普遍如來) in the center. This invocation is to be followed by twenty recitations, in the ten directions, of the name of Ānanda Tathāgata (Anan rulai 阿難如來). Moreover, in this therapeutic version of the Kitchens, the expression "Three Kitchens" occurs neither in the title, nor in the text itself. Although the method of fasting it advocates remains basically the same, the much more "buddhicized" style of this Dunhuang medical recension would indicate that it was produced in a different context, perhaps by local Buddhist healers.

The Method of the Kitchens

Whether taught by the Buddha or by Laozi, whether requiring adherence to the Three Jewels or described as an esoteric Taoist tradition, the practice of the Kitchens remains in any case a psychophysical technique centering on the recitation of the Five Kitchens poem, a recitation that has no doubt a mnemotechnical function. Each of its five strophes corresponds to one of the five directions (east, south, center, west, and north) and, for the Buddhist apocrypha, to each of the five agents (wood, fire, earth, metal, and water), as well as to a sensation or virtue (longevity, warmth, hunger, cold, and thirst). The sensation of warmth is associated with the heart, hunger with the spleen, cold with the lungs, thirst with the kidneys, while long life relates to the liver. This all conforms to the traditional Chinese theory of correspondences. We find here no reference whatsoever to the five elements according to the Indian Tantric system, which, let us recall, are earth, water, fire, wind, and space and are thus quite different from those belonging to the Chinese system.[76] The ritual modalities of the recitation of the five strophes of the Kitchens, which permit the ordering of the meditator's internal space and its synergy with the environment, remain unaltered in their Buddhist transposition.

The *Scripture of the Five Kitchens* gives no information about the technical aspects of the meditation process. Only some of Yin Yin's introductory lines extol, somewhat abstractly, the virtues of the Kitchens:

> Meditation that harmonizes the primordial breath (*yiqi*)[77] with the supreme [cosmic] harmony (*taihe*) permits one [to obtain] the fullness of the viscera, calm, and rectitude of the five spirits (*wushen* 五神).[78] The fullness of the five viscera brings about [the sensation] of repleteness. Quietude of the five spirits permits one to dispel attachments and desires.[79]

And concerning the goals of the Method, we have seen that Du Guangting attributes a similar explanation to the same Yin Yin: it brings about "the spontaneous harmonization of the Five Breaths" of the five viscera, abstention from food, and the attainment of "supreme harmony" (*taihe*). These terms in fact derive from the four characters used in the Five Kitchens' first verse: "Primordial breath in harmony with the supreme harmony" (*yiqi he taihe* 一氣和太和).

The harmony and plenitude of the five viscera allude concretely to the functioning of the digestive system, as it is conceived in traditional Chinese medicine in accord with the system of the five agents. In effect, it is held that digestion is governed by the spleen (corresponding to the center). The five flavors

---

76. On the adaptation of the Chinese system by Tantrism, see Yoritomo (1997). See also Demiéville (1974a): 251, who explains that Mahāyāna Buddhism claims a "phatogénie à base quaternaire." Tantric Buddhism, however, prefers the system of five elements.

77. The primordial breath is defined by Yin Yin, in his commentary of the first verse, as the "original breath" (*yuanqi*), which is made both of a celestial (*yang*) and terrestrial (*yin*) part and creates life.

78. The *Zhen'gao* 真誥 (Dz 1016. 5/10b, fifth century) defines the five spirits as the spirits of the hands, the feet, and the head. It seems, however, that the term more commonly designates the spirits inhabiting the five viscera and governing them. The *Taishang Laojun neiguan jing* 太上老君內觀經 (Dz 641. 2a; also edited in *Yunji qiqian,* 17/2a), for example, explains that "the five viscera conceal the five spirits" (五藏藏五神) and that they are the celestial souls (*hun* 魂) residing in the liver, the terrestrial souls (*po* 魄) inhabiting the lungs, the spermatic essence in the kidneys, the determination in the spleen, and the mental faculty located in the heart. See also the commentary of the *Yunji qiqian* (14/3b), which also attributes to the five viscera the same function of being the "residences" (*fu* 府) of the five spirits.

79. Dz 763. 1a.

(sweet, acrid, salt, bitter, and sour) inherent in foodstuffs become, once they are ingested and transformed in the stomach through the action of the spleen, the *qi* of five distinct types (plain, rancid, flavorful, burnt, and fetid). This process is alluded to in the fifth verse of the poem of the Kitchens, which says: "The different *qi* [consubstantial with] foodstuff (*shiqi* 食氣) condense [to form] *qi*." The five breaths thus produced nourish the five viscera (lungs, heart, liver, spleen, and kidneys) corresponding to the five agents, to the five directions, et cetera. So it is that the spleen is vital to the four other viscera. The perfect condition of the digestive functions it controls ensures synergy and equilibrium among the organs of the body.[80] Although extremely succinct, these technical explanations help us catch a glimpse of the manner in which psychophysical disciplines such as the "absorption of the yellow breath" (the color yellow corresponding to the spleen) and the Method of the Kitchens function. The process of sublimation involved consists of the replacement of the partially refined breaths produced by nutrition with the pure and subtle breaths generated alchemically in the practitioner's body. This is how he is supposed to attain "absolute harmony" and to realize health, long life, and, eventually, immortality.

The Method of the Five Kitchens anonymously presented in the *Fundamental Treatise for the Absorption of Pneuma* mentioned earlier describes these expected benefits but also provides the details of biological and psychological secondary effects, which the adept may endure in the successive phases of his apprenticeship. They are divided into ten periods of ten days, and then three periods of three years. The first three ten-day periods are times of pathological symptoms: the diminution of the *qi,* yellow complexion, vertigo, difficulties with bowel movements, reddish urine, cramps, and weight loss. Having passed this barrier of thirty days, the practitioner finally begins to recover his physical health. Psychological depression might occur during the seventh period, however, after which he will enjoy continuous well-being during the last three ten-day periods, until he attains, within the first one hundred days, a full mastery of the technique. His *qi* is then at its maximum, his thoughts are clear, his perceptions expanded, and he experiences a sensation of great peace. Three years of this ascesis assuredly bring him to rejuvenation, six years to strong vitality and clairvoyance, and nine to invulnerability and perfect control over the gods and spirits. The adept of the Kitchens has then become a "perfected man," a *zhenren.*[81]

The *Fundamental Treatise for the Absorption of Pneuma* also seems to suggest

---

80. See Maspero (1971): 484–487; and Sivin (1987): 220–223.

81. Dz 830. 9b–10a; also edited in *Yunji qiqian,* 57/10a–11b. Neither of these two versions mentions, properly speaking, the Kitchens, but there is no doubt that they are dealing here with the Method of the Five Kitchens, for the *Yunji qiqian,* which is the more complete, quotes the poem in extenso. The five stanzas must be recited in the five directions—east, south, cen-

that the practice of the Five Kitchens may be assimilated to the avoidance of grains or cereals. Abstinence from cereals (*duangu* 斷穀 or *bigu* 辟穀), whether absolute, partial, or reserved for the legendary saints, was a constant among Taoist dietary prescriptions and a fundamental rule of its asceticism.[82] The damaging effects of cereals were already denounced in the third century B.C.E. in the documents of Mawangdui.[83] Zhuangzi too evokes an inhabitant of a paradisiacal mountain who "does not eat the five cereals, but breathes wind and drinks dew."[84] The abstinence from grains, combined with techniques for the circulation and absorption of *qi*, gymnastics (*daoyin* 導引), the use of mineral drugs,[85] and other methods of longevity, was part of the Taoist path for becoming an Immortal. Huijiao 慧皎 (497–554), in his *Biographies of Eminent Monks* (*Gaoseng zhuan* 高僧傳), relates how some Buddhist monks were also involved, like the Taoist adepts, in ascetic rejection of cereals.[86] Observing an extreme frugality, they consumed only mineral and vegetal substances: wild fruits, mushrooms, and pine seeds, resin, or needles. The attributes of the *zhenren*—lightness, luminescence, levitation—are effectively incompatible with a grain diet, which is heavy and produces fecal matter and putrid exhalations and which therefore appeals to the Three Worms (or Three Corpses), the demonical spirits that live in the body and bring about its decrepitude and death. According to Ge Hong, the Taoists affirm:

> To attain longevity, the intestines must be clean. To achieve immortality, they must be free from residues.[87]

Referring to the *Huainan zi* 淮南子, Ge presents a quadripartite classification of diets (vegetarian, carnivorous, graminivorous, and ascetical) together with the personality types associated with them:

ter, west, and north—respectively, 90, 30, 120, 70, and 50 times in order to defeat *qi* disorder, hunger, heat, cold, and thirst.

82. See Lévi (1983). As explained by Despeux (1989): 247–248, the term "cereal," in the context of the practices of longevity, can be understood as the usual diet of the ordinary people, which consisted of course essentially of grains. The abstinence from cereal was then a synonym for fasting. See also Campany (2002): 22–24.

83. See Lévi (1983): 5; Harper (1998), sec. 4; and Campany (2005): 152–169.

84. *Zhuangzi,* chap. 1 (ed. *Zhuangzi jishi,* by Guo Qingfan 郭慶藩 [Beijing, 1961)]: 28), quoted by Lévi (1983). The five cereals are usually rice, millet, wheat, barley, and beans of different kinds.

85. In particular the "powder of cold meal" (composed, among others things, of substances derived from arsenic), which was highly fashionable during the third century. See Wagner (1973); and Obringer (1997).

86. *Gaoseng zhuan* 高僧傳, Zhonghua shuju ed. See, for example, the biographies of Shan Daokai 單道開 (chap. 9: 360–362) and She Gong 涉公 (chap. 10: 373–374). See also Jacques Gernet (1998): 20–21.

87. *Baopuzi neipian,* chap. 15, Wang Ming, ed.: 266.

Herbivores are good walkers, but they are stupid. Carnivores are strong, but irascible. Graminivores are intelligent, but not long-lived. Those who nourish themselves with breath are inspired and do not die.[88]

Such is the prerogative of the Taoist saint who is never harmed by fire or water and who never suffers from hunger or thirst. The *Fundamental Treatise for the Absorption of Pneuma* advocates a similar way and goal through the practice of the Five Kitchens. At its most basic level, this is a discipline for hygiene and well-being: the sensations of biological imbalance, hunger and thirst, heat and cold all disappear, giving way to a state of plenitude. Followed more assiduously, the cure leads the adept to eternal youth and long life and, after a relatively brief period (one speaks of a span of nine years[89]), to immortality and to the supreme objective of the Taoist quest: the state of the *zhenren*. Health, longevity, and immortality—the three stages of the Taoist salvatory creed are all present here.

For the Buddhists, the Method of the Kitchens is similarly assimilated to the practices of *qi* for perfecting the self. Though recommended above all as a recipe to eliminate hunger and thirst, it is moreover a technique for rejuvenation—white hair becomes black again, the teeth grow anew—as well as a means leading to the attainment of *bodhi,* to meeting Amitābha, and even to immortality. The practical indications given by the Buddhists are similar to the instructions presented by the Taoist documents, notably the physiological manifestations that may arise in the course of the practice: reddish urine and passing fatigue followed by renewed energy. The rules concerning the recitation of the five stanza poem are also identical. The numerical order of recitations specified for each stanza—90, 30, 70, and 50 for the directions—is undoubtedly inspired by the sequence 3, 5, 7, 9 that one finds in a great many Taoist practices for "nurturing life," which similarly rely upon sessions of visualization, respiration, and incantation.[90] Further technical details are specified by the *Sūtra of the Three Kitchens:* rotations of the tongue, swallowing, and meditation postures (one is seated with legs crossed, eyes closed, teeth lightly touching, the tip of the tongue glued to the palate). We learn also that the adept who has trained sufficiently succeeds, during his medita-

88. Ibid. On the abstinence from cereal in Ge Hong's work, see Campany (2002): 22–24.

89. Nine can be understood in its emblematic meaning, evoking a cycle of transformation, a period of gestation.

90. See, for example, the *Nüqing guilü* 女青鬼律 (Dz 790. 1/8a), which mentions the "great Dao of three-five-seven-nine for long life," *Sanwu qijiu changsheng zhi dao* 三五七九長生之道. In the Heavenly Masters' tradition to which this work belongs, 24, the sum of these four numbers, represents the 24 divinities or 24 breaths of the body. It represents a totality. See also the "Three, Five, Seven, Nine" method for absorbing the breaths in the *Fuqi jingyi lun* (Dz 830. 10b–11b; also edited in *Yunji qiqian,* 57/13a–b), which mainly consists in exhaling through the mouth the morbid breaths.

tion, in bringing about dream-visions of exquisite dishes that serve as substitutes for the "five flavors of food and drink" (*yinshi wuwei* 飲食五味), that is, the vulgar, material food whose abuse is denounced.[91] But these subtle, oneiric aliments, despite their high quality, are still regarded as "worldly delicacies " (*shijian shangwei* 世間上味). At a higher stage of asceticism, the practitioner abandons these virtual meals in favor of a genuinely transcendent diet composed of "celestial aliments and beverages" (*tianshang yinshi* 天上飲食), which come forth from the Heavenly Kitchens. The adept has no further need or desire to consume any real foodstuff for a considerable length of time: periods of a hundred or even three hundred days of total privation are mentioned. A passage found at the end of the Kōyasan manuscript provides additional details about this prolonged diet and the means to endure it:

> Even though deprived of all terrestrial nutrition, [the practitioner] acquires considerable energy. Spontaneously satiated, he [no longer] knows hunger and decrepitude (death). He who can assiduously persevere also ceaselessly sees nutriments appearing in dreams, which is a sign of the progress attained. If ever he feels his forces diminishing, he goes out to look at the sky and to visualize nourishment, while turning the tongue three times in the mouth. His energy will remount without further decline. After a practice of one hundred days, without any food or drink, he is sustained quite alive (literally, he does not die). If he [wishes then] to ingest something forthwith, he will suffer neither disorder nor harm.[92]

To the five-strophe poem that forms the ritual heart of the Taoist tradition of the Kitchens, the Buddhists have added an arsenal of invocatory formulae and *dhāraṇīs* (*zhou* or *tuoluoni*), giving to some of them the label of "supplementary" practices. The visualization of divinities with Sanskrit-like names (i.e., the divinities of the Kitchens, *chushen* 廚神), and the ritual involving a vessel of water consecrated with the aid of a willow stem, manifestly emanate from a Tantric background.[93] As we shall see in chapter 5, the willow twig was used in medi-

---

91. They are considered as a sign of the end of the world by the *Tingchu jing* (P. 2637 and P. 2703 R°).

92. Makita (1976): 359.

93. See Strickmann (1996): 151 who speaks of this rite in the connection with the Tantric fire ceremony, *homa*. It is of interest to note that, in this context, grains of the five cereals are placed in a vase filled with consecrated water, along with other symbolic substances. See also Demiéville (1974b), which describes the ritual in these terms: "[O]ne fills [the ritual vase] with filtered water, which one perfumes with varied fragrances. . . . In the opening, one plants branches with their leaves, flowers, and fruits, which fall in disorder from the lip; and around the lip one ties ribbons, to which flower garlands are affixed" (267). The exorcistic value of the willow sprig, moreover, is evident in Tantric therapeutic rituals, where it is em-

eval times in Buddhist Tantric therapeutic rituals and also for ceremonies of consecration and rituals of fire (*humo* 護摩, Skt. *homa*). Adapted here to the needs of the Kitchens, the individual rite of consecration through the "liturgical water pot" combines sacramental with charismatic dimensions: the vase is the almsbowl in which the symbolic food of the Kitchens is placed as an offering.[94] An analogous rite is found in the Kōyasan version: facing the north, the adept holds in his left hand a vessel of water over which he performs *mudrās* with his right hand while reciting two different types of incantations: one in pseudo-Sanskrit called the "Nazhi incantation" (*nazhi zhou* 那知咒), or the "*dhāranī* of the Kitchens" (*chu shenzhou* 廚神咒), and another one entitled the "*gāthā* of immortality" (*changsheng* [*busi*] *jie* 長生[不死]偈), or the "*gāthā* of the five directions" (*wufang ji* 五方偈), that is, the five-stanza poem. He then swallows this consecrated water, which, says the text, allows him to overcome all obstacles encountered during his practice.[95]

The divergences that appear in the apprenticeship program of the Method between Buddhist and Taoist recensions deserve to be underscored. We have seen that, for the Taoist *Fundamental Treatise on the Absorption of the Pneuma,* a basic mastery of the practice requires a hundred days. A period of nine years of assiduous training is necessary to reach the door of immortality. Assuming that it is not merely an error of transposition, the Buddhists seem to have deliberately and considerably reduced the time for preliminary apprenticeship.[96] They provide, however, much pragmatic information, in particular on the timing of the meditation. The recitations are to be practiced thrice daily, beginning at the *yin* hour (between three and five a.m.). The apprenticeship, which must be undertaken on a *ren* day of the sexagesimal calendar, should be adapted to the practitioner's horoscope, or "personal destiny" (*benming* 本命), an important concept of Chinese astrology that will be examined in chapter 4.[97] To illustrate the rule, the Kōyasan version gives this example: one born under the sign of water must practice facing the north and depends on *ren* and *gui* 癸 days (corresponding to water and to the north).

The consistency of these practical data, which are familiar overall to a disciple of the Taoist arts of longevity, does not succeed in masking the proselytiz-

---

ployed to whip the face of the patient (Strickmann (1996): 152) or to sprinkle consecrated water (Demiéville (1974a): 244).

94. Food blessing by means of incantations is inscribed within the framework of Tantric magico-religious procedures. See Strickmann (1993).

95. The reading of the text is uncertain due to missing characters: see the edition as given by Makita (1976): 359.

96. The initial phase of negative symptoms is reduced to three days, while the second step characterized by regaining one's energy comes to term in seven days instead of seventy.

97. P. 3032.

ing character of the *Sūtra of the Three Kitchens*. The method of absolute abstinence that it advocates, in spite of its technicity and hermetic character, requires neither the support of a master, nor any physical preparation besides a preliminary period of seven days of purification. A few recommendations and warnings are given, though the work insistently declares that it is possible for everyone to achieve, definitively and rapidly, the faculty to extinguish all desire and even the need to eat. In view of all this, it is difficult not to be perplexed about the seriousness of the sūtra, which resembles more a thaumaturgical recipe than an expedient process of self-perfection.

The resolute missionary vocation of the apocryphon is also obvious. It proclaims at the outset that the required condition for receiving initiation is unwavering faith in Buddhism. The Method is to be transmitted exclusively to adepts who have taken their refuge in the Three Jewels and whose faith is thereby certified. Traitors and impostors are threatened with the heaviest postmortem punishments, including infernal torments and rebirth among the hungry ghosts or animals. The rigorous control of the transmission is further restricted by the probationary period of seven days during which the devotee, having made an act of contrition so as to repent of his faults, is constrained to silence and isolation (all contact with women and animals being expressly forbidden), either in a meditation room or a place of retreat.

For their part, the Taoists do not insist upon any religious adhesion, nor do they publicize the merits of the practice of the Five Kitchens or its universal accessibility. The Method is unveiled, in the manner of other longevity techniques, in esoteric terms. The poem of the Five Kitchens might well have been the written expression of a teaching transmitted orally and directly from master to disciple.

It must be stressed nevertheless that, in the absence of the Buddhist versions of the Kitchens, however suspect they may be, we would have remained entirely ignorant of the ritual modalities of this medieval tradition. Buddhist apocrypha, which frequently stem from a religious reframing or didactic elaboration of "original" ritual and conceptual elements, are precious tools for the understanding of affiliated (Taoist or other) scriptures whose hermeticism bars even the most knowledgeable readers. And the *Sūtra of the Three Kitchens* is, as we shall see, by no means a unique case.

ALIMENTARY PRESCRIPTIONS, rules of abstinence, and purificatory fasts are of universal importance for traditional ritual customs and religious asceticism.[98]

---

98. For medieval Europe, see Bynum (1987).

The grain-free diet recommended by Taoism and the vegetarianism preached by Buddhism were the best-known examples in the Chinese world, where, as elsewhere, such dietary interdictions have been maintained and often justified by furnishing them with medical or ethical interpretations.[99] Hygienic arguments and theological presuppositions remain, in most such cases, closely linked. When examined from a socioeconomic perspective, however, the alimentary precepts also reveal more materialistic grounds, though these need not diminish the role of sanitary criteria or religious belief. For the Taoist, abstinence from cereals may be envisaged as an ecological reaction to agricultural policies, carried out at the beginning of the empire, which radically transformed Chinese lifestyle and diet in the process of settling the population.[100] The peasants were principally nourished with grain, so that when immense famines periodically took place owing to natural disaster, war, and insufficient state granaries,[101] they were left only with the prospect of seeking refuge in the wilderness, the mountains beloved of the hermits and Taoists, who established there, during the first centuries of the common era, their sanctuaries and parishes.[102] The nutrition privileged by the Taoist saint, whether mountain-dwelling ascetic or drug-taking alchemist, might have been, for ordinary mortals, devoid of all but the merest hint of a subsistence diet.[103] Chinese botanists sought to bring some variety to its content: more than four hundred wild plants that could be cooked and consumed in lean times, for instance, were catalogued by Zhu Xiao 朱橚 at the beginning of the fifteenth century.[104] These "famine foods," as they were called by Joseph Needham, have been the object of constant care on the part of the Chinese people and governments.

Such is the sociological landscape in which the tradition of the Kitchens evolved. As R. A. Stein made clear, the nutrition of immortality is also the nutrition of crisis. There can be no doubt, he states, that "in their search for

99. See Douglas (1966) on this rationalizing tendency in general.

100. See Schipper (1982): 216–218.

101. On the big famines of the first dynasties, see Twitchett and Loewe (1986), vol. 1: 617–622; and Swann (1950). On the premodern period, see Will (1980).

102. See Stein (1963): 59–69, who indicates that these administrative centers of the Heavenly Master organization included inns and restaurants, or kitchens (chu).

103. The passage of the Mawangdui document dealing with the practice of abstinence from cereal specifies, for example, that only one particular plant can be eaten by the adept. See Despeux (1989): 248.

104. *Jiuhuang bencao* 救荒本草 (Botanic of survival) in *Nongzheng quanshu* 農政全書, *Collection of Treatises on Agriculture,* compiled by Xu Guangqi 徐光啟 (1562–1633), a preeminent scientist and politician who also promoted the production of sweet potatoes, corn, and tapioca among other alternative foodstuffs. See Needham (1986), vol. 6, part 1: 64–70, who notes that a third of Xu's work is dedicated to the "control of famines," *huangzheng* 荒政.

exceptional substitute nourishment, the Taoists were able to make incidental discoveries in pharmacopeia and dietetics."[105] Besides these two indissociable fields of medicine and alimentary hygiene, I wish to note also a third, complementary domain, that of the practices of breath circulation and self-perfection. It seems to me that we must situate the tradition of the Heavenly Kitchens at the meeting point of these three domains, for it represents the definitive survival technique, the ultimate expression of dietary rigor transfigured into a way of salvation. The Tang epoch, to which the sūtras of the Kitchens are assigned, had its share of terrible shortages wherein the survivors were often constrained to sustain themselves with all sorts of food substitutes: roots, leaves, mud cakes, and the like. Cases of cannibalism were not rare, its disastrous reality being denounced, as we have seen, by the *Tingchu jing*.[106]

The Kitchens of the Buddha, as attested by the central place of this same *Tingchu jing* in a Dunhuang collection of medical recipes, were entirely of a piece with Tang-period Chinese Buddhist therapeutics. They provide an excellent illustration of the development of an original Buddhist pharmacology, a medico-religious pseudoscience associated with techniques of meditation and the quest for enlightenment. Their manifestation coincides with the vogue in China during the same period for the foreign materia medica of India and Central Asia[107] and in this respect echoes the call of Mahāyāna Buddhist proselytism, which was particularly inclined to rely upon medicine as a proven propaganda instrument. Many Chinese Buddhist monk-thaumaturgists, looking for the spiritual salvation of the unfaithful, introduced themselves as healers of their bodies.[108]

The interest that sustained the Heavenly Kitchens, in this troubled age of Chinese history, may be thus in part explained by desperate efforts to find miraculous solutions to the problem of famine. The *Sūtra of the Three Kitchens,* an apocryphon of survival, undoubtedly had no great difficulty in seducing, for a time, distressed populations and encouraging their swift conversion to Buddhism. And hunger was by no means their sole preoccupation. Evils abounded, requiring a refuge that religion sought to provide. Sorcery, to which we shall now turn, offers a cardinal example.

---

105. Stein (1972): 497–499.
106. On Tang-period cannibalism, see Schafer (1963): 107–108.
107. See Needham (1986); and Schafer (1963): 176–194.
108. See Demiéville (1974a): 243–244.

CHAPTER 2

In Pursuit of the Sorcerers

May the three beams and six pillars turn back against their instigators!
May evil and calamity by themselves turn back against them to exterminate
 them!

The antiquity and virulence of sorcery in China are confirmed by both archeological evidence and dynastic histories. The manuscripts of Mawangdui already bear witness to this during the third century B.C.E.[1] Despite the
adoption of draconian juridical and penal measures, which were incessantly
amended by successive dynasties in the attempt at suppression, sorcery continued to afflict all classes of society. The ancient elite, far from sequestering
itself in solemn state ceremonies and the cult of the ancestors, willingly gave
itself over to sorcery. The ravages thus caused are described by the official historians, who detail the pathetic sequels to its calamitous effects on political
life.[2] Above all, it was the phobia of bewitchment by means of the poison
known as *gu* 蠱 that continuously brought about a reign of intrigue and black-
mail in Chinese society.

The modus operandi of *gu* is derived from a singular, millennial recipe that
involves filling a jar with insects, serpents, and other vermin and letting them
devour one another. The last survivor, which presumably has concentrated
within itself all the venom of the other pests, is called *gu*.[3] This diabolical creature, subject to its master, enables him to apply its sorcery against enemies, notably by drugging their food. In all events, the *gu* places in high relief a semantic
field that extends far beyond a rudimentary method of poisoning. As a nosological concept, rich with diverse connotations, it is synonymous with toxicology,
demonic pathologies, and witchcraft.[4] During the medieval period, medical
treatises devoted whole chapters to the careful characterization of its etiology

---

Epigraph: Dz 652. 2a and T. 2882, vol. 85: 1383c.
1. Harper (1998):152–153.
2. Feng and Shryock (1935); Loewe (1970).
3. Etymologically explained as "insects in a vessel."
4. Obringer (1997): 225–263.

and to the prescription of remedies promising to cure the horrible illnesses occasioned by this scourge.[5]

If the mysteries of bewitchment by the *gu* have been in part unveiled, Chinese sorcery remains a little-explored subject overall. Its history remains to be written.[6] Performed most often by socially marginal actors, its solitary rites are poorly documented. In order to comprehend it, scholars have had no alternative but to turn to the secondary sources that derive from its opponents. Historical annals, penal codes, and medical manuals have been frequently consulted on the subject. Little attention, however, has been paid to the perspectives of established Chinese religions concerning this enduring problem for medieval Chinese society. How did Taoism and Buddhism, the two great religious traditions, envision sorcery? What were the strategies they adopted in seeking to combat it?

Two sui generis works of the medieval period, one Buddhist and the other Taoist, provide us with substantial material with which to respond to these questions. The first, which I translate here in extenso, is entitled the *Sūtra for the Conjuration of Bewitchments, Preached by the Buddha* (*Foshuo zhoumei jing* 佛說咒媚經). This short apocryphon was produced during the early emergence of esoteric Buddhism in China, the period called "prototantric" by the late Michel Strickmann and roughly corresponding to the two hundred years prior to the maturation of the tradition in the eighth century. Several recensions of the sūtra were found at Dunhuang,[7] two of which served as the basis for the edition given in the *Taishō shinshū daizōkyō.*[8] More recently, a manuscript copy of this same sūtra was discovered at the Nanatsu-dera monastery in Japan. Like many other Chinese apocryphal sūtras, the *Zhoumei jing* presents itself as a teaching of the Buddha for the salvation of beings. Its focus and priority, however, are to free the faithful from the horrid torments conjured up by curses. The antidote to sorcery consists of a ritual counterattack against witches by means of a battery of *dhāraṇīs*, as well as evocations of bodhisattvas and other divinities capable of undoing evil spells and protecting the faithful from them.

---

5. See Unschuld (1985): 46–50, who explains that the concept of *gu* is described throughout the medical literature of the first and second millennia as one of the main pathological causes. Therefore, numerous therapeutic diagnoses and means existed that were intended to protect against this danger. On the pharmacological literature providing lists of drugs, plants, and minerals to fight against *gu* poisonings, see also Obringer (1997).

6. Neither has modern ethnology dealt very much with this subject. In *The Religious System of China* (1907), vol. 5: 826–928, and vol. 6: 1187–1341, de Groot treats several aspects of black magic as it was practiced in Amoy at the end of the nineteenth century and the beginning of the twentieth. For an anthropological study of black magic in modern Japan and its relation to Chinese sorcery, see Blacker (1975): 51–68.

7. S. 418 and S. 2517, S. 2088, S. 3852, S. 4311, S. 4524, S. 6146, P. 3689, Beijing 8265, Beijing 8266, Beijing 8267, Beijing 8268, and Beijing 8269.

8. T. 2882, vol. 85: 1383–1384 (based on S. 418 collated with S. 2517).

The second work with which I am concerned here has been published in the Taoist Canon under the title *Scripture for Unbinding Curses, Revealed by the Most High Lord Lao* (*Taishang Laojun shuo jieshi zhouzu jing* 太上老君說解釋咒詛經).[9] In this case, it is the deified Laozi who, in the manner of the Buddha, offers a ritual solution to the scourge of sorcery, which he describes as an acute symptom of the decadent age preceding the imminent end of the world. As the paraphrase and citations given below will make clear, this work belongs to the Taoist tradition of the "conversion of the barbarians" (*huahu* 化胡). Its thoroughly pragmatic role in the struggle against bewitchment is but a pretext for its self-proclaimed proselytizing mission: to convert the populations of the West, that is to say, Central and Southern Asia.

Besides their opposition to sorcery, the two Buddhist and Taoist sūtras bear similarities that, as we shall see, disclose their link. even if not concretely demonstrating direct affiliation. In contrast to the case of the Heavenly Kitchens, the question here is not one of plagiarism or appropriation in the strict sense, but a more subtle sort of textual exchange between the two religions, in fact an instance of delayed response in the relation of the Taoist scripture to the Buddhist sūtra. Before entering into exegetical considerations, however, it will be useful to outline the religiocultural background of the texts. Within the limits of this chapter, however, I restrict myself to general considerations.

Buddhism and Taoism in Confrontation with Sorcery

For the historian of Buddhism, witchcraft is an expansive subject. Owing to the sustained attention it lavished upon sorcery through its eschatological representations as well as through its exorcistic and therapeutic rituals, medieval Buddhism notably contributed to its inscription as a social and psychological reality. Tantrism, in particular, became its fiercest adversary and appointed healer. For was not illness the principal harm done by witchcraft? The social terrain lent itself perfectly to this assumption. Far from being the fruit of the deranged imagination, demonic possession was recognized to be a tangible reality and a serious priority by both physicians and pharmaceutical professionals. Hence, materia medica, rites of exorcism, and prophylactic measures all readily found their places among the branches of empirical knowledge pressed into service in the Buddhist campaign against this evil.

Buddhism's assiduous concern with the treatment of sorcery stemmed in part from eschatological speculations that were widely distributed in medieval China. If we are to believe Michel Strickmann, Tantrism in particular made sorcery a

---

9. Dz 652.

"department of theology." With his admirable provocativeness, Strickmann goes so far as to speak of a "Buddhist recognition of black magic."[10] He writes:

> The principal function of the prototantric rite consisted in assuring the survival of Buddhism's faithful in a world prey to demons at the end of time. Particularly dangerous circumstances justified exceptional measures. Thus, anticipating the situation in the future, the Buddha consented to the use of murderous incantations.[11]

Such a paradox was rendered possible by the ambiguous nature of Tantrism's relations with techniques of bewitchment. In principle, contrary to the Buddhist ethic of respect for life,[12] the Tantric offensive as it appeared in rites of subjugation of enemies or domination (abhicāraka) manifestly made use of evil against evil, thus finding its raison d'être.[13] The boundaries between exorcism and the ars daemonum became on occasion so confused that only the hallmark of orthodoxy renders possible their differentiation, as will be demonstrated through the examples given in the last part of this chapter.

Sorcery, syndrome par excellence of the abject condition and suffering of humanity, naturally entered the frenzied domain of apocalyptical beliefs in which the Buddha's devotees rivalled the adepts of the Dao in bidding up predictions of the end of the world. For Buddhism, bewitchment was perceived as one of the flagrant signs foretelling the final age.[14] In prophesizing the decline of the Dharma (mofa 末法), the fifth-century Buddhist apocryphal Sūtra of Consecration (Guanding jing 灌頂經), for example, offers a list of the moral failings that stand at the origin of the painful reentrenchment of sorcery:

> The Buddha proclaimed: "In this world, ignorance and stupidity [are the lot] of generations, [with their complement] of duplicity and quarrel, injury and insult, suspicion and hatred."[15]

---

10. Strickmann (1996): 42, 152.

11. Ibid., 112–113.

12. Witchcraft is explicitly forbidden in the Vinaya. Consider, for instance, the twenty-ninth command, "against the use of condemnable means to gain one's livelihood," of the fifth-century Fanwang jing 梵網經 (T. 1484, vol. 24: 1007a23–27), the translation of which is attributed to Kumārajīva. There it is stipulated that it is reprehensible to turn to the methods of curses and to make toxic drugs and gu poisons. See de Groot's translation (1893): 61.

13. Some of these Tantric practices of sorcery are described in Duquenne (1983a): 610–640; and (1983b): 652–670.

14. Seidel (1970); Zürcher (1982); Mollier (1990).

15. Book 12 of the Guanding jing (T. 1331, vol. 21: 533). This book 12, which is entitled "Eliminating Faults and Transcending Life-and-Death," presents the most ancient extant version of the Sūtra of Bhaiṣajyaguru (Yaoshi jing 藥師經). The paragraph translated here is mentioned by Miyai (1996): 736. On the Guanding jing in general, see Strickmann (1990): 82–83.

FIG. 2.1. Guanyin saving the faithful from the peril of sorcery: details from Dunhuang paintings MG 17665 and EO 1142 (both tenth century). Courtesy of the Musée Guimet.

The *Lotus Sūtra* (*Saddharmapuṇḍarīkasūtra, Fahua jing* 法華經) had already ranked sorcery as one of the characteristic afflictions of the final years of the Dharma. Its celebrated twenty-fifth chapter, the "Universal Gateway of Guanshiyin" (Guanshiyin pumen pin 觀世音普門品), to which we shall return in the last chapter of this volume, enumerates the perilous situations in which the bodhisattva Avalokiteśvara (Guanyin) benevolently intervenes for the express salvation of the faithful: fire, shipwreck, aggression, imprisonment, demons, storms, and so on. Bewitchment, which is counted among these dangers (fig. 2.1), is evoked as follows in one of the *gāthās* given in the translation of Kumārajīva, dating to 406:

> If you are a victim of curses (*zhouzu* 咒詛) and poisons
> On the part of a being who wishes to harm you,
> Invoke the power of Guanyin,
> And [the harm] will return to its instigator (*huanzhao yu benren* 還著於本人).[16]

This chapter of the *Lotus* became so popular in China that, soon after the dif-

---

16. *Miaofa lianhua jing* 妙法蓮華經, T. 262, vol. 9: 58a. The most ancient extant Chinese translation is the one by Dharmarakṣa, dating to 286 C.E.

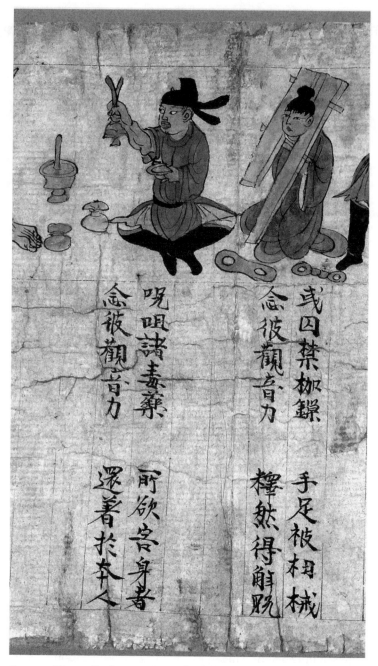

或囚禁枷鎖

念彼觀音力

手足被杻械

釋然得解脫

咒詛諸毒藥

所欲害身者

念彼觀音力

還著於本人

念彼觀音力

FIG. 2.2. The peril of sorcery in an illustrated Dunhuang manuscript of the *Guanyin jing* (P. 2010). Courtesy of the Bibliothèque nationale de France.

FIG. 2.3. The peril of sorcery in a tenth-century illustrated booklet of the *Guanyin jing* (S. 6983) from Dunhuang. Courtesy of the British Library.

fusion of Kumārajīva's translation, it began to circulate in the form of an independent text called the *Guanyin Sūtra* (*Guanyin jing* 觀音經),[17] which was depicted through an abundant iconography, as evidenced by the murals of the cave temples and the mobile paintings of Dunhuang.[18]

Also discovered in Dunhuang were several tenth-century illustrated scrolls

17. Murase (1971); Yü (2001): 37–38, 75–77.

18. In Dunhuang, the first representations of the *Guanshiyin pumen pin* date from the Sui period (Mogao caves 303 and 420), the latest from the Northern Song dynasty. See *Dunhuang shiku quanji* (1999), vol. 7, *Fahua jing huajuan* 法華經畫卷. For the mobile paintings, two may be mentioned from the Pelliot Collection housed in the Musée Guimet, EO 1142 and MG 17665, which depict only four perils (Giès et al. [1994]: 343–345 and plates 72 and 73), as well as several paintings of the Stein Collection kept in the British Museum: Stein paintings 2, 24, and 28 (see R. Whitfield 1982–1985, vol. 1: plates 18, 25, and 21). Other paintings of the *Guanyin Sūtra* are housed in the Arthur M. Sackler Museum (Cambridge, MA), the Rijksmuseum of Amsterdam (see Yü 2001: 82), and the Provincial Museum of Chengdu (see Giès et al. [1994]: 343–345).

and votive booklets of the *Guanyin Sūtra* with meticulous representations of the bodhisattva as savior from perils.[19] In these, the drawings that accompany the verses on sorcery show either a person seated on the ground wielding vials and a mortar (and so evidently engaged in the fabrication of *gu* poison), or else two men at table, one of whom, the victim of sorcery, vomits into the dishes (figs. 2.2 and 2.3),[20] a motif that has been continuously depicted up to the present day in Buddhist monastery paintings and publications (fig. 2.4). The theme of the bewitched supper was also treated by Song-dynasty sculptors. Among the perils depicted in bas-relief surrounding the famous Water-Moon (*shuiyue* 水月) Guanyin of cave 19 at Pilu monastery 毘盧寺 in Anyue 安岳, Sichuan, for instance, one can distinctly recognize the same motif (fig. 2.5).[21]

Buddhist literature often mentions enemies (*yuanren* 怨人) or evildoers (*e'ren* 惡人), namely, sorcerers and witches who trifle with life and death, enter into pacts with malefic demons (*e'gui* 惡鬼), and cause a great variety of demoniacal illnesses (*guibing* 鬼病), of which the most spectacular are no doubt the attacks of dementia. Demonic possession spares no one, not even members of the *saṃgha*. In the sixth-century *Sūtra of the Bodhisattva Ākāśagarbha's Questions on the Dhāraṇī of the Seven Buddhas* (*Xukongzang pusa wen qifo tuoluoni zhou jing* 虛空藏菩薩問七佛陀羅尼咒經), the Buddha deplores a case of witchcraft whose victims are monks. Lost in the heart of a forest, the two *bhikṣus* (*biqiu* 比丘) manifest all the signs of delirium: one screams obscenities, while the other, half-naked and with arms held up to the heavens, mutters strange noises.[22] Ānanda (Anan 阿難), the Buddha's closest disciple, is also said to have had a hard time getting rid of the bewitchment (*gu*) cast by a mother wanting to force him to marry her daughter, Mātaṅgī (Modeng 摩鄧), who was madly in love with the handsome *śramaṇa*.[23] For the laity, the devastating effects of sorcery are even more fearsome: they often strike not just the person intended but also, following the widespread Chinese principle of familial solidarity, his entire household. Repercussions can be felt all the way down to his domestic animals, estates, and cultivated fields, as is indicated in the *Zhoumei jing*.

---

19. See Drège (1999): 124–137.

20. These booklets are Pelliot (P.) 2010 and Stein (S.) 6983. See R. Whitfield (1982–1985), vol. 2: 92–93 and fig. 92. According to Giès et al. (1994): 345, the sorcerer depicted in the illustration of S. 6983 would be the person from whose mouth some lines are seen going out. These lines, they say, represent the evil incantations that he casts upon the victim sitting in front of him. I think that it is in fact the contrary; it is the victim who is vomiting (blood?). Vomiting, in particular of blood, is one of the main symptoms of bewitchment in China.

21. The sculpture dates back to the Northern Song, but according to Howard (1990): 57, the scenes of perils placed around the statue of Guanyin were restored under the Qing dynasty.

22. T. 1333, vol. 21. Xukongzang, i.e., Ākāśagarbha or Gaganagañja, is the bodhisattva of the center, also identified as Venus 明星.

23. *Foshuo Modeng nü jing* 佛說摩鄧女經, translated by An Shigao 安世高 (second century C.E.), T. 551, vol. 16.

FIG. 2.4. The peril of sorcery in a series of recent paintings of the *Guanyin jing* in the Guanyin hall of the Wenshu yuan 文殊院 monastery, Chengdu (Sichuan). Photograph by the author, 2001.

FIG. 2.5. The peril of sorcery at Pilu monastery, Anyue County (Sichuan). Photograph by the author, 2001.

Spectacularly exhibited in the Buddhist gallery of worldly evils, sorcery was equally implanted in the *imaginaire* of death as conveyed by the numerous textual and iconographic depictions of postmortem terrors. Death by bewitchment was included in two of the major Buddhist eschatological systems classifying the principal causes of a violent decease (*hengsi* 橫死), each of which is placed under the patronage of a great protective figure of the Mahāyāna—namely the buddha Bhaiṣajyaguru, Master of Medicine (Yaoshi 藥師), and the bodhisattva Guanyin. The first, that of Yaoshi, is set forth in the *Sūtra of Bhaiṣajyaguru* (*Yaoshi jing* 藥師經), where death caused by witchcraft is classed as the eighth in a series of nine violent ends (*daheng* 大橫):

> The eighth type of sudden death is brought about vengefully by bewitchment through talismans, curses, and the coercion of malefic spirits. Deprived of all merits, assaulted by suffering, [the victim] is taken prematurely to death.[24]

---

24. T. 1331, vol. 21: 535c. On Bhaiṣajyaguru and the sūtras dedicated to him, see Birnbaum (1979); and Kuo (1994a): 145 et seq.

The second classificatory system, relating to Guanyin, presents up to fifteen evil deaths (e'si 惡死) and distinguishes no less than four types of fatal bewitchment. The *Vast, Perfect, Unobstructed Dhāraṇī Sūtra of the Great Compassion Heart* [*Taught by*] *the Thousand-Armed, Thousand-Eyed Bodhisattva Guanyin* (*Qianshou qianyan Guanshiyin pusa guangda yuanman wu'ai dabeixin tuoluoni jing* 千手千眼觀世音菩薩廣大圓滿無礙大悲心陀羅尼經)—or, in short, the *Sūtra of the Thousand-Armed*—gives a detailed list of them: death brought about by *gu* poison (*wei gudu haisi* 為蠱毒害死); death caused by maledictions cast by a nefarious being (*wei e'ren yanmei si* 為惡人厭媚死); death following an evil illness (*e'bing* 惡病); and death inflicted by perverse and malefic demons (*xiegui e'gui* 邪鬼惡鬼).[25]

From the Tang dynasty on, these violent deaths also became objects of visual representations at Dunhuang and in Sichuan.[26] Cave 96 of the Qianfo zhai 千佛寨 at Anyue, for instance, which is devoted to Bhaiṣajyaguru, contains in its right section (to the Buddha's left) a bas-relief of the nine types of violent death, with mortality by witchcraft eighth among them. In Dunhuang, Northern Song painters placed Guanyin and Bhaiṣajyaguru side by side, both in their roles of protector from sudden death. One can see, for example, on the north face of Mogao chapel 76, a triptych in which an eleven-faced, eight-armed Guanyin is surrounded by a series of labelled, miniature narrative tableaux depicting the fifteen painful deaths, while Bhaiṣajyaguru is situated in the center of the nine violent deaths, including, of course, witchcraft as the eighth, as is confirmed by a corresponding cartouche that quotes verbatim the *Sūtra of Bhaiṣajyaguru*.[27]

---

25. T. 1060, vol. 20: 107. The *Sūtra of the Thousand-Armed* is an important Tantric work whose translation in Chinese is attributed to Bhagavaddharma (second half of the seventh century). See Yü (2001): 59–61.

26. On the mural paintings of Dunhuang (dating from the Tang–Northern Song period) inspired by the twenty-third chapter of the *Lotus sūtra* dedicated to Yaowang, "The Past Conduct of the Bodhisattva King of Medicine" (Yaowang pusa benshi pin 藥王菩薩本事品), see *Dunhuang shiku quanji* (1999), vol. 7, *Fahua jing huajuan*. A painting on silk from Dunhuang (Stein painting 36), which dates from the ninth century and depicts the Paradise of Bhaiṣajyaguru, also bears in its right-hand panel the nine types of violent deaths. See R. Whitfield (1982-1985), vol. 1: 302–306 and plate 9. See also Soymié (1981): 190–191. A similar painting from Dunhuang is shown at the National Museum of New Delhi.

27. See the reproductions in Lin (1991): 523 (plate 2); and *Dunhuang shiku quanji* (1999): vol. 25, *Minsu huajuan* 民俗華卷: 243, 244 (plates 3, 4). The illustration relating to the peril of sorcery in the painting of Bhaiṣajyaguru remains quite enigmatic. One can see a woman playing the *pipa* and dancing in front of a three-story altar on which stands a horse with a ram head mounted by a rider who has also a ram head. Could the strange mount and its minotaur rider be representations of the hemp horse effigies and their riders described in the *Zhoumei jing* as being pierced by the sorcerers (see below)? Paintings of caves 358 and 360 dating from the mid-Tang period and of cave 9 of the late Tang period show the same type of scene. See *Dunhuang shiku quanji* (1999): vol. 25, *Minsu huajuan*: 246–250.

All these artifacts plainly demonstrate that medieval Buddhism had expressly stigmatized sorcery as one of the major calamities afflicting humanity. The *Sūtra for the Conjuration of Bewitchments* and other contemporary or somewhat later writings permit us to specify, as we shall see, the expedients believed to have been used by the evildoers to target their victims and the religious techniques imagined to counterattack them.

In contrast with Buddhism, medieval Taoism did not devote much attention to sorcery. It could be said, without too much exaggeration, that the topic was passed over in silence. The apocalyptic literature, which flourished during the Six Dynasties, denounced the proliferation of demonical illnesses at the dawn of the end of time but did not consider them to be exclusively the result of the misanthropic activities of a few professional evildoers.[28] Demons were produced by an infinitely more extensive evil than basic witchcraft. Their omnipresence and enmity were entirely due to the blood sacrifices that they received and that were perpetuated by the common, "nameless" religion[29] observed by the great majority of the Chinese at all levels of society. For the theologians of the Dao, "shamans" (*wushi* 巫師) and sorcerers (*wuxi* 巫覡) were but a single noxious faction, for one no less than the other maintained illicit and risky relations with demonic spirits, that is to say, with the gods of the traditional pantheon that had been decreed to be outmoded and malevolent by the orthodoxy.[30] This amalgamation of sacrificial cults with sorcery per se explains to some extent why Taoism, despite its pronounced taste for exorcism, did not feel a pressing need to single out witchcraft in particular. With the exception of a medieval breviary, the *Penal Code of the Mysterious Metropolis* (*Xuandu lüwen* 玄都律文), which expressly prohibits recourse to sorcery (*gudao* 蠱道),[31] witchcraft was generally treated by Taoist moralists under the same rubric as all the other problems imputed to demons. To my knowledge, only one single text among the numerous exorcistic procedures found in the Taoist Canon dedicates a specific rite to the issue of sorcery. Thus, in its "Petition for Returning to Normality by Exteriorization of the Officers" (Huishan zhang chuguan 迴善章出官), the

---

28. On medieval Taoist Apocalypses, see Mollier (1990).

29. To adopt the expression of Rolf A. Stein.

30. For the Taoists the appellations "religion of demons" (*guidao* 鬼道) and "deviating methods" (*daofa* 倒法) are in fact used to designate the "vulgar" or "perverse cults" (*susi* 俗祀 or *yinsi* 淫祀)—that is, the sacrificial religion of the shamans (*wushi* 巫師), condemned as heterodox and dangerous by theologians of the Dao. See Stein (1979); and Mollier (2006).

31. Dz 188. This seventh-century work sets out the moral laws and the religious and ethical rules of behavior for the benefit of the faithful of the Way of the Heavenly Master's community. On the basis of thirteen precepts (1a–1b) and thirteen interdictions (3a–3b), the text lists in detail the good (*shan* 善) and the bad (*e* 惡) actions, as well as the benefits or the maledictions directly entailed by them.

Zhengyi chuguan zhangyi 正一出官章儀, a work of the Tang-period Heavenly Master tradition, advocates a ritual of petition, which, with the help of talismans and spells, can neutralize or even destroy the evil persons who perform witchcraft.[32] It should be noticed, however, that this seems to be a late elaboration of the "Petition for Unbinding Maledictions" (Jie zhouzu zhang 解咒詛章), which is just one among a large number of minor Taoist rites given in the *Petition Almanac of Master Red Pine* (*Chisongzi zhangli* 赤松子章曆) and performed for the deliverance of the faithful from sickness and other demonic afflictions by the Way of the Heavenly Master's clerics.[33] It would not be until long after, under the Song, that Taoism, probably influenced by Tantrism and in accord with the official tendency to demonize the shamans (*wu*) native to the numerous ethnic minorities of southern China, would adopt a more specific interest in the treatment of cases of bewitchment.[34]

In the context of medieval Taoism, the *Scripture for Unbinding Curses, Revealed by the Most High Lord Lao,* which is centered on the struggle against sorcerers, is thus something of an exception. Supreme evil and the height of moral turpitude, sorcery is denounced there as the undeniable sign of the end of the world (*moshi* 末世). The inventory of iniquity that issues forth from the mouth of Laozi seems to echo that of the *Sūtra of Consecration* cited above. The Taoist deity deplores the ravages caused by a depraved humanity obsessed with settling scores and destruction. Instead of doing good and respecting the Dao, people hand themselves over to heterodox gods and pass their time dispatching baleful spells, the effect being the proliferation of demonic forces. But, Laojun quickly reassures the faithful, this disastrous moral account and the alarming predictions are in fact not addressed to the Chinese people in particular but rather to the inhabitants of lands to the West. The Old Master is in effect far from the civilized world of China's central plains. His revelation takes place in Khotan (Yutian guo 于闐國), the Central Asian kingdom situated at the empire's frontier, a stage on the route leading to India (Zhuguo 竺國), where his mission is to convert impious populations to the true religion: Taoism.

The *Scripture for Unbinding Curses* is an unusual work that thus presents two specific arguments: it is at once an eschatological messenger as well as a ritual manual opposing sorcery. In the pages that follow, I seek to shed light upon its

---

32. Dz 795. 4b–5a.

33. Dz 615. 3/8a–10a. This work, dated by specialists to the mid-Tang dynasty, is essentially composed of earlier materials belonging to the liturgy of the Way of the Heavenly Master. It consists almost entirely of models of requests or petitions that the Taoist masters sent to the celestial authorities in order to free the faithful from all kinds of problems and calamities. See Nickerson (1997); and Verellen (2004).

34. See Boltz (1993): 271–272.

double vocation and to introduce some elements that help us understand the relationship, inasmuch as this can be established, between this Taoist sūtra and the Buddhist *Sūtra for the Conjuration of Bewitchments*. My translation of this latter and paraphrase of the former will be preceded in each case by a brief analysis of the texts in question.

The *Sūtra for the Conjuration of Bewitchments*, Preached by the Buddha

The *Foshuo zhoumei jing* no doubt dates to the end of the Six Dynasties or the beginning of the Sui,[35] for it is indeed listed in the Buddhist bibliographical catalogues of the late sixth century.[36] At the beginning of the seventh century, Yanzong 彥悰, in his *Zhongjing mulu* 眾經目錄, includes it in the category of "50 percent false apocrypha" (*wufen yiwei* 五分疑偽), also defined as "manmade" 人造.[37] The "one *juan*" sūtra will continuously be labelled as an apocryphon, a "fake" (*wei* 偽), by later Buddhist bibliographers.

Taking stock of the number of copies of this sūtra found among the Dunhuang manuscripts (no less than thirteen), one has the feeling that during the eighth and ninth centuries it enjoyed considerable success in the western regions of the Chinese Empire (refer to the list of manuscripts in note 7).[38] The manuscript preserved at the Nanatsu-dera attests also to its early importation to Japan.[39] This Japanese recension of the *Zhoumei jing* should date, according to the specialists, to some two centuries following the sūtra's Chinese creation,[40] an age during which sorcery was a leading preoccupation for all Japanese society, including the nobility.[41]

It should be underscored that the diffusion of the *Zhoumei jing* in Dunhuang was not due solely to its role in opposing witchcraft. In the last of its colophons, the early tenth-century manuscript Pelliot 2055 R° hints at another

---

35. Miyai (1996) considers it to be contemporaneous with Buddhist sūtras such as the *Guangting jing* (second half of the fifth century).

36. It does not figure in the *Chu sanzang jiji* 出三藏記集, by Sengyou 僧祐 (ca. 515; T. 2145, vol. 55), but is found listed among the "suspect" (*yi* 疑) sūtras of the *Zhongjing mulu* 眾經目錄, compiled in 594 by Fajing 法經 et al. (T. 2146, vol. 55, 138).

37. T. 2147, vol. 55: 4/174.

38. See Masuo (1996): 823–824. On the edition given in the *Taishō shinshū daizōkyō* (T. 2882), see above. There also exists a Korean impression of the sūtra dating to the seventeenth century.

39. Makita and Ochiai (1996), vol. 2: 701–742.

40. Miyai (1996) dates it to the eighth century. Though it is not clear, he writes, just how the *Zhoumei jing* was transmitted to the Nanatsu-dera, there can be no doubt the text was in circulation during the Nara period (710–794), an epoch that saw the full blossoming of Tantrism in China as well as the active importation of Buddhism to Japan.

41. See Miyai (1996); and Masuo (1996): 842–845.

function of the apocryphon. Like the famous *Sūtra of the Yulan Bowls* (*Yulan pen jing* 盂蘭盆經), related to the widely celebrated Buddhist Ghost Festival,[42] the *Sūtra for the Conjuration of Bewitchments* is listed among ten Buddhist scriptures of which copies were made for the traditional liturgy for the salvation of the dead, the seven week-period of mourning known as "seven seven feasts":[43]

> The faithful Zhai Fengda 翟奉達, Acting Vice Director of the Ministry of Public Works in the Department of State Affairs, had a copy of a sūtra in one scroll made on the occasion of each of the funerary ceremonies for the blessing of Lady Ma 馬, his departed wife: for the ceremonies of the first seven-day feast, the *Sūtra on Impermanence* (*Wuchang jing* 無常經); for the second feast, the *Sūtra on the Water-Moon Guanyin* (*Shuiyue Guanyin jing* 水月觀音經); for the third feast, the *Zhoumeijing;* for the fourth, the *Sūtra on the Questions Asked by a Deity* (*Tian qingwen jing* 天請問經); for the fifth feast, the *Sūtra of King Yama* (*Yanluo jing* 閻羅經); for the sixth feast, the *Sūtra for Protecting All Children* (*Huzhu tongzi jing* 護諸童子經); for the seventh feast, the *Heart Sūtra of the Prajñāpāramitā* (*Duoxin jing* 多心經); for the hundredth day (after death), the *Sūtra of the Yulan Bowls* (*Yulan pen jing*); for the first-year anniversary of her decease, the *Sūtra on the Buddha's Mother* (*Fomu jing* 佛母經); and for the third-year anniversary, the *Sūtra on Good and Evil Causes and Results* (*Shan'e yinguo jing* 善惡因緣經).[44]

The colophon informs us that the offering of these various sūtras was intended for the generation of merits to be transferred to the deceased, Mrs. Ma. At her husband's request, *nāga*s, *devarāja*s, and *vajrasattva*s, as well as the great bodhisattvas Guanyin and Dizang 地藏 (Kṣitigarbha), the protectors of dead souls, were solicited to assure the success of this mission and to guarantee her salvation.

The copying of the *Zhoumei jing* was thus commissioned by a well-known Dunhuang dignitary and Buddhist devotee, Zhai Fengda, for the third funeral service (the "third of the seven feasts" 第三七齋) performed at the end of the third week after the death of his spouse.[45] (We shall return to the eminent role that Zhai played in Dunhuang cultural and administrative life in chapter 4.)

---

42. T. 685, vol. 16. See Teiser (1988).

43. A ceremony is performed at the end of each of the seven 7-day feast periods, during a period of 49 days of the deceased's intermediate existence, then on the hundredth day, and on the successive anniversaries of the death.

44. P. 2055 R°. See Gernet and Wu (1970), vol. 1: 39–40; and Makita (1976): 338–340. For an analysis of this colophon and the ten listed scriptures, see Teiser (1994): 102–117. On the copies of these "offering sūtras," see Kuo (2000): 692–694.

45. On the controversy concerning the question of this family relationship, see Teiser (1994): 102–103n2.

Unfortunately, none of the copies of the *Zhoumei jing* intended for Mrs. Ma has survived, but there is a possibility that two of the other twelve Dunhuang recensions that have come down to us were commissioned for a memorial service intended for another deceased. Manuscripts S. 6146 and S. 2517 both bear the inscription, apparently written in an identical hand, "Linghu Jinzi gong" 令狐 進子供, "offering of Linghu Jinzi."[46] We may speculate that this person, known from other records at Dunhuang, also sponsored these hand copies of the *Zhoumei jing* for the funeral services performed on behalf of a deceased family member, as Zhai Fengda had done for his wife.

Taken as a whole, the several versions of the *Zhoumei jing* form a homogenous group, whose variants are minor. Only the Beijing manuscript 8269 and the version from the Nanatsu-dera add, at the end of the text, a series of supplementary incantations. In the Beijing manuscript these consist of three *dhāraṇīs* in pseudo-Sanskrit: a "*dhāraṇī* of the names of diseased-demons," *binggui zhouming* 病鬼咒名; a "*dhāraṇī* of the bodhisattva Bhaiṣajyaguru to bind up the demons," *Yaowang pusa fugui zhou* 藥王菩薩縛鬼咒; and a *dhāraṇī* that the text erroneously attributes to the *Laṅkāvatārasūtra* (*Lengqie jing* 楞伽經).[47] As for the addition to the Nanatsu-dera manuscript, it is spoken of as a citation from the *Regal Sūtra of the Six-Syllable Mantra* (*Liuzi shenzhou wangjing* 六字神咒王經; refer to the end of the translation below), a short apocryphal sūtra dating to the first half of the sixth century.[48]

The *Sūtra for the Conjuration of Bewitchments, Preached by the Buddha*[49]

At one time the Buddha was staying at the marvelous Dragon palace in the land of Shewei 舍衛.[50] With eyes turned down upon the obscurity [of the world below], he observed living beings committing unspeakably many sins. He revealed then the

---

46. The inscription is found under the initial title in S. 6146 and under the final title in S. 2517. The same name and the same title appear among graffiti in another Dunhuang manuscript, P. 4019 C. V°. 2. See Soymié (1995), vol. 5, part 1: 16. Members of the Linghu family belonged to Dunhuang official society since the Six Dynasties period. See Shirasu (1980): 38.

47. *Lengqie aba duolou baojing* 楞伽阿跋多羅寶經 (T. 670, vol. 16).

48. The *Regal Sūtra of the Six-Syllable Mantra, Preached by the Buddha* (*Foshuo liuzi shenzhou wangjing* 佛說六字咒王經). There exist different recensions of this apocryphon in the *Taishō shinshū daizōkyō* (T. 1044–1045, vol. 20). See Strickmann (1983): 434.

49. The version that I have selected is the one from Stein manuscript 2088. The manuscript presents an integral and meticulous version of the text. (The version of Beijing manuscript 8265, also complete, is less readable. For the Nanatsu-dera version, which is similarly complete, see Makita [1976] and Miyai [1996]). The most important variations, notably found in the *Taishō* canon and this Nanatsu-dera edition, are indicated in the footnotes.

50. Śrāvastī, ancient kingdom east of Kapilavastu.

means for all to be delivered from the paths of death and of suffering.[51] "Today," [he said,] "I will speak to you of things past as of things future. I see that once upon a time, in the Jetavana garden 給孤獨園,[52] during the age of the Buddha King of Emptiness (Kongwang fo 空王佛),[53] there was an old woman[54] who, at the entrance to a fox's den,[55] burnt animal fat in the middle of the night under the stars,[56] and so prepared bewitchments (*meigu* 魅[媚]蠱). She thus constrained (*qian* 牽) the celestial divinities above and the Five Emperors below as well as the gods of the mountains,[57] the General of the River (Hebo jiangjun 河伯將軍), and the god of the Five Ways (Wudao shen 五道神),[58] while imploring all the spirits to put her machinations into action. She made dolls of straw, human effigies, and talismans; [prepared] imprecations and curses (*yandao zhouju* 厭禱咒咀); usurped the names and patronyms of people; and armed herself with pins, needles, and clods of yellow earth.[59] Facing the stars, she soliloquized in a state of trance. She took possession of garments and belts, cloth of silk or of five-colored threads, jars or earthenware utensils [belonging] to a household, [and she also seized] horse- or mule-hair, cow-hair or wool, [and] pig- or dog-hair;[60] [in short, she used] all sorts of objects[61] [that belonged] to a family in order to assemble her [sorceress'] kit. She put to use even the door wedges,[62] even the spoons and chopsticks of the house, to make her witchcraft. Besides that, [she fabricated] horses in hemp or madder[63] with riders mounted upon them, [which she] pierced through the heart and liver, pinning the hands, feet, eyes, kidneys, and back. With the aid of hair and of clay, of five-colored silk, clothing, underwear, and belts, she cursed pastures and fields.[64] She grasped hold of a dress and waved it above a cliff

51. I follow here the Nanatsu-dera edition.
52. The garden of Prince Jeta in the kingdom of Śrāvastī, where Śākyamuni preached.
53. Dharmagahanābhyudgatarāja, the Buddha King of Immateriality. See Forte [(1976): 159 et seq., 271–280.
54. Some versions, like Beijing 8266, give "two old women." The edition of the *Taishō shinshū daizōkyō* omits two characters, consequently inducing an error in the punctuation and reading (as "an old fox").
55. Lit. "wild fox's den."
56. Lit. "the sun, the moon, and the five planets."
57. S. 3852 adds "the god of the tree," *shushen* 樹神.
58. This is a divinity of the infernal realm in charge of the five paths of rebirth, or five *gati*. See Dudbridge (1996–1997), who mentions the *Zhoumei jing*, p. 95.
59. The clod of earth is found several times as a vehicle for moving while remaining invisible in the novel *Investiture of the Gods* (Fengshen yanyi 封神演義), by Xu Zhonglin 許仲琳 (sixteenth century), Shanghai guji chubanshe ed. (1989), chaps. 44 and 48.
60. The Nanatsu-dera edition mentions only the hair of pigs, sheep, and dogs.
61. Lit. "of the Five Elements." The Nanatsu-dera edition gives the character 形 instead of 行, which does not make sense.
62. I follow here the *Taishō shinshū daizōkyō* edition.
63. *Masou ma* 麻蒐,馬. Other versions give *mazou ma* 麻鄒馬. The meaning of the character *zou* remains obscure in this expression. See Miyai (1996): 723n13.
64. I follow here the *Taishō shinshū daizōkyō* edition.

while monologuing. She utilized, moreover, statues of human heads, or, [under the influence] of demons, she prepared talismans, imprecations, and baleful spells. She fabricated human images and uttered senseless words. She thus bewitched the cows, sheep, horses, chickens, dogs, and pigs of a household, provoking maledictions to befall the folk. She realized images of horses and demonical deities, or of cows, sheep, pigs, or dogs, and [thus] she bound their proprietors with curses. Attaching no more value to life than to death, brutally[65] slaying the virtuous and the good, she acted by herself[66] or by teaching another [how to bring about] a thousand calamities and ten thousand sins.

"May the three beams and six pillars[67] turn back against their instigators! May evil and calamity by themselves turn back against them to exterminate them![68] Post-haste, may they flee 3,610 li away and [thus be put] beyond the state [of doing harm] and this without delay!

"I invite the divine kings of the Green Emperor of the east to come and devour the sorceress' belly. I call upon the divine kings of the Red Emperor of the south to come and devour the sorceress' feet. I invite the divine kings of the White Emperor of the west to come and devour the sorceress' head. I invite the divine kings of the Black Emperor of the north to come and eat her eyes. I call upon the divine kings of the Yellow Emperor of the center to come and devour her hands."[69]

In the assembly, there was a bodhisattva named Great Force (Dali 大力, Mahābala) who adjusted his garments in order to prostrate himself [at the feet] of the Buddha and to address him: "[Your] disciples, O world-honored one, [are incapable] of distinguishing merit from sin. I have ascertained that in the world there are numerous beings [who commit] the five mortal sins (wuni 五逆) and give no credit to the pathways of good. [They entice one another] with pleasures and diversions[70] and are constantly motivated by bad thoughts. They are ignorant of the means to be reborn in the celestial paradise in order to enjoy happiness there, and they do not know of the torments that exist in the infernal dungeons. They devour one another and bewitch the virtuous and the good. I beseech [you] with all of my vows, O world-honored one, [that you may furnish] your disciples with clarifications and explications. For in attaining the Way, [we may be up to] saving the whole world."

The Buddha then informed the bodhisattva Great Force: "Down to this day,

---

65. Other versions give "indifferently."

66. I follow here the Nanatsu-dera edition, which adds "acts by herself" 若自作.

67. The meaning of this sentence, which remained incomprehensible for Miyai (1996; 723n22), becomes clear only thanks to an analogous expression in the *Scripture for Unbinding Curses, Revealed by the Most High Lord Lao* (see below).

68. For Miyai, this passage is also hardly understandable; see Miyai (1996): 723n23.

69. The Nanatsu-dera edition only lists three among the Five Emperors (east, north, and center).

70. Versions S. 418 and S. 3852 give "[They encourage] each other to eat fish and meat."

you have not yet understood. I will therefore clarify and develop [my teachings] for you. Listen attentively![71] I have sent to earth the four celestial kings (*devarājas*) and other [divinities] so that they will [strive] without respite in order to cure all evils, [so that they] will expel them in haste to a distance of thousands of *li* and be [forever] rid of them, [thanks to] the incantation that says:

"'Sire sorcerer Panshidu 槃市都, Mother sorceress slave Panshinu 槃市奴,[72] I know your names, I know your names! If you fabricate evil spells, they will return against you. If you teach anyone [to make them], you will be automatically annihilated.

"'On this day I invite the *deva*s of the four heavens to come and register[73] the names of the sorcerers. I curse these latter, that their heads be broken into seven pieces like the branches of the Ali tree 阿梨![74]

"'I call at once a Brahman (Poluomen 波羅門) that he come to curse the sorcerers so that their heads be broken into seven pieces like the branches of the Ali tree!

"'I invite the *nāgarājas* of the four heavens, that they come to curse the sorcerers so that their heads be broken into seven pieces like the branches of the Ali tree!

"'I invite here the bull-headed Abang 牛頭阿滂,[75] that he come to curse the sorcerers. May they not remain here; otherwise may their heads be broken into seven pieces like the branches of the Ali tree!

"'The Buddha possesses great *dhāraṇīs* to curse the sorcerers[76] so that their heads . . .[77]

"'I call here the bodhisattva Universal Virtue (Puxian 普賢, Samantabhadra), that he come to curse the sorcerers so that their heads . . .

"'I call upon the bodhisattva Changing Light (Gengming) 更明, that he come to curse the sorcerers so that their heads . . .

"'I call upon the bodhisattva Great Knowledge (Dazhi 大智), that he come to curse the sorcerers so that their heads . . .'"

(*Following is a lengthy enumeration of bodhisattvas, with the same formulae of invitation and exhortation imposing the sanction. I abridge it here, preserving only the list of bodhisattvas. The variants found in the edition of the* Taishō shinshū daizōkyō *are given in brackets.*)

---

71. I follow here the *Taishō shinshū daizōkyō* edition.

72. Version S. 418 and *Taishō shinshū daizōkyō* give Panyongdu 永 and Panshinu 石.

73. The *Taishō shinshū daizōkyō* version gives *lailu* 來錄 instead of *laishe* 來攝, "to come and collect."

74. The Ali tree or *arjaka* bears perfumed white flowers. When they fall, its branches break, it is said, into seven pieces. See Demiéville et al. (1929), vol. 1: 37.

75. Guardian of hell, represented with the head and hooves of a bull. See Demiéville et al. (1929), vol. 1, "Abō."

76. The text here seems corrupted; therefore I follow the other Dunhuang versions (S. 2882, S. 418, etc.).

77. Each of the following invocations ends in the same manner: ". . . so that their heads be broken into seven pieces like the branches of the Ali tree."

" 'I call upon the bodhisattvas: Xiangguang 象光 [Delicate Light, Mengguang 蒙光], Great Light (Daguang 大光 [Fire Light, Huoguang 火光]),[78] Variegated Light (Huaguang 華光), Moon Light (Yueguang 月光, Candraprabha), Dragon Light (Longguang 龍光), Venus (Mingxing 明星),[79] Thousand Yang (Qianyang 千陽), Valiant Force (Yongli 勇力), Universal Light (Puming 普明, Samantaprabha), Great Brightness (Daming 大明), Zhuanlun 轉輪 (Cakravartī), Uniform Light (Tongguang 同光), Midday (Rizhong 日中), Tree King (Shuwang 樹王), Celestial Dragon (Longtian 龍天), Earthquake (Didong 地動), and Established (Jianli 建立).[80]

" 'I invite here the divine kings (shenwang 神王) of the Green Emperor of the east to come and devour the sorceress' belly.

" 'I call upon the divine kings of the Red Emperor of the south to come and devour the sorceress' feet.

" 'I invite the divine kings of the White Emperor of the west to come and devour the sorceress' head.

" 'I invite the divine kings of the Black Emperor of the north to come and eat her eyes.

" 'I call upon the divine kings of the Yellow Emperor of the center to come and devour her hands.

" 'May they [scourge them] incessantly!

" 'I call here [the divinities] of the sun and the moon, of the Five Stars and the Twenty-eight Lunar Mansions. May they apprehend the sorcerers and chase them for a thousand li!

" 'May the giant beasts of the east come to devour the sorceresses' bodies!

" 'May the millipedes and centipedes of the south come to eat the sorceresses' eyes!

" 'May the white elephants of the west come to devour the sorceresses' heads!

" 'May the black birds[81] of the north come to peck at the sorceresses' hearts!

" 'May the dragon-kings of the Yellow Emperor of the center come to devour the sorceresses' bodies!'

" 'I see the sorceresses with their bulging eyes. In a frenzy, having lost all semblance of humanity, they run amok, whether at people's doors, or in their homes, or while [perched] atop a millstone, or in the open fields where they bolt about without respite. On the first or the fifteenth day of the first month, or on the days that begin the four seasons,[82] they burn fat and recite interminable spells.

---

78. Other versions give also Huoguang pusa.

79. The Nanatsu-dera edition gives "the bodhisattva Bright Sovereign," Minghuang 明皇 (the character huang is probably a mistake for the character xing).

80. The Nanatsu-dera edition gives "Established Cloud," Jianyun 建雲.

81. The Taishō shinshū daizōkyō edition gives "black elephants" for "black birds."

82. Shijie ri 時節日.

"'I know your names, so move on![83] Make haste to disappear![84] Whether sitting or turned upside down,[85] may you be annihilated! And may your head be split in seven pieces like the branches of the Ali tree!

"'As soon as they provoke malefactions,[86] the incantations of the bodhisattvas will exterminate them on the spot, irremediably and without possible recourse!'"

The World-Venerated One spoke again: "Today, for all beings of the ten directions, and for all you good men and good women, I have pronounced this Sūtra for the conjuration of spells."

All of the Buddhas of the Ten Directions and the Seven Buddhas of the Past, the Sixteen Princely Buddhas,[87] the great heavenly bodhisattvas, the celestial arhats, the great kings of the four heavens, the *nāgas*, the eight categories [of beings], all the divinities of the different heavens and men [who have attained] the four stages [leading to] *nirvāṇa* are gathered together under the Dragon-Flower Tree[88] on the summit of Mount Sumeru. [All the members of] this innumerable assembly[89] request [the path of] salvation.

May the monks and nuns, *upāsaka*s and *upāsikā*s [laymen and -women], and men and women of goodwill burn incense and venerate the Buddha, receive this sūtra, and make it the object of an uninterrupted cult. Thus will they obtain grace. If those who are afflicted or in pain can give rise to good thoughts, they will attain all the happiness of paradise. Before reciting this sūtra, [one must] bathe, practice the rites, burn incense, and worship it. In this way, one will be able to deliver oneself from bewitchment. Seven recitations are necessary to break the heads of the sorcerers into seven pieces like the branches of the Ali tree and to dispel all sufferings.

All the members of the great assembly hearing this sūtra rejoiced and, prostrating themselves [before the Buddha], swore their allegiance.

(*In Beijing 8269 [on which see above] this last sentence is omitted, as it also is in the version from the Nanatsu-dera, where it is replaced by the following passage:*)

Quzhi quzhu 佉知佉注, *qukunzhi* 佉昆知, *jianshou jianshou* 緘壽緘壽, *duozhi pozhi* 多知波知!

---

83. Lit. "you may not stay here!" 不得停止.
84. The *Taishō shinshū daizōkyō* edition gives "hurry up and vanish in the world beyond" (lit. "other places," *tuofa* 他方).
85. The *Taishō shinshū daizōkyō* gives "standing," *li* 立.
86. Lit. "they produce red mouths and red tongues" 生赤口赤舌. The expression "red tongues" seems to be a synonym for "curses"; see Miyai (1996): 727.
87. Shiliu wangzi 十六王子. The buddhas reigning over the eight directions: see Mochizuki (1936–1963), vol. 3: 2406.
88. *Nāgapuṣpa,* the bodhi tree.
89. The expression 平(評)量冢生, which figures in all the versions (except in S. 3852), is incomprehensible. Perhaps the character *ping* is erroneous and one should read *wuliang* 無量 or *xuliang* 許量, as suggested in note 14 (p. 1383) of the *Taishō shinshū daizōkyō*. As for S. 3852, it gives the characters 謫稱矣云, which do not make any more sense in this context.

And why is it so? There is nothing in this world that surpasses the accumulation of good deeds and the fields of merit.

Quzhi quzhi 知, *qukunzhi, jianshou jianshou, duozhi pozhi! zhidoudi* 知兜帝, *amidi* 阿彌帝, *agudi* 阿固帝!

As for the incantations, [in case of] malefic ones, these are the incantations that one uses subversively.

Moxiupo 摩休破, *wumotuo* 烏摩陀, *tutuomi* 徒陀彌,

Quyu potuoti 佉傴波陀提, *tutuomi* 徒陀彌, *pintoumodi* 頻頭摩帝!

Zhidizhi duopoti 至帝至多波提!

Apai zhantuo paixi pohe 阿箄旃陀箄悉波呵!

May one observe and recite the *Regal Sūtra of the Six-Syllable Mantra* (*Liuzi shenzhou wangjing* 六字神咒王經). This mantra has the power to bring back to life the branches and foliage of dead trees and so, a fortiori, protects men from all suffering and unhappiness.[90]

The "Conversion of the Barbarians" and the Taoist Strategy against Sorcery

As the paraphrase presented below will demonstrate, the true raison d'être for the *Scripture for Unbinding Curses, Revealed by the Most High Lord Lao* would appear to be more ideological than ritual. It declares its message to be intended, above all, for the "barbarians of the West," of whom it already knows that only the smallest minority ("six in ninety") possess an affinity (*yuan* 緣) with Laojun's teaching and so will be able to comprehend it. Thanks to the diffusion of this scripture and of Taoist rituals, these rare, privileged individuals may hope to be rid of the scourge of witchcraft and to obtain salvation. The *Scripture for Unbinding Curses* is therefore clearly inscribed within the "conversion of the barbarians" (*huahu*) tradition, which was mentioned in the introduction.

Does our knowledge of the surviving *huahu* literature permit us to determine to what period our *Scripture for Unbinding Curses* should be assigned? Comparative data are too meager to situate it precisely. The eschatological message of our anti-sorcery scripture and its theory of "three ages of antiquity" (*sangu* 三古)[91] resemble those of another Taoist work of the *huahu* tradition discovered at Dunhuang, the *Marvelous Scripture of Supreme Lingbao on Laozi Converting the Barbarians* (*Taishang lingbao Laozi huahu miaojing* 太上靈寶老子化胡妙經, S. 2081),

---

90. This last sentence is found in almost identical form in the *Regal Sūtra of the Six-Syllable Mantra* (see below).

91. In the *Scripture for Unbinding Curses*, Laojun's intervention is placed during "mid-antiquity" (*zhonggu* 中古), which follows the golden age of "high antiquity" (*shanggu* 上古).

which dates to the end of the sixth century.[92] But our text seems closer, with respect to the setting of its revelation, to another, slightly later version of the "conversion of the barbarians" legend, one that has also come down to us thanks to the preservation of the Dunhuang collections, and that dates at the latest to the second half of the seventh century. Like our Taoist sūtra, this *Laozi huahu jing* (P. 2007) places its action in Khotan. There, in 1028 B.C.E., at the monastery of Pimo 毘摩 Laozi, with his disciple Yin Xi's aid, teaches the *Book of the Conversion of the Barbarians* to an assembly of divinities and Central and Southern Asian sovereigns.[93] In all events, it seems plausible that the *Scripture for Unbinding Curses* dates to the early Tang dynasty. Following, I offer a detailed paraphrase of its contents, with some verse passages given in translation.

The *Scripture for Unbinding Curses,* *Revealed by the Most High Lord Lao*

It is in Khotan, at the site of Salvation by immortality (Xiandu zhi suo 仙度之所), that Lord Lao reveals this "sūtra" to Yin Xi, the Guardian of the Pass. He explains to him that moral purity, religious rectitude, and the harmony of High Antiquity (*shanggu* 上古) have given way to the moral decadence characteristic of the end of the world (*moshi* 末世). Human beings are false-hearted. Instead of doing good, they perpetuate evil. Instead of respecting the Dao, they turn to perverse divinities and devote themselves to sorcery (*zhouzu* 咒詛) in order to bring harm to the lives of others, whence the proliferation of demons.

Laojun exhorts Yin Xi to listen to him, arguing that these people of the "intermediate age" (*zhonggu* 中古) have thus propagated the practices of sorcery (*yandao* 厭禱). They utilize the demons of heaven and earth by drawing images of them, writing their names in temples and sanctuaries, and forming secret pacts with them. They spit water, leap, and gesticulate, with bulging eyes and wide-open mouths. In this way, "they do harm to good people and teach others how to do evil."

Faithful men and women, who are victims of these bewitchments (*zhouzu yandao*), after taking the indispensable aromatic bath, must install an altar and invite a Taoist of the Three Grottoes (*Sandong daoshi* 三洞道士) to recite this sūtra in order to generate some merit. In this way, their illnesses will be cured. The faithful who have

---

92. See Anna Seidel's study and translation (1984).

93. T. 2139, vol. 54. See Zürcher (1959): 303. Khotan and its Pimo monastery were already associated with Laozi's "conversion of the barbarians" in the *History of the Northern Dynasties* (*Beishi* 北史), compiled during the years 630–650 by Li Yanshou 李延壽 and covering the years 368–618. The text reads: "Five hundred *li* to the west of Khotan, there is the Pimo monastery. It is said that this is the place where Laozi converted the barbarians and became Buddha" (*Beishi*, chap. 97, 3209). See also Zhang and Rong (1993): 291–292.

been cursed can also be delivered by rendering a cult to the Emperors of the Five Directions, who, invited with their following of nine million horsemen, arrive from the four cardinal points and the center, from the zenith and the nadir, in order to chase away evil spells and to assure well-being and longevity. To this end, one must recite this rhymed incantation:

> The Law is great and majestic.
> The sky is round and the earth square.
> In the sky are the nine pillars,
> On earth the nine beams.
> Let the sorcerers suffer their own villainy!
> Six pillars, three beams,
> Bewitchments evaporate,
> Three beams, six pillars,
> To return to their instigators.
> Six *jia* 甲, six *yi* 乙,
> That bewitchments depart in haste.
> Six *bing* 丙, six *ding* 丁,
> That bewitchments circulate no more.
> Six *wu* 午, six *si* 巳,
> That bewitchments appear no more.
> Six *geng* 庚, six *xin* 辛,
> That bewitchments are ineffective.
> Six *ren* 壬, six *gui* 癸,
> That bewitchments self-destruct,
> That maledictions resolve themselves quickly.
> In haste, in haste, in accord with the Law!

The Generals of the Three and the Five (Sanwu jiangjun 三五將君), the Emissaries of the Eight Winds (Bafeng shizhe 八風使者), and the Vassal Lords of the Nine Regions (Jiuzhou she 九州社) are also called to assemble at the head of ten thousand generals and tens of millions of troops in order to halt the sorcerers: "May their heads be broken into seven pieces!"

Laojun reveals the method of this *Scripture to Unbind Maledictions and Bewitchments* (*Jiechu zhouzu yanmei jing* 解除咒詛厭魅經). The faithful for whom it is recited see their illnesses cured; their misfortunes and calamities are dissipated. They know harmony and health, happiness and longevity. Laojun recites a *gāthā* (*jie* 偈):

> Formerly I traveled in China
> And I ascended to unsurpassed heaven.
> Today I betake myself to India (Zhuguo 竺國)
> To convert all beings.

Among ninety, there are but six

Who have an affinity [with my teaching].

One must bring those who are faithful

To transmit it until it spreads by itself.

Pure and exalted hearts will never slide back.

They obtain rebirth in unsurpassed heaven.

Wherever this sūtra is recited,

People will gain longevity,

The ten thousand transcendent beings protect them,

All diseases disappear.

Happiness is assured in this life,

The body is strong like gold and stone.

One attains the realization of the unsurpassed Law.

Calamities evaporate and felicity arrives by itself.

Laojun concludes his sermon. The sages assembled around him prostrate themselves and retire with great satisfaction.

The Two Sūtras for Undoing Spells

Though not perfectly echoing one another, the Taoist *Scripture for Unbinding Curses* and the Buddhist *Sūtra for the Conjuration of Bewitchments* contain many analogies that demonstrate their proximity. One notes first of all that the two texts recommend the use of the exorcistic formula "May their heads be broken in seven pieces!" (*tou po zuo qifen* 頭破作七分) hurled against the sorcerers.[94] Also significant is the presence in our texts of the injunction "May they [male sorcerers or female witches] who cast [the bewitchment] themselves or who instruct others to cast it suffer in return its noxious effects."[95] Finally, let us turn our attention to another element that is even more striking, an enigmatic expression that appears in identical fashion in both sources: "May the three beams and six pillars turn back against their instigators!"[96] If the second part of the phrase, "turn back against their instigators," seems relatively common—one finds it in the passage on sorcery from the *Guanyin Sūtra* to which I have referred above[97]—the occurrence in each work of a formula so unusual as "three beams and six pillars" cannot be the result of sheer coincidence. Incomprehensible in the Buddhist sūtra, its sense is somewhat clearer in the Taoist work, as

---

94. To this formula, the *Zhoumei jing* always adds "like the branches of the Ali tree!"

95. Version S. 2088 of the *Zhoumei jing* gives (汝)若作魅蠱者反受其殃汝教他作身自滅亡, while the Taoist version (p. 1b) more succinctly says: 若自作若教他作者令受其殃.

96. Dz 652. 2a: 三梁六柱還其主. *Zhoumei jing*: 三梁六柱還著本人.

97. The *Guanyin jing* says: *huanzhao yu benren* 還著於本人.

may be seen in the foregoing passage, which seems to suggest that one summons the support of heaven and earth by invoking the earth's beams and the sky's pillars to chase away evil and send it back to its author.

Not only do these stylistic indicators disclose an unmistakable genetic connection between the two scriptures, but so too do the ritual elements common to them. Both works advocate the invocation of the same exorcistic pantheon as the panacea against bewitchment. The markers of the Ten Celestial Stems of the sexagesimal calendar, on the one hand, and the Five Emperors governing the five directions, on the other, are the deities that the *Scripture for Unbinding Curses* summons to drive away curses. If the *Zhoumei jing* relies on *deva*s and bodhisattvas to expel the witches' evil, it also "invites" the Emperors of the Five Directions and their divine escorts to a less noble mission—that is, to aggressively devour the witches. It goes without saying that this phalanx of anthropophagous deities is not of Buddhist extraction. The Five Emperors together with the deified calendrical signs were in fact already assigned an anti-sorcery function in the Way of the Heavenly Master's "Petition for Unbinding Maledictions," from the *Petition Almanac of Master Red Pine*. There, the five "lords" (*jun* 君) of foreign ethnicities (Yi 夷, Man 蠻, Rong 戎, Di 狄, and Qin 秦) were regrouped in five pairs corresponding to each of the five directions and to the four seasons, with the addition of all four taken together, and charged with the expulsion of witchcraft. It was indeed crucial to solicit the proper seasonal divinity in order to determine the period of the year during which the curse was cast.[98] For the *Zhoumei jing* as well, each seasonal change was indeed a time acutely favorable for bewitchments.

The precise filiation of the *Scripture for Unbinding Curses* and the *Sūtra for the Conjuration of Bewitchments* remains an open question, but taking account of the historical, philological, and ritual evidence that I have produced, one may reasonably speculate that the Taoist scripture is a Tang-dynasty, *huahu*-genre response to the Buddhist anti-sorcery sūtra, whose relative ancestry is

---

98. *Chisongzi zhangli* (Dz 615. 3/9a–b). A more ancient Taoist work, the *Scripture of the Divine Cinnabar of the Nine Cauldrons of the Yellow Emperor* (*Huangdi jiuding shendan jing* 黃帝九鼎神丹經), cited in the *Baopuzi neipian, juan* 4, Wang Ming ed.: 74), alludes also to the same calendrical pantheon, which it places under the government of the Five Emperors. The edition of this work in the Taoist Canon presents a set of "talismans of the Five Emperors" (*wudi shenfu* 五帝神符), each of which is associated with a sexagesimal binomial (Dz 885. 19/6a–8b). An ancient Shangqing text, the *Shangqing gaoshang yuchen fengtai qusu shangjing* 上清高上玉晨鳳臺曲素上經, bears also talismans for the five celestial branches (Dz 1372. 15a–22a). These calendrical divinities are found, much later, during the Ming period, in the pantheon of the Heavenly Masters organization of Mount Longhu 龍虎山. See the *Secret Register One and Orthodox of the Most High for Unbinding Curses of the Five Tones* (*Taishang zhengyi jie wuyin zhouzu bilu* 太上正一解五音咒詛祕錄, Dz 1217. 1b–2a), mentioned below.

confirmed and which had drawn some of its materials from still earlier medieval Taoist sources. This type of Buddho-Taoist exchange, consisting of responses over a short span of time, well illustrates the complexity and diversity of interactions between the two traditions.

Offensives and Counteroffensives: Sorcery and Exorcism

It seems to me to be appropriate, in the final parts of this chapter, that we distance ourselves to some degree from the materials that I have just introduced in order to envision, from a more global perspective, sorcery and the religious expedients created to combat it during the medieval period. I have chosen to present the material below with reference to three types of ritual action: action by image and writing, verbal action, and action by means of drugs.

As is clear in the translation of the *Zhoumei jing* given above, in the eyes of the medieval Chinese, the manufacturer of evil spells is before all else a woman. She is a demented and obscene creature who displays all the signs of the savage: she officiates in solitude on crucial dates and at night, out in the open in a remote wilderness, at the entry to a foxhole, or on the edge of a precipice. She exposes herself in the very midst of the fields or else perched on a grain mill. When in trance, "having lost all semblance of human appearance" and "with bulging eyes," she monologues, yells out "senseless words," and recites "interminable spells," while brandishing the possessions and clothing of the members of the household that is the target of her venomous deeds. Such is the witch as conforms to a universal cliché: she is marginal, enraged, and lascivious, at the borderline of madness. To reinforce this stereotype, the *Zhoumei jing* associates the witch with the fox or, worse, the "wild fox."[99] The female fox, a tantalizing succubus who preys upon the male essence, is a theme that has always captivated the Chinese imagination. The amalgamation of the woman's supposed sexual perversity and propensity for evil is manifest in the lexical ambiguity of terms like *mei* 媚 and *yao* 妖, which signify "sorceress" as well as "to charm" or "to seduce."[100] The official annals have also contributed to underwriting the assimilation of sorcery to femininity. It is certainly not a coincidence that, among the cases of bewitchment related in the *History of the Han,* the majority of those accused are female. These include both professional shamans (*wu*) like Li Ruxu 李女須, who, during the first century B.C.E., offered her malicious services to the

---

99. On the term "wild fox" in the context of Tantric sorcery, see Strickmann (1996): 157.

100. The version of Nanatsu-dera gives the characters *meigui* 媚鬼, "sorcerer-demon" (col. 41), to designate the witches. Versions S. 2088 and T. 2882 prefer the homophonic character *mei* 魅, which originally meant "demon of the forests and mountains" (often depicted as a quadruped with a human face) but means, in this context, "to bewitch."

prince Liu Xu 劉胥 in order to facilitate his attempts to succeed to the imperial throne, as well as amateur witches such as the dowager empress Chen and her daughter, who in the second century C.E. were severely chastised for their "women's witchcraft" (*furen meidao* 婦人媚道).[101] Twelfth-century China would continue to imagine the sorceress concocting the *gu*, naked and dishevelled, busy with a nocturnal sacrifice.[102]

These witches' sabbaths *à la chinoise* have the allure of a grotesque profanophany, an indecent transgression of liturgy. In fact, in the trappings of the Chinese sorcerers, the historian of religions, as also the anthropologist, will not fail to recognize the ordinary tools of the shaman or the exorcist. As in other civilizations, where "black magic" and the officially recognized "orthodox magic" are close relations and represent two faces of one and the same tradition, the medieval Chinese instigator of evil and his opponents have recourse to analogous weapons, whether symbolic representations such as images, effigies, and talismans, or else verbal formulae: incantations, *dhāraṇīs*, prayers, injunctions, and imprecations.[103] In soliciting the agency of supernatural beings, they all serve the malefactors just as well as the exorcists who oppose them. The same drugs may operate, too, as poisons or antidotes, according to need. In addition to the *Scripture for Unbinding Curses* and the *Zhoumei jing,* the works from which I draw extracts here disclose the concrete procedures of bewitchment and exorcism in medieval times and so permit us to demonstrate the veracity of these principles of similarity and reciprocity.

Generally speaking, the techniques of sorcery, inasmuch as they are succinctly described by their detractors, are close to those picturesquely related by our Buddhist sūtra throughout. The *Sūtra of Consecration,* for instance, offers a concise overview of the sorcerers' work, which, at this point of our investigation, will appear familiar to us:

> There are some who use the divinities of the mountains and the demonic spirits of the trees, the gods of the sun and moon, or the spirits of the Southern and Northern Dippers and enter into pacts with them in order to realize all sorts of bewitchments. They make use of peoples' names, fabricate effigies of them, creating talismans and spells whose aim is to bewitch them.[104]

---

101. See Loewe (1970); and Twitchett and Loewe (1986): 170–171. Harper (1998): 158–159, without providing further evidence, relies on a Mawangdui document to affirm that, in antiquity, "the compound *wugu* reflects the perception that women's magic was inherently dangerous (especially for men)."

102. See Obringer (1997): 248.

103. See, for example, for medieval Europe, Schmitt (2001), chap. 13.

104. Chap. 12 (T. 1331, vol. 21: 523b). The passage is mentioned by Miyai (1996): 736.

The Taoists evoke witchcraft's methods, broadly speaking, in the same terms. We have seen that the *Scripture for Unbinding Curses* denounces the utilization of the demons of the heavens and earth (i.e., the pagan divinities venerated in temples and sanctuaries, *miaoshe* 廟社), as well as the fabrication of effigies, misappropriation of individuals' names, and pacts with occult forces (*zhoushi* 咒誓). It decries those sorcerers who dance while in trance, with "bulging eyes and wide-open mouths," who leap, gesticulate, and spray water from their mouths. The aforementioned *Petition Almanac of Master Red Pine,* which is contemporaneous with the Buddhist *Sūtra of Consecration,* enumerates the same types of expedients for "bewitching" (*yandao* 厭禱): the constraining of celestial and terrestrial forces (*qianyin tiandi* 牽引天地), summoning of demons and divinities (*zhigui hushen* 指鬼呼神), and curses (*zhouzu* 咒詛). The sorcerer, whether he be a professional (that is, a heretical master, *xieshi* 邪師) with an army of demonical spirits in his service or an ordinary amateur (an evildoer, *e'ren* 惡人), uses the image and the name, as well as the tufts of hair or nail clippings of his victim to injure or kill him.[105] The impaling of human effigies with a knife, it should be noted, appears to have persisted throughout centuries. In their *Secret Register One and Orthodox of the Most High for Unbinding Curses of the Five Tones (Taishang zhengyi jie wuyin zhouzu bilu* 太上正一解五音咒詛祕錄), with which they exorcised those possessed, the Ming-dynasty Heavenly Masters of Mount Longhu 龍虎山 still denounced the sorcerers who, like their predecessors, "fabricate images of their victims and pierce them with the jabs of a knife."[106]

The same violent customs are described as well in premodern Chinese literature. The sixteenth-century novel *Investiture of the Gods (Fengshen yanyi* 封神演義), which endlessly depicts the power struggles among the rulers of antiquity, gives a vivid account of the manner in which the Prime Minister of the future Zhou dynasty was the target of a bewitchment ordered by his political enemies and conducted by the expert hand of a sorcerer, who

> had edified an earthen terrace where he established an altar. At its summit he strung up a straw dummy upon which he wrote the Prime Minister's name. . . . Afterwards, the sorcerer unknotted his hair, brandished a sword, and performed the step of the Great Dipper, all the while reciting incantations and pressing into the air talismans formed with his magical seal.[107]

---

105. Dz 615. 3/8a–10a. See Verellen (2004): 320.
106. Dz 1217. 3a (fifteenth century C.E.).
107. Xu (1989), chap. 44. Chapter 48 of the same novel describes in similar terms another case of bewitchment. I warmly thank Danielle Éliasberg for having drawn my attention to these passages.

Manifestly, nothing ever changed in the realm of witchcraft traditions, and all the ingredients of the basic Chinese exorcism were distorted for evil ends, including the famous apotropaic choreography of the Great Dipper ritual, of which more will be said in chapter 4 of this volume and which has been turned here into a murderous weapon.

Effigy, Icon, and Writs

It may seem astonishing to encounter, among the crude equipment of Chinese sorcery, such universal tools of witchcraft as puppets and needles. Nevertheless, we know that in China the ritual utilization of effigies is ancient and that it is not, no more than the other techniques mentioned above, the instrument of evildoers alone.[108] By means of symbolic action upon a statuette, the exorcist is able to expel a demon or cure the person represented. The Taoist rites of "replacement bodies" (*tishen* 替身), intended in particular to undo cases of possession due to ancestral vengeance, are well known.[109] Chinese Tantrism, too, made abundant use of human figurines in order to chase away evil, but equally, as we shall see, to transmit it within the context of ritual procedures considered to be "orthodox."

In contradistinction to funerary statuettes (the figurines of substitution, *yong* 俑) placed in tombs to assure the protection of the deceased,[110] the puppets created by the sorcerer as by the exorcist were not destined to endure. They were, as attested in numerous Tantric texts, ephemeral icons, owing both to the nature of the material from which they were fabricated and to the harsh treatment to which they were subjected.[111] We have seen that, as was the case of the dummy of the Prime Minister of the Zhou, the effigies made by the sorcerers of the *Zhoumei jing* were in straw (reed or hemp). The witch pierced the anatomy of the puppet with her pins and needles, thereby reaching at a distance the neuralgic or vital zones of the victim's body. The physical integrity of the target being in this way symbolically altered or disordered, he would fall ill and succumb.

Complementing the effigy of substitution, Chinese sorcery took recourse

---

108. On several occasions, wooden effigies are mentioned in the Mawangdui manuscripts. See Harper (1996): 244 et seq.

109. See Schipper (1985a).

110. Such wooden funerary effigies (notably in peach wood) have been discovered in Mawangdui as well as in later tombs. One statue in cypress wood has also been excavated in the grave of a woman belonging to a local noble family from Jiangxi, dating to 1090: see Hansen (1996): 286.

111. See the example of a Tantric exorcism of the Tang, cited by Davis (2001): 122–123, in which a puppet made of straw is beaten and then imprisoned and buried in a sealed jar.

to other ruses in order to act upon its victims. For this, it employed their organic waste (hair of the head and body, nail clippings), materials they had worn (clothing, threads, and patches), various "bodily extensions" such as objects of everyday utility (kitchen utensils, chopsticks, spoons, pieces of furniture, etc.), as well as hairs from their domestic animals. All such elements having direct contact with the person targeted could serve as the vehicle for transmitting him ill.

Now, the strategies elaborated for opposing sorcery by medieval Chinese Tantrism called upon just the same techniques to turn a hex back upon its promulgator. Exorcists fabricated dolls of clay, wax, dough, or other fragile substances, which they consecrated prior to inflicting upon them their final ill treatment. Stabbed or beaten, flayed or slashed, crushed or broken, these icons were violently reduced to debris. The *Collection of Dhāraṇī Sūtras* (*Tuoluoni ji jing* 陀羅尼集經), one of the first collections of Tantric rituals diffused in China, announced the three specific types of bewitchments currently reported in the nosographies given in the medieval materia medica and proposed methods to eradicate them through the maltreatment and destruction of statuettes:

> To cure those illnesses caused by *gu* poisons (*yangu* 厭蠱), the "savage path" (*yedao* 野道), and the "demon cat" (*maogui* 貓鬼), one models a human effigy in dough made from wheat flour. One consecrates a *vajra* staff (*jingang zhang* 金剛杖) to smash the statuette. Its fragments are burnt like incense, and all the bewitching demons who plant trouble are destroyed and made incapable of doing injury![112]

Other objects even more unusual were also imagined to neutralize the sorcerer or to return his evil to him:

> In case of bewitchment induced by any malefic person whosoever, having as its consequence the [victim's] losing his mind, one should procure the bone of a male human being, make a stake from it, and consecrate it with a mantra recited 1,008 times. One then drives it into the earth, at the door of the bewitcher.[113]

One detects in this stake of bone as recommended in this morbid procedure an analogy to the *kīla* (dagger) frequently used in the Tibetan world, as well as to the wooden spikes sculpted or painted with a human face, such as those unearthed in the regions of Dunhuang and Gaochang 高昌, in Xinjiang. Some twenty centimeters in length, in some cases bearded, these stake-effigies were

---

112. T. 901, vol. 18: 8/860; see also 2/797 and 8/858 on wax effigies. On the three specific types of bewitchment, see below.

113. T. 901, vol. 18: 5/833.

buried, apparently for exorcistic ends, as confirmed by the inscriptions "substitute person" (*dairen* 代人) or "peach man" (*taoren* 桃人), with which they are sometimes inscribed.[114] Endowed with a strong demonifuge potential in the Chinese religious imagination, peach wood was already used in antiquity, as attested in the Mawangdui manuscripts, to fabricate figurines destined to be hung on doors for the protection of children.[115]

Whether manipulated for macabre practices of sorcery or used in the frame of Tantric *abhicāraka* orthopraxis, stakes and figurines are identical in terms of their forms and their ends. Numerous Tantric works reveal how effigies may be transformed into veritable assassins. A ritual procedure translated by the great Tantric Master Vajrabodhi (669–741) describes, for instance, how an icon of the terrifying Vajrayakṣa, duly fabricated and consecrated, can become an infallible long-range murder weapon and made operational in less than three days.[116] An effigy of the wrathful bodhisattva Vajrakumāra (Jingang tongzi 金剛童子) modelled in the powder of a human skull (*jiepoluo* 劫波羅, Skt. *kapāla*) could similarly, according to another illustrious eighth-century Tantric figure, Amoghavajra (Bukong 不空), succeed in the elimination of a persona non grata. The officiant had simply to place it on a triangular altar, raise his little finger in the *vajra mudrā* (*jingang quan* 拳), and jab it right in the heart. Vajrakumāra, armed to the teeth, made himself manifest through the body of his icon and pronounced a pitiless death sentence against the targeted undesirable person:

> "I have been mandated to put an end to your fate. [Henceforth,] you exist no longer." On hearing these words, [the victim] begins to vomit hot blood and takes his last gasp.[117]

The same fearsome Vajrakumāra could also, with even more modest materials and a basic seven-syllable incantation, willingly supervise the eradication of a human being by means of the ill treatment of his image:

---

114. The origin of these stakes in China goes back at least to the first century C.E. See Whitfield and Farrer (1990): 174–175. A dozen or so wooden stakes of approximately the same dimension, but dating from around the sixth century, have been also excavated in the region of Gaochang. They are thought to have had a funerary function, but some of them bearing the inscription *dairen* would rather suggest an exorcistic use. Another specimen inscribed with the characters *taoren* 桃人, "peach man," has been discovered in a *stūpa* in the same region. See Liu Hongliang (1986).

115. See Harper (1998): 169–170.

116. *Jingang yaosha zhennuwang xizai daweishen yan niansong yigui* 金剛藥叉瞋怒王息災大威神驗念誦儀軌, T. 1220, vol. 21.

117. *Shengjiani fennu jinggang tongzi pusa chengjiu yi gui jing* 聖迦柅忿怒金剛童子菩薩成就儀軌經 (abbreviated here as *Vajrakumāra tantra*), T. 1222, vol. 21: 1/122, "translated" or compiled by Amoghavajra. On other Tantric rites for perpetrating murders, see Duquenne (1983a).

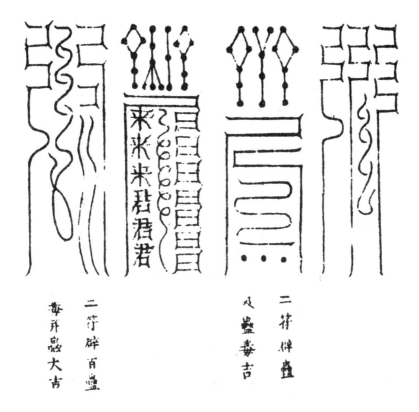

Fig. 2.6. Four Taoist talismans to expel the *gu* poison (Dz 673).

> One fabricates a human effigy with a protuberance. Clasping a knife between the teeth, one utters [the following formula]: *"didi zhazha jiangjiangjiang."* One then presses the knife into the protuberance and smashes the doll.[118]

Besides effigies, there is another, more specifically Chinese image-type device that was sometimes exploited for nefarious ends: talismans (*fu* 符). Indispensable tools for wonder workers and religious officiants since early antiquity, talismanic writs possess, as will be seen in more detail in the next chapters, a coercive influence on the invisible world, due to the intrinsic powers attributed to their archaizing runes and characters. Witches' talismans are mentioned, without further specification, by the *Zhoumei jing*. Curiously, neither this last, nor the *Scripture for Unbinding Curses* prescribes any counter-talismans—that is, talis-

---

118. *Dhāraṇī of the Heart of Vajrakumāra* (*Jingangtongzi xinzhou* 金剛童子心咒), Dunhuang manuscript P. 3914, quoted by Gao (1993): 267.

mans whose purpose is to overcome witchcraft. Nevertheless, they may be found elsewhere in Buddhist and Taoist literature. Examples include the two talismans of the Zhengyi "Petition for Returning to Normality by Exteriorization of the Officers," mentioned above, and a group of four talismans to expel the *gu* and its poisons issued among many other apotropaic *fu* in the Tang-dynasty *Three Talismanic Sections of the Original Chaos, by the Most High Lord Lao* (*Taishang Laojun hunyuan sanbu fu* 太上老君混元三部符) (fig. 2.6).[119]

Other anti-sorcery *fu* included in later Taoist works deserve to be pointed out as well—for instance, the talismans to vanquish the venomous effects of the *gu* poison and other forms of witchcraft, which are included in the *Guide of the Golden Lock and the Moving Pearls* (*Jinsuo liuzhu yin* 金鎖流珠引), an important ninth- or tenth-century ritual compendium.[120] Two scriptures likely dating to the Ming dynasty—the *Transcendent Talismans for Stabilizing Houses, from the Secret Method of the Most High* (*Taishang bifa zhenzhai lingfu* 太上祕法鎮宅靈符) and the *Secret Register One and Orthodox of the Most High for Unbinding Curses of the Five Tones,* mentioned earlier—propose as well a series of four talismans for solving problems due to curses (*koushe* 口舌) and opposing seasonal bewitchments, respectively.[121]

As for the Buddhist talismanic war against witchcraft, one example is particularly worth noting. It is a *fu* for the "expulsion of the *gu* poison" (*gudu zichu* 蠱毒自除) inscribed on the back of a small tenth-century Dunhuang Buddhist booklet, which is accompanied by *dhāraṇīs* and a pharmacological recipe (fig. 2.7). The directions for use adjoined to this talisman are as precise as they are awkward. They stipulate that it should be written before sunrise, on a *duanwu* 端午 day (the fifth day of the fifth month), with "black mud" (*heitu* 黑土) diluted on an ink stone. A little bit of this same substance should be kept in the calligrapher's mouth during the writing process, and the rest, mixed with a remedy, has to be rubbed on the body of the bewitched person, who is advised to stay at home and to eat seven or eight apricots and three jujubes every day.[122]

Before closing our inventory of the written expedients meant to release spells and cases of possession, I must also underline a typically Taoist ritual

119. Dz 673. 3/27.
120. Dz 1015. 20/6a and 25/9a. On this work falsely attributed to the eminent mathematician and Tang court astronomer Li Chunfeng 李淳風 (602–670), see Strickmann (1996): 232–236; Barrett (1990); and Poul Andersen in Schipper and Verellen (2004), vol. 2: 1076–1079. About Li Chunfeng, see the *Xin Tang shu* 新唐書, *juan* 204, 5797–5798; and *Jiu Tang shu* 舊唐書, *juan* 79, 2717–2719.
121. Dz 86. 11a and Dz 1217. 2a–3a.
122. P. 3835 V°. See Gao (1993): 317–318. Other talismans meant to be swallowed for curing "demonic diseases" (*guibing*) appear also in a Dunhuang manuscript, S. 2498, dealing with minor Tantric apotropaic rites.

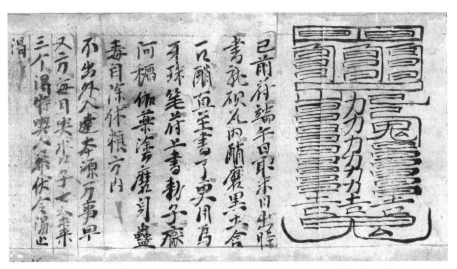

Fɪɢ. 2.7. A Buddhist talisman for the expulsion of the *gu* poison (P. 3835 V°). Courtesy of the Bibliothèque nationale de France.

item—namely, "petitions" (*zhang* 章). As was already indicated, this mode of communication with the celestial bureaucracy was privileged in the Heavenly Master's tradition. Transcribed in good and proper form after a diagnosis achieved by means of divination (*zhanshi* 占筮), the Zhengyi "Petition for Unbinding Maledictions," for instance, was directed in the name of the patient to solicit the aid of the seasonal divinities who enable the evacuation of the "perverse energies" (*xieqi* 邪氣) that have been maliciously introduced into his body and so to facilitate the restoration of the "correct" ones (*zhengqi* 正氣). After scrupulously discharging the payment of a certain number of tokens of faith in order to fulfil his debt to the celestial authorities, the beneficiary of the ritual might thereby be released from the demons that possess him and finally enjoy the pacification of his souls. The omnipotent power of talismanic writing is here reinforced by the irresistible authority of the bureaucratic procedure.[123]

The Energy of Words

For the *Scripture for Unbinding Curses* as for the *Zhoumei jing,* there is, however, no need for recourse to effigies, talismans, or writings in order to combat bewitchment,[124] for they rely exclusively on verbal offensives to expel it and to

123. Dz 615. 1/3a, 1/13a–13b, and 3/8a–10a.
124. Curiously, though we know that *fu* were adopted to a great degree in Buddhism and in Tantrism above all, the *Zhoumei jing* proposes no talismans whatsoever.

put to rest the nuisance of sorcerers and witches. The *Zhoumei jing* threatens them by unceasingly iterating—according to the ancestral Chinese method of reciting an entity's name, whether divine or demonical, in order to subjugate and control it—"I know your names, I know your names," and it makes clear that deities have been dispatched to "register them." Like the demons to which they are assimilated, the sorcerers are held at bay and paralyzed by the simple evocation of their names. The technique was equally deployed by Tantric exorcists. The *Vajrakumāra tantra,* for instance, explains how to get rid of an undesirable being by burying toxic drugs beneath the threshold of his house while pronouncing his name.[125] Mastered in the esoteric Buddhist circles, the strategy was no doubt also appreciated by the apostles of sorcery. To usurp the names of people was one of the expedients used to curse a victim according to the *Zhoumei jing.*

Even more widespread and dependable than the use of names and patronymics, the recitation of ritual formulae was recognized as the method ne plus ultra by clerics, exorcists, and sorcerers during medieval times. Repeatedly, the *Scripture for Unbinding Curses* insists that its *dhāraṇīs* and incantations (*zhou* 咒) work wonders to counteract bewitchments. Oral formulae such as "May the three beams and six pillars turn back against their instigators! May evil and calamity by themselves turn back against them to exterminate them!" are altogether unambiguous in their intention to do injury to sorcerers. We have also seen in the translation given above that the *Zhoumei jing* is particularly violent in its oral offensive on witches. By verbally designating the choice bits of their anatomy, one casts them as fodder to the gods. The witch is thus literally dismembered by words that, in this ritual context, are transformed into sharp-edged weapons. Her belly, her feet, her head, her eyes, her hands, and her heart become prey to the Five Emperors and their divine emissaries, who are summoned together to partake this macabre feast in the company of elephants and birds, millipedes and centipedes. We may note, too, that a similar genre of exorcistic injunctions inviting benevolent divinities to devour evil creatures and demons existed already under the Han.[126]

The certitude that spells, incantations, mantras, and *dhāraṇīs* were omnipotent and invincible was by and large shared throughout the different religious currents. Taoism and Buddhism made prodigious use of them in various forms,

---

125. T. 1222, vol. 21: 1/122.

126. See, for instance, the formula accompanying an apotropaic talisman on a plank exhumed in 1957 in Jiangsu, which stipulates that a demon suspected of intruding upon a family has to face the following ultimatum: "If you do not flee to a distance of three thousand *li,* you will be devoured by the deity so-and-so of the southern mountain." Refer to Wang Yucheng (1991).

including mnemotechnical poems and pseudo-Sanskrit formulae.[127] Tantrism was of course so prolific in this domain that its officiants were frequently titled "master of mantras" (*zhoushi* 咒師, which is probably equivalent to Skt. *mantrin*). It is sufficient to peruse manuals such as the *Collection of Dhāraṇī Sūtras* in order to gain an idea of the overwhelming quantity and diversity of mantras and *dhāraṇī*s employed in Buddhist esoteric rituals of exorcism and therapeutics. Like the written sign, sound possesses an inherent vitality and coercive power. It is this "energy of the word," to borrow the fine expression of André Padoux, that gives the practitioner, in the appropriate setting, the opportunity to communicate directly with occult entities.[128] "It is the *qi*," explains Ge Hong, "which permits one to subjugate (*jin* 禁) spirits and divinities." As soon as words are correctly pronounced, their *qi* is set in motion and the forces that they designate are materialized and mobilized.[129] Rendered thus tangible, they may be summoned for help or else banished according to need. Donald Harper has underlined, too, the use of what he terms "breath magic" in pre-Han medico-religious practices whereby the officiant had to spit, sputter, or blow before or just after uttering his incantations.[130]

The *Scripture for Unbinding Curses,* the *Zhoumei jing,* and the other works I have cited clearly demonstrate that incantations may act either to provoke evil or to expel it. As a verb, *zhou* means "to consecrate" or "to breathe power into," but it also signifies "to exhort" or "to conjure,"[131] while in its nominal and negative uses, it may be combined with different characters to denote "curses," "imprecations" (*zhouzu* 咒詛), or "maledictions" (*e'zhou* 惡咒).[132] The term *yan* 厭, whose primary senses are "to detest" and "disgusting," is also associated with orality in the context of sorcery, notably when it is combined with the character *dao* 禱, "prayer," becoming equivalent to "to curse," "to put under a

---

127. Strickmann (1996), chap. 1. See also Sawada (1992 [1984]).

128. Padoux (1980).

129. *Baopuzi neipian,* chap. 5, Wang Ming, ed.: 114.

130. Harper (1998): 164–165. The action of spitting or puffing water with the mouth is still currently performed in rituals today by Taoists and mediums in order to expel demons.

131. The same, almost homophonic character, preceded by the radical 示 (*zhu* 祝), signifies "to pronounce an incantation" (whether positive or negative).

132. The compounds *zhouzu* 咒咀 and *zhoushi* 咒誓 seem equivalent in the *Guanding jing* (chap. 12, T. 1331: 533). The expression *wu zhuzu* 巫祝詛 is already attested for the Han period as a synonym of bewitchment. See Harper (1998): 158, who quotes the *Hanshu* and translates the expression as "shaman curses." On the use of *zhou* in Buddhist sorcery, see Strickmann (1996): "Le même verbe *tchou* 'prononcer une incantation,' s'appliquait aux deux formules (dhāraṇī et mantra) ainsi qu'aux charmes et aux envoûtements par les sorciers profanes" (70). "Les 'dhāraṇī' taoïstes sont étroitement associées à la riche tradition chinoise de malédiction, et jusqu'à une époque récente les invectives profanes partageaient le vocabulaire et la conception du monde des ensorcellements taoïstes" (120). Sorcery is also labelled as a "way of curses by perverse demons" (*xiegui zhoudao* 邪鬼咒道).

spell." Other technical nomenclature belonging to sorcery, such as "red mouth" (*chikou* 赤口) or "evil mouth" (*e'kou* 惡口), obviously alludes to the despised linguistic weapons of the sorcerers, as well as to the injurious potential of their words. It is not rare to see all of these terms run together to designate sorcery in general, as they are in the phrase *dugu yandao zhouzu e'kou chishe* 蠱毒厭禱咒詛 惡口赤舌.[133] Spells that the witches "recite interminably" for "calling the demons" (*hu baigui* 呼白鬼), explains the *Zhoumei jing,* are in fact the "incantations used subversively" (*luanyong zhou* 亂用咒). In other words, they are formulae that have been soiled and vitiated for malevolent ends. For inducing evil, sorcerers rely on the vocabularies of hate, toxicity, and crudeness. Derogatory and repugnant phrases attract the wicked forces and bring about bewitchment. With their *zhou,* witches can also constrain "orthodox" divinities, the gods of the traditional Chinese pantheon. The *Zhoumei jing* is entirely of a piece with the *Sūtra of Consecration* on this subject: the celestial deities—the astral divinities and the Five Emperors—as well as the mountain gods, the General of the River, the gods of the trees, and the god of the Five Ways, are subdued and channelled by the magnetism of these noisome recitations, and they are thereby irremediably coerced into committing malefic deeds.[134]

The same divinities of the stars and of nature, set off course by the witch, are the very ones invoked by the Buddhists of the *Zhoumei jing* so as to reestablish order. Irrepressible, the ritual word is capable of turning them alternatively into agents of evil or supporters of good. Whatever their function is, however, it leaves nothing to envy. Recalled to the right path by the *Zhoumei jing*'s litanies, these divinities (who are regarded in Buddhism, it must be said, as inferiors) are nevertheless assigned a lamentable mission: they must "break the witches' heads into seven pieces like the branches of the Ali tree" or, worse, devour them.[135] The *Zhoumei jing* thus stands here in the line of medieval Buddhist and Taoist demonological manuals, which address rebel demons with just the same kind of merciless summons mingled with threats of corporal punishment and extermination. "Your head will be smashed into pieces" is an imprecation endlessly repeated to dangerous spirits, and thereby the choice of expulsion or conscription into the ranks of the Dao.[136] We have seen that the *Scripture for Unbinding Curses* uses the same stereotypical formula.

---

133. See, e.g., T. 1333, quoted below.

134. See the *Guanding jing,* 12/523.

135. Similar injunctions may be seen, for example, in the *Scripture of the Divine Incantations of the Abyssal Grottoes* (*Taishang dongyuan shenzhou jing* 太上洞淵神咒經, Dz 335); see Mollier (1990): 103 et seq.

136. See Miyai (1996): 725–726, who gives several examples in Buddhist apocryphal sūtras of the Six Dynasties period.

Though serving as an injunction or ultimatum when addressed to the ambivalent or malfeasant creatures one seeks to eliminate, the *zhou* takes on, by contrast, the polite and respectful tones of invitation and prayer when offered to the orthodox and superior deities to whom one turns for assistance. The *Zhoumei jing* thus solicits the aid of the entire hierarchy of the trustworthy Buddhist pantheon: the *nāga*s, *deva*s, arhats, buddhas, and bodhisattvas are all convened so as to join forcefully in the witch hunt. In the tight battle between good and evil, only these venerable figures offer a real and solid surety to the faithful.

Many other medieval Buddhist works also proclaim their incantations as being the magisterial means to put an end to sorcery. For the aforementioned *Regal Sūtra of the Six-Syllable Mantra, Preached by the Buddha* (*Foshuo liuzi shenzhou wangjing* 佛說六字咒王經), it is the all-powerful Six-Syllable Mantra that does miracles,[137] in all places and circumstances, against the ill effects of bewitchments.[138] Recited seven times in succession, following an offering of incense and invocations to Guanshiyin, Mañjuśrī, and Maitreya,

> it has the power to revivify the branches and foliage of the dead tree, and a fortiori it can [act] on human beings so as to assure longevity up to a hundred years. They will thereby know a hundred autumns.[139]

Two sūtras placed under the patronage of the Seven Buddhas (for more on whom, see chapter 3) praise their *dhāraṇī*s as real panaceas for countering sorcery, above all its pernicious illnesses. The "*dhāraṇī* of Yamāntaka" (*daweide tuoluoni* 大威德陀羅尼), recommended by the *Sūtra of the Bodhisattva Ākāśagarbha's Questions on the Dhāraṇī of the Seven Buddhas,* among an abundance of therapeutic recipes, consists of an invocation of the names of the Seven Buddhas to vanquish evil illnesses and annihilate the problems engendered by "black magic."[140] The *Sūtra of the Great Dhāraṇī Pronounced by the Seven Buddhas and Eight Bodhisattvas* (*Qifo bapusa suoshuo da tuoluoni shenzhou jing* 七佛八菩薩所說大陀羅尼神咒經) is similarly capable of delivering victims from bewitchments (*gumei* 蠱魅)

---

137. T. 1044, vol. 20. It is not clear to what this "Six-Syllable Mantra" 六字咒 refers. There is no allusion here to the well-known Guanyin Mantra. The sūtra in fact consists of seven mantras, six of which are pseudo-Sanskrit formulae also called "real and true mantras" (*zhenshi zhangju* 真實章句), plus one *dhāraṇī* (*tuolouni*), which is an invocation to the bodhisattvas and divinities.

138. Three types (or schools ?) of sorcery are listed: the sorcery of Śakra 帝釋咒道, the sorcery of Brahmā 梵王咒道, and the sorcery of the four *devarāja*s 四天王咒道.

139. T. 1044, vol. 20: 40.

140. T. 1333, vol. 21. On Yamāntaka, the "Annihilator of Death," whose Chinese name is *daweide mingwang* 大威德明王, see Duquenne (1983b).

and dispelling poisons.[141] Venerated as they were in medieval China for their curative and exorcistic talents, the Seven Buddhas, whom we will meet again in the next chapter, were no doubt thought to be perfectly suited to triumph in the anti-sorcery campaign.

The incantations may be pronounced upon a material or virtual support to which they confer an apotropaic power. The *Collection of Dhāraṇī Sūtras,* for instance, teaches the recitation of a mantra for consecrating a cord made of cowhair.[142] Tied to the feet of the patient's bed, it liberates him from "demonic illness that nothing else succeeds in curing."[143] Knotted around someone's neck, it guarantees him divine protection.[144] Water vessels may similarly be consecrated and so acquire exorcistic properties against the "demon of sorcery" (*yangu gui* 厭蠱鬼). It suffices to recite a *dhāraṇī* twenty-one times upon a copper or porcelain jar filled with three *sheng* (升; about three liters) of water, to cover it with a white cloth and seven willow twigs, and to place it inside the latrine.[145] More will be said in chapter 5 about these Tantric rituals for the consecration of a water vessel by means of a willow branch. Here, other liturgical accessories should be mentioned, in particular branches of acacia, a wood that, like peach and willow, seems to have been favored for its apotropaic virtues and could also be easily invested with exorcist powers by means of mantras:

> The Master of incantations constructs a square altar (*jiejie* 結界) around which are planted four sprigs with eight branches in acacia wood (*qutuoluo* 佉陀羅, Skt. *khadira*), which he consecrates with a mantra recited 108 times.[146]

One last rite, also found in the *Collection of Dhāraṇī Sūtras,* merits citation in order to illustrate the cogency of the word in the war against sorcery. The esoteric manual expounds how, through the energy of a highly aggressive mantra, one can definitively neutralize an enemy, whether or not he is a practitioner of sorcery, by means of a sophisticated, if gloomy procedure, which requires ashes from a cremated corpse:

> On a moonless night one tosses this ash into the (ritual) fire, pinch by pinch, one hundred and eight times. The evil person is thereby annihilated.[147]

---

141. T. 1332, vol. 21: 2/545. It was compiled in the fifth century. See Kuo (1994a): 89.
142. On the "incantation cords," see below, note 157.
143. T. 901: 2/787.
144. T. 901: 8/860.
145. T. 1332: 4/560. See Demiéville (1974b),
146. T. 901: 5/833.
147. Ibid.

Poisons and Antidotes

To close our inventory of the witchcraft practices and the counteroffensives to them, I would like to return to bewitchment through poison, the infamous *gu,* whose semantic range I evoked at the beginning of this chapter. The various measures, imagined and experienced, to oppose the "way of *gu*" (*gudao* 蠱道) or "*gu* poison" (*gudu* 蠱毒) are legion. Both religious experts and men of science mercilessly fought against it and persistently proposed remedies to cure the damage it wrought. Medieval physicians, who had to deal with this problem on the twin fronts of treatment and etiology, recognized three types of bewitchment, the same types that we have seen above enumerated in the *Collection of Dhāraṇī Sūtras:* the *gu* poisons, the "savage paths" (*yedao*), and the "demon cats" (*maogui*). Each of them was generally known as causing terrible and even fatal sufferings, often accompanied by hemorrhaging from the mouth and anus, symptoms graphically depicted by medieval illustrators, as we have seen earlier too. We have to rely on the distinguished seventh-century *Treatise on the Origin and Symptoms of Illnesses* (*Zhubing yuanhou lun* 諸病原後論) in order to find more precise nosological descriptions of these fearful malefactions. The *gu,* the treatise explains, is carried by a serpent, frog, lizard, or beetle; the "savage path" is a "masterless *gu,*" a sort of orphan bewitchment that loiters in nature and strikes by chance; while the "demon cat" is raised under the eye of a sorcerer.[148] According to another contemporaneous medical manual, the famous *Essential Priceless Prescriptions for All Urgent Ills, by the Perfected Sun* (*Sun zhenren beiji qianjin yaofang* 孫真人備急千金藥方), attributed to the renowned Sun Simo 孫思邈 (581–682), *gu* poisons and demon cats belong to the same category as foxes and old things (*laowu* 老物), also favored as vectors for sorcery. A long section of the work treats the ravages that they provoke and provides various pharmaceutical recipes together with moxibustion techniques capable of uprooting them.[149]

The phobia of ensorcelment was exploited to good advantage by Buddhism as well. Daily ritual prophylaxis was recommended to the faithful in order to avoid the risk of contamination, notably by means of food and

---

148. *Zhubing yuanhou lun,* chap. 25, as translated in Obringer (1997): 264–273. See also Strickmann (1996): 156–157, who mentions the same passage. Obringer indicates elsewhere that the Penal Code of the Tang sanctions the practice of the "demon cat" with the penalty of death by strangulation (ibid., 251).

149. Dz 1163. 74/1a–10a. Conforming to the tendencies of the epoch, the author of the *Prescriptions for All Urgent Ills* ascribes to southerners an unfortunate penchant for morbid practices. I refer here to a passage (74/2b), which says, in summary, that people from the mountains of the Jiangnan region know well the practice of *gu* by means of snakes. Absorbed in food or beverages, it causes mortal cases of dysentery. On the *gu* as a southern China practice, see Obringer (1997): 244–249.

drink.[150] Diagnosed cases of bewitchment were purged by rites, but also by drugs prescribed by the *saṃgha*. Religion and medicine entered in league with one another to chase away evil, assisted in this by the great upsurge of Indian materia medica in medieval China. A fine example of the medico-religious consensus, which prevailed at the time, is found in a small Buddhist pharmacological treatise discovered among the Dunhuang manuscripts that presents a "Recipe for Expelling the Poisons of Bewitchment" (Chu gudu fang 出蠱毒方), wherein parasitology, demonology, and sorcery are closely related. The remedy consists in the preparation of drugs according to a very precise posology, which, accompanied by the recitation of a mantra divulging the sorcerers' names (father "beetle," *qianglang chong* 蜣蜋虫, and mother "demon Yeshe," Yeshe gui 耶闍鬼), is supposed to cleanse the perverse consequences of ensorcelment.[151] Medication and ritual formulae combine, in this case, their vermifuge and demonifuge effects to overcome witchcraft.

Other Buddhist sūtras also rely on materia medica to concoct antidotes to sorcery. The *Dhāraṇī Sūtra of the Thousand-Armed, Thousand-Eyed Bodhisattva Guanyin,* mentioned earlier, suggests:

> For one who suffers from the bewitchment by *gu* poison, one powders camphor and bdellium incense (*jujuluo* 柜具羅, Skt. *guggulu*).[152] Mixed with well water and heated, the remedy is placed before the image of Guanyin while reciting a mantra 108 times. Consumed [by the patient], it assures his cure.[153]

"Malign illness" (*e'bing*) is the generic term employed in Buddhist literature to designate demonical pathologies induced by curses. Drugs and medical beverages, aromatic baths, inhalations of incense smoke, and rubdowns with phytotherapeutic oils are recommended by the *Sūtra of the Bodhisattva Ākāśagarbha's Questions on the Dhāraṇī of the Seven Buddhas* in order to suppress them.[154] In association with liturgical prescriptions—the construction of an

---

150. See the *Sūtra of the Bodhisattva Ākāśagarbha's Questions on the Dhāraṇī of the Seven Buddhas,* T. 1333: 564), which advises the recitation of a *"dhāraṇī* of the Seven Buddhas," every morning and evening and before each meal in order to be immunized against bewitched food or beverages.

151. P. 2637 and P. 2665. Harper (1996): 243 underlines the tight connection already existing in the Shuihudi materials (third century B.C.E.) between insects, "bugs," and malefic demons. Unschuld (1985): 46–50, insists also on the link between the *gu,* "worm spirit," infectious parasites, and demonological concepts. See also Obringer (1997).

152. Bdellium, or *gum gugul,* is an aromatic resin of Southeast Asia, which had a demonifuge reputation in Tang China. See Schafer (1963): 169–170.

153. *Qianshou qianyan Guanshiyin pusa guangda yuanman wu'ai dabeixin tuoluoni jing,* T. 1060, vol. 19: 110.

154. T. 1333, vol. 21.

altar, performance of a fire ritual (*humo* 護摩, *homa*),[155] recitation of *dhāraṇīs*, aspersion with consecrated water, and fabrication of "incantation cords" (*jie-zhou suo* 結咒索)[156]—they deliver patients "possessed by an evil demon" (*e'gui suo chi* 惡鬼所持) and above all by the terrible *wangliang* 魍魎 mainly responsible for cases of mutism.[157] Leprosy (*lai* 癩) and epilepsy (*xian* 癇) were also among the illnesses typically caused by bewitchment. The *Vajrakumāra tantra* recommends a special curative therapy:

> [The practitioner] undertakes a *homa* rite in the direction of the door of Heaven and recites a mantra 1,008 times. He then takes the ashes of the *homa,* which he puts in four jars full of water. He consecrates them 1,008 times. Someone who is afflicted by an evil demon, or who has leprosy or epilepsy caused by ensorcelment, should bathe and then dress in new and clean clothes. A circular altar is constructed in a pure place. One prepares a bed on which the patient is put. The four jars of consecrated water are placed before him [and the practitioner] sprinkles his crown and body with this water while reciting the mantra ceaselessly.[158]

The *Collection of Dhāraṇī Sūtras,* for its part, is not sparing in its elaborations of measures designed to annihilate "perverse demons" (*e'gui* 惡鬼), toxic drugs (*duyao* 毒藥), and "demonic pathologies" (*guibing* 鬼病) inflicted by sorcery. Fumigations, inhalations, aromatic baths, and varied posologies, together with rites and perpetual incantations, may be counted among the noninvasive therapies for eliminating evil. But other harsher cures are also prescribed: entire immersion of the possessed in water during a moonless night,[159] or a séance of fustigation with mustard seeds, well known in the Indian world for their apotropaic qualities:

> In case of illnesses due to bewitchment by a fox 狐魅, by a mountain spirit 山精鬼魅, or by a *gu,* one consecrates grains of white mustard with a mantra recited twenty-

---

155. On *homa* rituals, see Strickmann (1983), (1996): 337–368.

156. These amulet cords of different colors on which the incantation must be chanted are then tied (bound, *xi* 繫) around the neck, the waist, or another part of the body of the patient. See T. 1333: 562, 564.

157. T. 1333: 564. When a possessed person is afflicted by mutism 口噤不矣, says the text, this means that he is victim of the demon Pishedu 毘舍闍 (i.e., Piśāca, the chief of demons). He suffers also from dyspepsia or rheumatism. One must take some Buddha flowers (from the Buddha's altar?), reduce them to powder, and dissolve it in peach alcohol and rice wine. The mixture should then be poured into a silver cup and placed in front of the Buddha's image. One recites the incantation 1,008 times and gives the beverage to the sick person.

158. T. 1222: 2/112.

159. T. 901: 5/833.

one times and then throws them into the face and chest of the patient. One burns incense while turning around him and makes him inhale the smoke twenty-one times.[160]

Still more vigorous were treatments by flagellation, inflicted no longer upon the effigy but upon the patient himself by means of twigs of peach wood, a substance whose exorcistic virtues that have already been mentioned. The séance was then orchestrated as follows:

> One first strikes [the patient] under the right arm, on the left elbow, between the kidneys, and on the thighs. His illness will thereby be cured.[161]

The alliance of rites and medicine was not the sole prerogative of religious institutions. To combat sorcery, the medical manuals did not disdain the know-how of priests and shamans. Materia medica was generously spiced with ingredients borrowed from exorcists, as can be seen in this curious technique for hunting down a sorcerer-poisoner, from the illustrious Sun Simo:

> There are some persons who practice poisoning by the *gu* in order to provoke illnesses. If, besides providing medication, one [adds] knowledge of the name of the "master of the *gu*" 蠱師, one can, by calling him, cause him to flee. One who wishes to learn his name must tear the skin head of a drum, burn it, and ingest a spoonful of the ashes. The sorcerer's name will immediately make itself known.[162]

Though this method may strike us as quite eccentric, it probably did not seem at all aberrant to professionals charged with communicating with spirits. We have seen that to proffer the name of a person, divinity, or demon is a stratagem of coercion frequently adopted by exorcists and sorcerers. As for the drum whose ingested head unexpectedly serves to bring forth the evildoer's name, how can we avoid finding here an allusion to the privileged instrument of the shaman-exorcist?

As our anti-sorcery sūtras and the few examples given above make clear, the exorcist's remedy is often of the same nature as the evils it is supposed to chase

---

160. T. 901: 2/792.
161. Ibid.
162. *Qianjin yaofang,* Dz 1163. 74/2b.

away. The strategies for neutralizing witchcraft are essentially forms of counter-malediction. The fire of fat fed by the witch of the *Zhoumei jing* in order to prepare her misdeeds can be seen as a simulacrum of the Tantric fire ritual, *homa;* and the talismans and incantations that she employs, as distortions of the basic rites of Chinese exorcism. Even the confection of the *gu* drug and the malevolent acupuncture that she practices on the substitutional bodies of her victims resemble masquerades of traditional cures.

It should be underscored that medieval Taoism distinguished itself radically from the medicalized approach privileged by Buddhism for dealing with exorcism. It was not that the Taoists were not convinced that there was a direct relation between certain illnesses and sorcery. Quite the contrary. The *Petition Almanac of Master Red Pine,* cited above, enumerates in detail the physical and psychological pathologies caused by witchcraft: heaviness in the limbs, loss of vitality, confused dreams and thoughts, mental disorders.[163] In any event, the explicit interdiction of all forms of genuine medical exercise as stipulated in the theology of the early Way of the Heavenly Master was uninterruptedly maintained throughout the medieval period:

> [The Taoist Master] must not, in order to care for the ill, take recourse to acupuncture or to moxibustion, nor to infusions and other remedies, but exclusively [make use of] the ingestion of talismans and [consecrated] water, the confession of sins, the rectification of conduct, and the presentation of petitions.[164]

The treatment of ensorcelment was no exception to this rule. The *Scripture for Unbinding Curses,* the "Petition for Unbinding Maledictions," and the *Secret Register for Unbinding Curses from the Five Tones* all demonstrate that it was exclusively by rites, and by writings in particular, that the Taoists of medieval China exorcized the bewitched.

---

163. Dz 615. 3/8b. The entourage of the victim presenting these symptoms is also afflicted: the family suffers from misfortune, strange phenomena, and repeated calamities.

164. Anonymous commentary on the work of the renowned theologian Lu Xiujing 陸修靜 (406–477), the *Abbreviated Code of Master Lu to Enter the Dao (Lu xiansheng daomen kelüe* 陸先生道門科略) Dz 1127. 8a.

CHAPTER 3

Augmenting the Life Account

In the time of the Yellow Emperor, people of superior longevity lived for 120 years, those of moderate longevity for 100 years, and those of the least longevity for 80 years.

There is no more patent case of purloined scripture, among the examples presented in this volume, than that of the *Sūtra to Increase the Account* (*Yisuan jing* 益算經).[1] This short text of one *juan,* known from many examples discovered among the Dunhuang manuscripts, has been labelled an apocryphal, or "suspect" (*wei* 偽), sūtra in Buddhist catalogues since the end of the seventh century. It has continued to be classified as such by specialists down to the present day, notably by Makita Tairyō, even though the term "apocryphon" cannot be considered, in this case, to be more than a euphemism.[2] Makita himself seems to have overlooked the existence of two Taoist *Yisuan jing* printed in the Ming Taoist Canon, one of which evidently served as the model for the Buddhist sūtra, which replicates it almost to perfection. More than a classic apocryphon, therefore, the *Sūtra to Increase the Account* may be rightly described, once again, as an appropriation, even an outright copy of a Taoist work.

The Taoist *Yisuan jing* and its Buddhist "clone" consist in essence of an invocation of the Generals of the Six *jia* (*liujia jiangjun* 六甲將軍), a list of the stars and planets, a litany for personal protection, and fifteen talismans. The aim of all of this is to assure the health and welfare of the faithful so that they may surely reach, without adversity, the full term of existence, whose optimal

---

Epigraph: *Almanac for Organizing Rituals of Petition According to the Original Stars* (*Yuanchen zhangjiao licheng li* 元辰章醮立成曆), Dz 1288. 1/12a (Six Dynasties).

1. For a preliminary study of this scripture, see Mollier (2003). A French version of the present chapter has been published as Mollier (2007).

2. Makita (1976): 83–84.

span is estimated at 120 years. For, as the title allows us to divine, the *Yisuan jing,* whether in its Taoist or Buddhist version, has the objective of preserving or, better still, prolonging the lives of the faithful. Thus, the expression *yisuan* 益算—"to increase the life-capital" or "to add to the account"—articulates by itself a forceful approach to longevity.

"Increasing the Life-Capital"

Under the Han dynasty, the term "account," *suan* 算, designated a monetary tax payment but also carried a metaphorical significance, that of the "celestial account," the span of life allotted to each individual.[3] This double sense would be conserved during the medieval period, when the *suan* were, materially speaking, the sticks used by diviners for calculations and equally the temporal units serving to quantify destiny.[4] The famous fourth-century alchemist Ge Hong provides an illuminating explanation of this system for calculating fate:

> Everyone has a "personal endowment" (*benshu* 本數) based on the initial length of existence he receives with his life span. If this endowment is significant, then his *ji* 紀 and *suan* will be difficult to exhaust. Consequently, he will die in old age. If [on the contrary] his original endowment is meager, and if, a fortiori, he commits numerous infractions, his *ji* and *suan* will quickly come to the end. He will then die in the flower of life.[5]

As Ge Hong specifies elsewhere:

> In heaven as on earth, there are divinities charged with the assessment of faults who subtract [a period of time] from the life-account (*suan* 算) of culpable individuals in proportion to the gravity of the transgressions they have committed. As their life-account diminishes, people fall into poverty and illness, and they become frequently prone to afflictions and misfortune. When their *suan* is finally exhausted, they die. The causes of the *suan*'s being cut back are so numerous that it is impossible to expose them all. . . . Grave faults are punished by the deduction of one *ji* 紀, equivalent to 300 days. Minimal faults count a *suan,* which is to say, 3 days.[6]

---

3. See Hou (1975): 100.

4. They served both in hemerological divination and cleromancy. See Kalinowski (2003): 226, 309.

5. *Baopuzi neipian, juan* 3, Wang Ming, ed.: 53.

6. Ibid., *juan* 6: 125. According to Wang Ming, one *ji* would be equal to 12 years (he cites, in particular, a commentary on the *Shangshu* 尚書). On the other hand, Wang considers that we should read 100 days, and not 3 days, as the cost of one *suan.* According to him, the character 百, "hundred," would have been omitted and we should therefore read "one" 一, and not "three" 三 (ibid., 132nn27–28).

As an account or unit of measure within the account, the value of the *suan* is variable. It evidently differs among individuals, for we are not all endowed with the same quotient of existence at the point of departure. A life span of 120 years, termed "celestial longevity" (*tianshou* 天壽) in the *Book of Great Peace* (*Taiping jing* 太平經), is estimated as the ideal length of life in medieval Taoism. The author of the extensive, synthetic Taoist treatise entitled the *Lingbao Scripture of the Most High Concerning Karmic Retribution* (*Taishang dongxuan lingbao yebao yinyuan jing* 太上洞玄靈寶業報因緣經, hereafter *Lingbao Scripture of Karmic Retribution*), dating from the sixth or the beginning of the seventh century, went so far as to evaluate down to the day the extent of this ideal span: 43,200.[7]

Taoism and, sometime later, Buddhism offered a concrete, even economical image of the ratio of existence allotted to each person. The life-allocation was conceived to be a celestial granary placed at the disposal of each human individual in order to assure his survival during his earthly sojourn. Consisting of cereals, the Chinese staple, this metaphorical provision is initially determined according to the subject's horoscope. When this personal reserve granted by heaven is consumed in its entirety, his vital energy can be sustained no longer; the hour of his death has thus arrived. The *suan* is similarly thought to be equivalent to a treasury, a sort of celestial bank account that may be credited and refinanced through offerings of sacrificial paper money or other goods entered into exchange, in order not to bring to ruin one's vital inheritance.[8] A fine example of such transactions with the divine accountants is found in the *Petition Almanac of Master Red Pine* (*Chisongzi zhangli*), emanating from the Heavenly Master tradition. Besides pieces of silk and cash, the scripture recommends an offering of twelve bushels of the "rice of destiny" (*mingmi yidan erdou* 命米一石二斗) to "increase the account" (*yisuan*)—that is to say, one's longevity—and to traverse safe and sound the trials of existence.[9] We know from historical sources that the rice tax—which the faithful of the Heavenly Master community, during the late Han dynasty, had to donate to their parishes and which lent to its religious organization its famed sobriquet, "Way of the Five Bushels of Rice" (Wu doumi dao 五斗米道)—served to fill its coffers with food. However, the material value of this tithe was doubled, in all evidence, by its symbolic significance: in acquitting himself of this obligation, the adept had occasion to reimburse or, better, to augment his personal fund, his metaphorical account, or *suan,* held in trust in the beyond. The rice offering allowed him to hope in return for the betterment of his ma-

---

7. Dz 336. 8/4b. "Medium longevity" is 80 years, and "inferior longevity" is only 60 years. See *Taiping jing hejiao*, Wang Ming, ed.: 723; Kaltenmark (1979): 41; and Penny (1990).

8. Hou (1975): 98–102.

9. Dz 615. 3/20b. See also Hou (1975): 111.

terial life and suitable longevity. It is no accident that the three great annual assemblies during which this payment of the grain tax was made were at the same time the periods for updating the civil registers maintained by the Heavenly Master clergy, registers in which the adepts' births, deaths, and major religious life events were recorded.

Whether as "life-capital" or as the "unit of the account" serving to quantify the duration of existence, the *suan* refers back to the notion of predetermined destiny (*ming* 命), a pervasive idea throughout ancient China and one fully exploited by the Taoists.[10] Thus, every individual, as a function of a number of variable parameters—genetic inheritance as well as moral (whether karmic or ancestral), cosmic, and astrological configurations—is programmed to live for a certain time in a certain fashion. But, as Ge Hong stresses, this life-capital is not immutable and is in no case acquired once and for all. Life span may be lengthened or shortened in connection with moral conduct and religious ethics. For Ge Hong, as for the Taoists who succeeded him, the exercise of free will weighed heavily in the scales of destiny. Each one had to choose to follow good or evil paths and thus to provide himself with prospects for a long life or, on the contrary, "not to complete the account" (*bu man suanji* 不滿算紀), that is to say, to die prematurely.[11]

How does this system of "direct" retribution operate? Its agents are thought of as divinities who are forever surveying our deeds. No one escapes the omniscient, vigilant policing of these censors and clerks of the world beyond, collectively known as the Directors of Destiny (Siming 司命), who supervise the course of existence and methodically maintain the registers of life and death in which the names of all human beings are inscribed. One of the fourth-century Shangqing writings helps us get an idea of the titanic work incumbent upon the celestial administration:

> In order to inventory the dead and the living, the Great Yin (the realm of the dead) possesses black records and white registers [formed] of bound tablets in vermilion. The list of the living is organized in chronological order, just as the dead are enregistered, in succession, for comparison. As many as six thousand tablets are [sometimes required] to maintain the register of a single individual.[12]

---

10. Hou (1975): 106–126.

11. Dz 336. 8/5a.

12. *Annals of the Lord of the Dao, Sage of the Latter (Heavens) of Shangqing* (*Shangqing housheng daojun lieji* 上清後聖道君列紀, Dz 442. 12a), belonging to the ancient Shangqing canon revealed to the visionary Yang Xi 楊羲. See Robinet (1984), vol. 2: 107–110; and Bokenkamp's translation (1997): 339–362.

Merits and faults are thus scrupulously noted and quantified by the divine bureaucracy, to assure that no moral debt will remain unpaid. This implacable machine surveying our faults also coordinates a penal routine intended to sanction the guilty.[13] The divine censors of morality are equally judges invested with the right to chastise. From the period of the Six Dynasties on, the Taoists created breviaries providing lengthy tables of sins and infractions of the ethical and religious rules, with the corresponding sanctions threatening the culpable. Control, calculation, and retribution are the three keys in their system of repression and justice. Consider, for instance, the aforementioned *Petition Almanac of Master Red Pine:*

> Within the human body, there are always present the divinities of the "office of faults" (*siguo zhi shen* 司過之神), who, at opportune times, depart and return in order to report good and evil actions on high. One hundred twenty faults are subject to a "notch" (*ke* 刻), of which the consequence for the guilty party is the diminution of his advantages and the multiplication of his troubles.[14]

This rigorous and fearsome penal policy was fortunately leavened by positive incentives. Following the same sure logic, divine reward was granted no less than punishment. In the early-Tang *Penal Code of the Mysterious Metropolis* (*Xuandu lüwen* 玄都律文), for instance, one is consoled in discovering that virtuous acts are quantified according to a scale from one to a thousand: well-being and serenity for a simple good action, an ironlike constitution for twenty good deeds, and, to the degree to which one scrambles up the ladder of goodness, one may assure prosperity, fortune, and felicity for one's whole family and future generations. According to the same cumulative principle, faults, at least when limited to a few units, will not yield more than minor physical or material disadvantages, but should they surpass a certain quota, their ill effects will reach a crescendo in provoking severe disease, bankruptcy, or, even worse, the death of the guilty party and the extinction of his line.[15]

Thus, while those who commit sins and transgressions need not await postmortem judgment to expiate their crimes and can suffer a part of their penalty here below, the man of excellent behavior and probity might aspire to a foretaste of the fruits of his virtuous morality during his earthly sojourn. Or so, at least, he is left to

---

13. See, for example, the chapter "Interdictions and Taboos of the Laws of the Dao" (*Daolü jinji*) of the *Code of Nüqing for [Controlling] the Demons* (*Nüqing guilü* 女青鬼律, Dz 790. 3/1a–3b), which gives a list of rules followed by the number of *suan* that will be deducted from the individual's life span in case of transgression.

14. Dz 615. 2/29b.

15. Dz 188. For other examples on the Taoist systems of retribution, see Yoshioka, *Dōkyō to bukkyō,* vol. 2 (1970): 167–227, 290–339; and Kohn (1998).

believe. Whether positive or negative, human actions are inevitably paid in return. Sooner or later this will affect the individual's quality of life, and it will have inevitable consequences for what one holds most dear: the length of life itself.

The expedients that have been devised in China to push back the due date of death are beyond counting, and the Taoists have been, without challenge, the most inventive in this regard. Whether psychophysical, dietetic, alchemical, or ritual, the methods that they have espoused for achieving longevity or, better, immortality are legion. Less a preoccupation among the Buddhists, the question of long life is nevertheless not at all neglected by them. Does not the twenty-third chapter of the *Lotus Sūtra* (*Miaofa lianhua jing* 妙法蓮華經), for instance, promise to those who have the opportunity to hear it that they "will not age and will not die" (*bulao busi* 不老不死)?[16] What's more, the notion of a divine accounting of sins was part of the Buddhist heritage prior to its diffusion in China,[17] as was the idea of meritorious action being rewarded by an extension of one's existence.[18] Chinese Tantric Buddhism would also start, towards the beginning of the eighth century, to promote its own rites to prolong life. An example is found in the Taoist-inspired talismanic seals of the deity Ucchuṣma (*Huiji jingang* 穢跡金剛), which were swallowed by the faithful or applied to the body and which worked wonders by chasing off demonic emanations, diseases, and natural calamities, as well as by conferring long life.[19]

Human longevity became a focal preoccupation in Buddhist apocrypha such as the *Sūtra Preached by the Buddha to Extend Destiny* (*Foshuo yan shouming jing* 佛說延壽命經), rediscovered in several versions at Dunhuang.[20] Contemporaneous to the *Yisuan jing*, this short sūtra, whose title leaves no doubt as to the goal of its teaching, promises to the faithful who recite and worship it that the bodhisattva Prolongation of Destiny (*Yanshou pusa* 延壽菩薩) will accord them an extension of life.[21]

---

16. T. 262. *Yaowang pin* 藥王品, quoted by Makita (1976): 80.

17. See Kuo (1994a): 91, who notes that the first extant versions of the *Sūtra of Amitābha* translated into Chinese during the second and third centuries mention the "names' registers" to which the gods consign the bad deeds of individuals.

18. See Mochizuki (1936–1963), vol. 1: 315a, which gives, as an example, a quotation of the *Caityapradakṣiṇagāthā* (*Zuorao Fota gongde jing* 左繞佛塔功德經), the "Sūtra of the Merit of Circumambulation" (T. 700), translated by Śikṣānanda (652–710).

19. See in particular the section "Divine Rites to Prolong Life" (*Shenbian yanming fa* 神變延命法) of the *Rites of the Vajra-Being of Impure Traces* (*Ucchuṣma*) *for Exorcising the Hundred Weirds* (*Huiji jingang jin baibian fa jing* 穢跡金剛禁百變法經, T. 1229, vol. 21: 160). On this apocryphal work, see Strickmann (2002): 158–161; and Davis (2001): 134–136.

20. The work is labelled as apocryphal in Mingquan's late seventh-century catalogue (T. 2153, vol. 55: 15/474), in the same category as the *Yisuan jing* (see below).

21. S. 2428. A different version of this sūtra, with the same title (P. 2171), advocates the recitation of the names of seventeen divinities. See Makita (1976): 80–83.

With greater complexity, the *Sūtra to Increase the Account* sets forth a selection of ritual processes that, as will be seen later on, also aim at the consolidation and augmentation of the life-capital for its practitioners. The formulae, invocations, and talismans advocated here, both apotropaic and prophylactic, are considered infallible guarantees of the security and health without which one could not attain a respectable old age.

The Buddhist *Yisuan jing*

A half-dozen copies of the *Sūtra to Increase the Account*—or, according to its full title, the *Sūtra of the Divine Talismans of the Seven Thousand Buddhas [to Increase the Account], Preached by the Buddha* (*Foshuo qiqian fo shenfu [yisuan] jing* 佛說七千佛神符[益筭]經)—are preserved in the collections from Dunhuang.[22] A fragment of the text was also discovered among the manuscripts of Turfan (Ch. 2190 R°). The edition of the sūtra in the *Taishō shinshū daizōkyō* is based upon Dunhuang manuscript S. 2708, but this edition,[23] as well as that established by Makita Tairyō, supply only a fragmentary version. They evidently do not take into account manuscripts P. 2558 R° and P. 3022 R°, in which the beginning of the work is indeed present and which therefore permit us to reconstruct the integrality of the text.

In its variant versions, the sūtra bears the title *Sūtra of the Divine Talismans of the Seven Thousand Buddhas, Preached by the Buddha* (*Foshuo qiqian fo shenfu jing* [P. 3022R°, S. 2708]), or the abridged title *Sūtra to Increase the Account* (*Yisuan jing*, or *Foshuo yisuan jing* [P. 2558 R°, P. 4667 V°]), or else a title combining the two: *Sūtra of the Divine Talismans of the Seven Thousand Buddhas to Increase the Account, Preached by the Buddha* (*Foshuo qiqian fo shenfu yisuan jing*, P. 2558 R°). In most cases, the sūtra is edited in the form of an independent work, but we also find it included in a manual of divinatory techniques (P. 4667 V°), to which we shall return. A copy of the text also occurs in a manuscript where it follows the Tantric *Dhāraṇī Sūtra for the Salvation of Preta with Burning Mouths* (*Foshuo jiuba yankou egui tuoluoni jing* 佛說救拔焰口餓鬼陀羅尼經), the translation of which is attributed to Amoghavajra 不空 (705–774).[24] Finally, we may note as well the curious presence of seven of the fifteen talismans of the *Yisuan jing* at the end of a Dunhuang manuscript copy of the *Sūtra for the Conjuration of Bewitchments, Preached by the Buddha* (S. 4524), which has been examined in chapter 2.

---

22. P. 2558 R°, P. 2723, P. 3022 R°, P. 4667 V° (P. tib. 2207), S. 2708, and S. 4524.
23. T. 2904, vol. 85: 1446.
24. P. 3022 R° and T. 1313, vol. 21: 464–465. Although belonging to the same manuscript, this text is from another hand.

There is no mention of the *Sūtra to Increase the Account* prior to the end of the seventh century. Mingquan 明佺 signals its existence in his Buddhist *Catalogue of Scriptures Authorized by the Great Zhou* (*Da Zhou kanding zhongjing mulu* 大周刊定眾經目錄), a bibliography compiled under the patronage of the empress Wu Zetian 武則天 in 695. The *Yisuan jing* may have then existed in three versions, for Mingquan gives three consecutive titles of the sūtra that are undeniably related as confirmed by later catalogues: a *Sūtra to Increase the Account* (*Foshuo yisuan jing* 佛說益算經一卷), a *Sūtra of the Divine Talismans of the Seven Buddhas* (*Foshuo qifo shenfu jing* 佛說神符經一卷), and a *Sūtra of the Divine Talismans to Increase the Account* (*Foshuo yisuan shenfu jing* 佛說益算神符經一卷).[25] In the view of this Tang bibliographer, these three works, like the other apocrypha he lists, are of little value. This, at least, is the impression he gives when he comments:

> These have been forever among the sūtras classed as false (*weimiu*). Although they lay claim to the name of the Buddha, their stylistic confusion, and the corruption and inconsistency of their contents, leave not the shadow of a doubt that this is in fact a question of human falsification.

Less than a century later, the Buddhist Zhisheng, in his *Record of Śākyamuni's Teaching, Compiled during the Kaiyuan Era* (*Kaiyuan shijiao lu*) of 730, mentions only a single *Yisuan jing* but specifies that the sūtra had indeed been registered under three different titles in the catalogue of his predecessor Mingquan.[26] Is it possible that, in the span of a few decades, three different sūtras had been merged into one, or that, since its origins, a single text had come to be known by three titles, as Zhisheng seems to have suggested? The variants in the titles of the sūtra known from the copies found at Dunhuang would incline us to the latter option if the question of the "two Taoist *Yisuan jing*" did not put this in doubt.

The Two Taoist *Yisuan jing*

If only a single Buddhist recension of the *Yisuan jing* has come down to us, we have indeed, as mentioned above, access to two different Taoist *Yisuan jing* in the Ming *Daozang*. The first is entitled the *Marvelous Scripture for Prolonging Life and for Increasing the Account, Revealed by the Most High Lord Lao* (*Taishang Laojun shuo changsheng yisuan miaojing* 太上老君說長生益算妙經, Dz 650), and the second is the *Marvelous Scripture of the Divine Talismans to Increase the*

---

25. T. 2153, vol. 55: 15/474c.
26. Zhisheng mentions a "one-*juan* Yisuan jing" 益算經一卷 (T. 2154, vol. 55: 18/677b).

Account, Revealed by the Most High Lord Lao (*Taishang Laojun shuo yisuan shenfu miaojing* 太上老君說益算神符妙經, Dz 672).[27] It is the first *Yisuan jing* that is, as we shall see, the near-perfect double of the Buddhist *Yisuan jing*.[28] As for the second Taoist *Yisuan jing,* it might have been a rewrite of the first, but one cannot entirely exclude the possibility that it could also have been the model for one of the two other Buddhist *Yisuan jing* mentioned by Mingquan and lost thereafter.

The close relationship of the two Taoist *Yisuan jing* is unmistakable. Besides their titles, the two works bear many other similarities, beginning with the unusual site of their revelation: a country called Chanli 禪黎國, situated in the Azure Heaven (*Biluo tian* 碧落天). The two texts inform us that it was here, on the Rampart of Red Stone (Chishi cheng 赤石城) in the city of Shudu 蜀都 (at present Chengdu 城都, in Sichuan) that Laojun taught them to the Heavenly Master Zhang Daoling 張道陵, some months apart during the first year of the mythical era Han'an 漢安. He confided to Zhang the mission of eradicating evil and increasing the longevity of human beings, while sparing them from calamity and illness. The transmission of each of the two works was made under a pledge: an "oath sealed with the help of a stone split [in two parts]" (*zheshi wei xin* 折石為信), each part being kept by one of the parties, in the case of the "first" *Yisuan jing;* and an oath "engraved in stone" (*keshi wei xin* 刻石為信) in the case of the "second," which adds that Zhao Sheng 趙昇 and Wang Chang 王長, the two favorite disciples of the Heavenly Master, were present as witnesses.[29]

The two Taoist works promise to their devotees the support of the astral officers (*tianxing guan* 天星官), the directors of long life (*changsheng siming* 長生司命), and other spatiotemporal deities, and they insist in particular upon the power of the Generals of the Six *jia,* also called the "divinities of the Six *jia* governing the account" (*liujia zhusuan shen* 六甲主算神). It suffices to invoke these Generals by their proper names in order to obtain their assistance and, above all, additions to the "account," that is, extensions of life.

Although the transmission of these two works to Zhang Daoling, the founder of the Taoist clergy during the second century C.E., is of course fic-

---

27. One should also add to these a third work that bears the title of *Marvelous Scripture of the Divine Incantations for Prolonging Life by the Most High* (*Taishang shenzhou yanshou miaojing* 太上神咒延壽妙經, Dz 358). But this third short text seems to be a later, abridged version of Dz 650.

28. Xiao Dengfu mentions the proximity of the two texts in his *Daojiao xingdou fuyin yu fojiao mizong* (1993): 31–35.

29. Dz 650. 4b and Dz 672. 2a. On Zhao Sheng and Wang Chang, see the translation of Zhang Daoling's biography in Ge Hong's *Shenxian zhuan* 神仙傳 (fourth century C.E.), in Campany (2002): 349–356.

titious, their affiliation to the "One and Orthodox" (Zhengyi 正一) Way of the Heavenly Master (Tianshi dao 天師道) is nonetheless perfectly credible. We will see that the central role of the Generals of the Six *jia* in the two texts and the recitation of the invocation dedicated to them are in effect derived from Zhengyi rituals of the Six Dynasties period.

Closely linked by their narrative frame and their religious origin, the two Taoist *Yisuan jing* reveal nevertheless a major disparity: their talismans are completely different. Although the eight *fu* of the "second" Taoist *Yisuan jing* (Dz 672) are talismans related to the seven stars of the Great Dipper (Beidou 北斗), with the addition of one *fu* relating to the constellation of the Three Terraces (Santai 三台), the fifteen talismans of the "first" *Yisuan jing* (Dz 650), to be examined below, are altogether sui generis. Why, then, given that they proclaim themselves to be products of a common revelation and promote the same practice, do our two Taoist *Yisuan jing* present two types of talismans? The most plausible explanation appears to be that these talismans are complementary. The *fu* "to increase the life-capital" and those of the Great Dipper would form part of a single ritual ensemble whose evident purpose is to guarantee the security and longevity of the initiates. We will see in the next chapter how the stars of the Beidou and the Three Terraces play a central role in Taoist, but also Buddhist, astrological conceptions and rituals and that, in fact, the talismans of the "second" *Yisuan jing* are found in a Taoist text related to the cult of the Dipper.

Before we examine in detail the varied ritual components of the method "to increase the account" and attempt to disclose the manner in which the Buddhist *Yisuan jing* was calqued on the basis of its Taoist model, we must first turn to the contents of the scriptures themselves.

Synopsis

I provide here a paraphrase of the Taoist version of the *Yisuan jing*. The Buddhist sūtra corresponds closely, with the exception of the introductory section and several short phrases (given in brackets in the text that follows), as well as a few additional variants analyzed below.

> [Once upon a time, in the land of Chanli (Chanli guo 禪黎國) in the Azure Heaven (*Biluo tian* 碧落天), the Most High Lord Lao, deploring the distress of men and women stricken with illness, tribulations and premature death, convoked the Celestial Officers of the Ten Directions (Shifang tianguan 十方天官), the Veritable Lords of the Five Peaks (Wuyue zhenjun 五岳真君), the Directors of Long Life (Changsheng siming 長生司命), and many other divinities to a special assembly. Because,

he explained, there are so few in the world who hold allegiance to the Dao, it is urgent to remedy the lack of instruction among human beings who, instead of preserving themselves, accumulate evil deeds and thus provoke disease and suffering.

The Most High has therefore ordained the convocation of the Divinities of the Six *jia* governing the account (of destiny) (Liujia zhusuan shen 六甲主算神), together with their cavalry, requiring that they patrol the world to promulgate his teaching there and to transmit his talismans. People should wear them, recite this scripture, and observe the interdictions. Respecting the Three Jewels and rendering a cult to them with offerings of incense, each will be able to escape from calamities and demons.]

The Generals of the Six *jia* are called by their personal names, together with their escort of officers, to come in order to protect and to shore up the life-allocation of the faithful. (*Refer to the full translation of this passage in the section "The Invocation of the Generals of the Six jia," below.*)

Thus, those who are in the throes of death may, thanks to these Generals and their 12,700 protective divinities, acquire a life-supplement of 2,999 units (*dao* 道). Similarly, those who suffer from illnesses and other demonic aggressions will be saved by the intervention of the thousands of divinities called upon to aid them. They will see their life-capital augmented by thousands of units and so will attain immortality and the Dao. The divinities of destiny not only exercise a protective function but equally confer wisdom and lucidity. They also chase off demons and fulfil one's wishes.

The Most High Divine Talismans (*taishang shenfu* 太上神符), also called divine talismans of the Six *jia* (*liujia shenfu* 六甲神符), have the power to hammer down demons, vermin, and poisons used in bewitchment, deities of mountains and forests, gods of the soil and of grain, gods of the wind and the stove, as well as the dragon deities. They can also sweep away nightmares and dementia, sorcery and malediction, devils and bloodsucking vampires.

This scripture, sovereign among all scriptures, must be maintained with great respect and must not be divulged lightly.

Each of the seven stars of the Northern Dipper controls a particular domain: the first, bad energies; the second, ghosts; the third, demons; the fourth, bad dreams; the fifth, maledictions; the sixth, administrative altercations; and the seventh, bankruptcy. [The two assistant stars of the Dipper respectively control persons' destiny and demonic spirits.] The stars of the Three Terraces protect human life, while the Five Stars (Wuxing 五星) have the power to eliminate calamity and adversity, to drive away epidemics, diseases, and prejudices due to treachery or jealousy, and to put to flight all demons. "May each in haste conform to the Law!"

Each of the five talismans possesses a specific power, whether protective or apotropaic (*discussed in detail below*). By simply wearing them, all evil creatures are disintegrated. "May each in haste conform to the Law!"

The Generals of the Six *jia* go into action beginning with the first among them on the first *jiazi* day of the first lunar month.

[It is in the fifth month of the first year of the Han'an 漢安 era, on the Rampart of Red Stone in the capital of Shu (Shudu), that the Most High Lord Lao has delivered this revelation to the Heavenly Master. On this occasion, an oath was sealed by means of a stone split (in two parts).]

The faithful who sense the arrival of the end of their existence may, after having bathed and taken the precepts, escape death by burning incense and meditating.

By the same token, those whose days are numbered may, by wearing these Divine Talismans of the Great Dao (*dadao shenfu* 大道神符), obtain celestial protection from suffering and calamity, as well as an augmentation of nine billion units of life-capital. With the "perfect energies" that nourish their three cinnabar fields thus maximized, a longevity of 120 years is guaranteed to them.

(*Here follows the beginning of a litany for personal protection* [*see the translation below*], *which is then interrupted to describe the beneficent effects of the talismans:*)

In this way, the disciples who wear the talismans placed under the defense of the Generals of the Five Peaks (Wuyue jiangjun 五岳將軍) become invulnerable.

(*The second part of the litany is then taken up again for three columns of the text.*)[30]

Each of the ten demonifuge talismans exercises control over a type of demon (*see the list below in the section "Talismans for Increasing the Life-Capital"*). "May each in haste conform to the Law!"

(*Here follow the models of the fifteen talismans.*)

Genesis of an Apocryphon

While the *Yisuan jing* relates, in the classic manner, how it was transmitted by Laojun to a celestial assembly charged with its diffusion on earth for salvific ends, the Buddhist sūtra remains completely silent regarding its divine origin. The text begins abruptly, without the usual narrative introduction (Skt. *nidānakathā*) indicating how the Buddha came to preach it.[31] Neglecting thus the stylistic conventions common to Buddhist sūtras, whether apocryphal or not, the author or authors were content with a brief phrase to point out the religious identity of the sūtra and assure faithful readers of its credentials as the Venerable One's words:

---

30. The litany begins at the last column of page 4b and is interrupted at the seventh column of page 5a. It starts again at the last column of page 5a and ends at the third column of this same page.

31. P. 2558 R° and P. 3022 R°.

The Buddha preached this Sūtra to save and protect life, to increase the account, and to save people from disease and affliction, [and the teaching was received] upon bent knee, with palms joined, and wholeheartedly, in order to expel disorder and annihilate evil.[32]

Without this hasty note and a peppering of Buddhist terms among the text columns, it would be absolutely impossible to distinguish our apocryphon from its Taoist double. In effect, with only a minimum of resources the Taoist persona of the *Yisuan jing* was erased so that the revelation of Lord Lao could masquerade as a Buddhist sūtra. A new title was thus effortlessly created by the simple addition of the three characters *qiqian fo* 七千佛, "seven thousand buddhas," to the characters *Yisuan jing*.[33] The adjustments effected in the body of the sūtra were similarly slapdash, and the substitutions of specialized vocabulary may be readily picked out: "buddhas" has replaced "immortals" (*xian* 仙), and "bodhisattvas" (*pusa* 菩薩) stands for "perfected ones" (*zhenren* 真人); the "orthodox way" (*zhengdao* 正道) has become the "way of the Buddha" (*fodao* 佛道); the Generals of the Six *jia* have abandoned their officer corps in favor of an escort of buddhas, while such Taoist appellations as Divine Talismans of the Great Dao or Most High Divine Talismans (*taishang shenfu*), designating the ensemble of the *fu* presented here, have been bartered for the ostensibly Buddhist label "talismans of the thousand (or seven thousand) buddhas" ([*qi*] *qianfo fu*). This is how, without further artifice, our Buddhist sūtra was made to see the light of day.

Easy and fast, the "cut-and-paste" method, whose results may be amply appreciated here, would have served more than one counterfeiter to fabricate sacred writ. It is again to Du Guangting that one must turn for a contemporaneous testimony of this singular editorial procedure. In his tenth-century *Record of Miracles in Support to Taoism* (*Daojiao lingyan ji*), referred to earlier, Du recounts how a Buddhist monk named Facheng 法成[34] came to withdraw a hundred Taoist manuscripts and then describes what he did next:

---

32. P. 3022 R°, cols. 1–2.

33. One notices here that the "seven thousand buddhas" who appear in most of the titles of the Dunhuang recensions seem to result from the stylistic inflation of the "Seven Buddhas," a fact confirmed by the list of titles given in Mingquan's catalogue. It is nonetheless interesting to note that the number "seven thousand" is also used in Taoism to designate the "seven thousand divine generals of the Northern Dipper" who come to earth to attend to the "delimitation of personal destiny" in the Taoist *Beidou jing* (*Taishang xuanling beidou benming yansheng zhenjing* 太上玄靈北斗本命延生真經, Dz 622).

34. It seems very unlikely that this figure mentioned by Du Guangting, and said to be of unknown origins, could be the famous Tang-dynasty Tibetan monk and translator of the same name.

He substituted their titles to give them the names of Buddhist sūtras. He replaced "Heavenly Venerable" (*tianzun*) with "buddha," "perfected ones" with "bodhisattvas" and "arhats" (*luohan* 羅漢). In many places, he modified dialogues and terminology, striking out and cutting [the texts] of some 160 scrolls.[35]

Such was the dishonorable fashion, in the eyes of Du, in which a good number of Buddhist sūtras were created. And as we have seen in chapter 1, in the same *Daojiao lingyan ji* Du denounces, in a more circumstantial manner, the fraudulent production by similar means of the *Sūtra of the Three Kitchens*.

Was the *Yisuan jing* a part of the plunder of 160 Taoist manuscripts pirated for a bargain by Facheng? Du does not breathe a word about this. But, in what concerns us here, the comparison that can be made between the "original" Taoist version of the *Yisuan jing* and its Buddhist "counterfeit," together with a close analysis of the method for "increasing the account," will permit us to evaluate with relative precision the manner in which the apocryphal sūtra was born.

The Method to Increase the Life-Capital

In one tradition as in the other, the ritual instructions concerning the conditions for the transmission of the *Yisuan jing* are meager. The Taoists indicate that the "disciples" (*dizi* 弟子) who receive the protective talismans must wear them, recite the sacred scripture, worship with incense offerings, and respect the Three Jewels as well as the precepts (*zhaijie* 齋戒), which are not, however, explicitly stipulated.[36] There is, in any case, a rule upon which the text insists— namely, that it must not be divulged lightly.[37] These bits of information give us to understand that the possession of the scripture was subject to an initiation. Might this have taken place within a framework of therapeutic rituals? The text promises on several occasions, in effect, miraculous remissions for the ill and the dying, bestowed by the divinities summoned to infuse them with an existential reprieve. It is possible that it was through the medium of curative rites that Buddhists or Taoists transmitted to these fortunate survivors the talismans that suited their problems and eventually the scripture as well as the oral directives for observing its worship and method.

The *Yisuan jing* resists stylistic linearity no less than doctrinal consistency, weaving together incantatory formulae and talismans. At first glance, the reader has the impression that it consists of a juxtaposition of disparate recipes. This ap

---

35. *Daojiao lingyan ji*, Dz 590. 12/1b; also edited in *Yunji qiqian*, 119/23a. See a summary of Facheng's story in Verellen (1992): 248–249.

36. Dz 650. 1b.

37. Dz 650. 3b.

parent absence of cohesiveness, however, is neither accidental, nor exceptional. It derives from the fact that the *Yisuan jing,* like many other ritual manuals, whether Taoist or Buddhist, responds primarily to practical requirements. The work nevertheless cannot be reduced to a mnemonic aid or an instruction manual. Whether preached by the Buddha or revealed by Laozi, it claims, in fact, to be eminently sacred and so demands respect and veneration. It is the "Sovereign among all sacred scriptures" (*zhongjing zhi wang* 眾經之王), says the Taoist version, and therefore the faithful must worship it.[38] The stereotyped expression "May each in haste conform to the Law!" (*jiji ru lüling* 急急如律令), which intermittently punctuates the diverse sequences of the text, its incantations, and invocations, suggests an oral, ritual use for the scripture. Parts of it must certainly have been chanted in order to put into action and to reinforce the efficiency of its talismans.

The various ritual components of the *Yisuan jing* are chained together in the following order:

> Invocation of the Generals of the Six *jia*
> List of the names of the seven stars of the Northern Dipper, the Three
>   Terraces, and the Five Stars
> List of five prophylactic talismans
> Litany for personal protection
> List of ten demonifuge talismans
> Models of the fifteen talismans

These ritual sequences, however disconnected they may appear, closely correlate with one another, as will be demonstrated in the course of our analysis.

The Invocation of the Generals of the Six *jia*

The Buddhist *Yisuan jing* and the two Taoist *Yisuan jing* are placed under the patronage of the divinities of the Six *jia* 六甲. The assigned role of the Generals of the Six *jia* is to supervise human destiny and to guarantee, thanks to the aid of their innumerable subalterns, the security and longevity of the faithful. For this purpose, too, they oversee the diffusion of the scripture and its prodigious talismans. Their function is, as a result, of the highest importance, and the invocation dedicated to them thus merits our attention.[39] Here I give a

---

38. Dz 650. 1b and 3b.

39. This invocation of the Generals of the Six *jia* is located at the very beginning of the Buddhist sūtra and just after the introductory scenario of the two Taoist *Yisuan jing* (Dz 650. 1b–2a and Dz 672. 2b–3a).

complete translation of it after the version found in the "first" Taoist *Yisuan jing*:

> The *jiazi* General 甲子將軍, Wang Wenqing 王文卿, and his following of 149 officers "bring forth my account" (*sheng wo yisuan* 生我益算) with [a deposit of] two thousand units (*dao* 道), protecting my person while permitting me to attain perfection of spirit, serenity of heart, and the expulsion of evil and illness.
>
> The *jiaxu* General 甲戌, Zhan Zijiang 展子江, and his escort of 135 officers "bring forth my account" with [a deposit of] two thousand units, acting so as to protect my person by expelling affliction and suffering from my body.
>
> The *jiashen* General 甲申, Hu Wenzhang 扈文長, and his following of 131 officers "nourish" (*yang* 養) my account of two thousand units and assure my protection by acting so as to put back in place [lit. "return"] my celestial and terrestrial souls (*hun* and *po*).
>
> The *jiawu* General 甲午, Wei Shangqing 衛上卿, and his escort of 139 officers "credit" (*yu* 與) my account of two thousand units, guaranteeing me a longevity of 120 years.
>
> The *jiachen* General 甲辰, Meng Feiqing 孟非卿, and his following of 135 officers "supplement" (*fu* 扶) my account of two thousand units, surveying my person and sparing me all adversity.
>
> The *jiayin* General 甲寅, Ming Wenzhang 明文章, and his 131 officers "guarantee" (*jiu* 救) my account of two thousand units and protect my person by intercepting all demons.[40]

The Six *jia,* as purveyors of vitality and invested here with the rank of general, are none other, to be sure, than the markers serving to indicate the beginning of each of the decades in the sexagesimal cycle of the Chinese calendar. Early on, due to the initial and pivotal positions of the *jia* in the temporal scale, they were assigned divinities to whom a determining role in the regulation of the cosmos was attributed. Systems of hemerological divination, such as the famous and abstruse technique of the "hidden periods" (*dunjia* 遁甲), which were dedicated to them, had applications in the military arts as well as in the occult sciences.[41] The talismans associated with the Six *jia* were endowed with extraordinary protective and exorcistic virtues. Conferred upon Taoist adepts who were sufficiently advanced in their training to "nourish life," they were special tools for attaining immortality. Thanks to them, Taoist initiates could,

---

40. Dz 650. 1b–2a.

41. On the *dunjia* method, see Ngô (1976): 190–195; Andersen (1989–1990): 33–34; and Schipper (1965): 34–42. On the *dunjia* in the *Baopuzi,* see also Campany (2002): 231–232. On the Six *jia* and their role in the Taoist hemerological systems, see Schipper and Wang (1986): 201–204.

after having retrieved the *jia* conjunctions in the sexagesimal cycle, slip across the calendrical interstices so as to pass beyond the time-space continuum. Thus "hidden" (*dun*)—invisible to the common run of mankind and invulnerable to the demonic attacks that were particularly acute during these critical moments—the adepts could merge with the divinities in the other dimension, the world of nonbeing that belongs to the immortals.

As suggested earlier, the talismanic tradition of the Six *jia* was connected with other means to achieve immortality, such as the practice of the Kitchens. The Six Dynasties Shangqing Taoists were great experts in this domain. In his *Declarations of the Perfected* (*Zhengao* 真誥), the illustrious hermitic scholiast and ninth patriarch of the lineage, Tao Hongjing 陶弘景 (456–536), makes several allusions to the "Yin and Yang talismans of the Six *jia* of the mobile Kitchens" (*liujia yinyang xingchu fu* 六甲陰陽行廚符) that the adept must swallow in order to obtain supernatural capacities.[42] But the transcendent Six *jia* prized by the Shangqing adepts were female deities, "jade maidens" (*yunü* 玉女), and therefore quite different from the male, martial *jia* of the *Yisuan jing.* In order to trace these Generals of the Six *jia,* one must turn to another Taoist pantheon: that of the Way of the Heavenly Master.

Among the myriad of divinities supposed to assure inalterable assistance to the Heavenly Master's initiates, a major place is accorded to the deities of the calendrical cycle and consequently to the Six *jia.* One finds them inventoried primarily in two types of Zhengyi sources: on the one hand, in the initiatory and protective registers (*lu* 錄) that the faithful received successively, at different stages of their lives, in accord with their spiritual elevation and, on the other, in the manuals of "petitions" (*zhang* 章), the written requests that were sent to the cosmic authorities in the course of curative or exorcistic rituals.

An excellent example of the first type of document is the "Purple Register" (Chilu 赤錄), or Tenth Register, which corresponds to the highest degree of initiation prior to clerical ordination in a Zhengyi parish.[43] In this important

---

42. Dz 1016. 20/7b. Tao Hongjing also mentions in his *Zhen'gao* a Method of the Flying Spirits of the Six *jia* (Lingfei liujia fa 靈飛六甲法, Dz 1016. 18/11b). See Robinet (1984), vol. 2: 207–212. For other talismans of the Six *jia,* see the *Marvelous and Mysterious Veritable Scripture of the White Monkey of the Dongshen [Canon]* (*Taishang dongshen xuanmiao baiyuan zhenjing* 太上洞神玄妙白猿真經, Dz 858) and the *Secret Scripture of the Talismans of the Luminous Mirror of the Liuren Talismans of the Most High* (*Taishang liuren mingjian fuyin jing* 太上六壬明鑑符陰經, Dz 861. 1/13a–16a and 2/5a–6a). The talismans of the Six *jia* are mentioned in the bibliographical passage of the *Baopuzi neipian,* chap. 19, Wang Ming, ed.: 335). See also Inoue (1992).

43. The faithful to whom it was transmitted, having reached the mastership of space and time, were authorized to practice the sexual rites of the "Union of Pneumata" (*heqi* 合氣) to obtain immortality, thanks to which they could conceive perfect children, or "seed children" (*zhongzi* 種子). On the Taoist sexual rites, see Yoshioka (1964); Strickmann (1981): 148–152; Kalinowski (1985); and Mollier (1990): 76–77.

register, the Six *jia* are, like the fifty-four other cyclical divinities, flanked by officers (*congguan* 從官), and their proper names are precisely those of the Generals of the Six *jia* of the *Yisuan jing*: Wang Wenqing, Zhan Zijiang, Hu Wenzhang, Wei Shangqing, Meng Feiqing, and Ming Wenzhang (fig. 3.1). Another Zhengyi register, the *Marvelous Scripture of the Talismans of the Six jia to Guard the Womb and Protect Life, Revealed by the Most High* (*Taishang shuo liujia zhenfu baotai huming miaojing* 太上說六甲真符保胎護命妙經), also presents the Six *jia* with the same patronyms, but in this case the temporal divinities fulfil a more specific task: the facilitation of childbirth.[44]

The Six Dynasties Zhengyi rituals of petitions also did not fail to call upon or, more precisely, to refer to the Six *jia*. We have seen in chapter 2 how the *Petition Almanac of Master Red Pine* relied upon the deified sexagesimal markers to oppose sorcery. But a better example of the use of the Six *jia* is found in another, less well-known Zhengyi calendar of petitions entitled the *Almanac for Organizing Rituals of Petition according to the Original Stars* (*Yuanchen zhangjiao licheng li* 元辰章醮立成曆). In a passage precisely designated the "Selection of the Names of the Divinities of the Six *jia* and the Number of Their Officers" (*Tui liujia shenming ji congguan shu* 推六甲神名及從官數), this calendar provides a complete list of the Six Markers, with their personal names and the exact number of officers in their escort.[45] The small hemerological treatise that serves as an appendix to this almanac furnishes the following indications, for example, concerning the pair formed by the fifth and third *jia*:

> *Jiachen* 甲辰 [who is called] Meng Feiqing 孟非卿 is escorted by fourteen officers; *jiaxu* 甲戌 [who is called] Zhan Zijiang 展子江 is escorted by fourteen officers. [Position of] the star Lucun 祿存 (the third star of the Beidou).[46]

Obscure as they are, astrocalendrical instructions such as these permitted the Taoist Masters to evaluate lucky and unlucky conjunctions and to calculate the periods of the intervention of the temporal deities and the propitious times for conjuring away evil and for sending the written petition to heaven. For this reason, the ascertainment of the positions of the Six *jia* was crucial. For it is precisely

44. Dz 50. 3a–7b. The text allegedly transmitted by Laojun to the Guardian of the Pass, Yin Xi 尹喜, includes a talisman called "stabilizer *fu* of the Six *jia*" (*liujia zhefu* 直符) to be placed close to the head of a woman in labor in order to drive away maledictions.

45. Dz 1288. 2/4a–6a. In addition, the text describes each of the sequences of the ritual and gives a complete list of the markers and symbols that compose the "original destiny" (*yuanchen* 元辰), that is, the origin and destiny of the individual.

46. *Sexagesimal Calendar of Personal Destiny and the Original Stars* (*Liushi jiazi benming yuanchen li* 六十甲子本命元辰曆), Dz 1289. 2a.

FIG. 3.1. The Generals of the Six *jia* at Mount Heming 鶴鳴山 in Jiange 劍閣, Sichuan. Late Tang dynasty. Photograph by the author, 2004.

at these moments that, as underscored by the *Petition Almanac of Master Red Pine,* the "gates of the heavens are open," so that it is entirely propitious to launch ritual missives into the divine spheres.[47] The petition was redacted with reference to the particular problem motivating it and to the patient's horoscope. The knowledge of the positions of the seven stars of the Great Dipper, which manages each person's destiny, was therefore also indispensable.

To take the full measure of the connection existing between these stars and the Six *jia* markers, we must rely upon later Taoist sources, notably the *Guide to the Golden Lock and the Moving Pearls (Jinsuo liuzhu yin),* already mentioned in chapter 2. The text, which devotes several chapters to rites centered around the Six *jia* and the Beidou, underlines the intimate filiations uniting them as well as other astrocalendrical elements: "The seven stars are the children of the Six *jia*" 七星六甲之子也, "the Six *jia* are the children of the Five Phases" 六甲者五行之子也, or else "the Six *jia* are the father and mother of the seven stars" 六甲是七星之父母.[48] More explicitly, the *Guide to the Golden Locks and the Moving Pearls* situates the Six *jia,* as active principles of the cosmogonic process, within a sequence conforming to the normal, even stereotypical, Taoist scheme of the creation of the universe: the Dao, it is declared, gives birth to the One, the One to the Two (Yin and Yang), the Two to the Three (the ten thousand things), the Three to the Four (the four seasons), the Four to the Five (the Five Phases), the Five to the Six *jia,* the Six *jia* to the Seven (the seven stars), and so on.[49] As regulators of the cosmic tempo—by the same token as Yin and Yang or as the Five Phases—the Six *jia,* which engender the seven stars of the Great Dipper, thus exercise ascendancy over these latter. Besides, the *Guide to the Golden Locks and the Moving Pearls* insists on the obligation of the Taoist adept to invoke the personal names of the Generals in Chief (*da jiangjun* 大將軍) of the Six *jia* (although it abstains from giving them) and stipulates the existence of hundreds and thousands of subaltern divinities, jade maidens, and youths, serving under their command.[50] And, as we have seen above, the *Yisuan jing,* evidently with greater care for precision, speaks of 12,700 divinities enrolled under the Six *jia* Generals' authority.

To this I must add that the dynamic relation among the Six *jia* and the seven stars of the Great Dipper does not act solely on a cosmic scale. In conformity with

---

47. Dz 615. 1/22a. See also Campany (2002): 74n200.

48. Dz 1015. 20/1a–1b.

49. Dz 1015. 16/1a.

50. Dz 1015. 16/2b–3a. In order to invoke these countless divinities, the commentary suggests that the practitioner of the talismanic ritual inscribe the names of the Generals, officers, and jade maidens (at least probably the most important among them) on a bamboo slip and hang it on a wall or a pillar. He can thereby be sure to put into action the entire exorcistic and protective pantheon of the Six *jia.*

Taoist principles of resonance and correspondence between the universe and the human body, the Six *jia* are also divinities residing in each of us, managing our anatomy. In his early eighth-century commentary on the *Precious Book of the Inner Landscape of the Yellow Court* (*Huangting neijing yujing* 黃庭內景玉經), Bo Lüzhong 白履忠, for example, holds the Six *jia* responsible for the opening and proper function (or the good "circulation," *tong* 通) of the "seven orifices," or "seven doors" of the body, a role usually assigned to the seven stars of the Beidou, as will be detailed in chapter 4.[51] Bo underscores as well the exorcistic mission of the Six *jia* within the human body and the necessity of reciting their personal names so as to prevent all forms of disease.[52] It comes as no surprise to learn that the six prophylactic patronymics enumerated by Bo are exactly those of the Generals of the Six *jia* of the Heavenly Masters' pantheon and the two Taoist *Yisuan jing*.

If it is impossible to affirm that the invocation of the Generals of the Six *jia* reaches back to the ancient Chinese longevity practices of which the *Book of the Inner Landscape of the Yellow Court* is one of the most salient representatives—Bo's commentary is late, and the *Book of the Inner Landscape of the Yellow Court* itself does not mention our divinities by name—it remains the case that it was a fundamental component of the Six Dynasties Zhengyi astrohemerological liturgy.[53]

Having concluded this long digression, we now must return to our subject proper and examine how this Taoist invocation of the Six *jia* survived in its Buddhist incarnation, the *Sūtra to Increase the Account,* where we find it, despite some emendations, preserved in its essentials. The first of the six invocations of the formula, for example, is rendered as follows:

> The *jiazi* 甲子 General brings forth my account and with the seven thousand buddhas (*qiqian fo* 七千佛) protects my person in bringing me to achieve unity of heart and in expelling evil and disease.[54]

As is evident, the suppression of the personal names of the Six Generals (perhaps considered too Chinese), and the replacement of their escorting offi-

---

    51. *Huangting neijing yujing zhu* 黃庭內景玉經註, Dz 402, commentary by Bo Lüzhong 白履忠, alias Liangqiu zi 梁丘子 (fl. 722–729), who is also the author of a commentary on the *Laozi* and was active during the Kaiyuan 開元 era under the emperor Tang Xuanzong 玄宗 (refer to his biography in the *Jiu Tang shu, juan* 192, Zhonghua shuju ed.: 5124).
    52. Dz 402. 3/8b–9a; also edited in *Yunji qiqian,* 12/11a.
    53. This Zhengyi inheritance, indirect as it may be, is also confirmed on the theological level. In perfect accord with the ideology of the Way of the Heavenly Master, which virulently condemns the worship of the carnivorous divinities of the traditional pantheon, the Taoist *Yisuan jing* promises a fatal end to the gods of the mountains and forests, of the soil and the cereals, and of the wind and the stove, as well as to all the other blood-eating demons (Dz 650. 5b).
    54. P. 3022 R° and P. 2558 R°.

cers by a following of seven thousand buddhas, permitted the Buddhist author(s) to adapt the formula to its new Buddhist context, and so too for the remaining five invocations. Thus, even though deprived of their patronyms and spruced up in the company of buddhas, our Six Generals were no less firmly ensconced in their respective roles as personal safeguards, regulators of energies, and exorcists of perverse forces. Once again, one can appreciate the degree to which the Buddhists, like their Taoist colleagues, and despite the haste with which they evidently fabricated this apocryphon, demonstrated scrupulous care for ritual formulae and procedures, the gold standard for all religious praxis.

Invoking the Stars

The second element in the ritual frame of the *Yisuan jing* is astrological in nature. It concerns two types of asterism supposed to ensure the safety and well-being of the faithful: on the one hand, the Five Stars, and, on the other, two Ursa Major constellations—namely, the Three Terraces (or Three Eminences) and the Great Dipper, whose close relationship to the Six *jia* we have just reviewed.[55]

It is not certain that the Five Stars, to which the *Yisuan jing* attributes considerable exorcistic potential, correspond to the Five Planets. With the exception of the fourth among them, which unambiguously designates Mars, the names of the four others do not at all correspond to the planets' usual designations:[56]

> Yuanxing 怨星, "star of hate"
> Liangxing 良星, "star of goodness"
> Bixing 辟星, "star of punishment"
> Yinghuo 熒惑, Mars
> Weixing 危星, "star of peril"

According to a widespread Chinese belief, the stars and planets, which generally bring luck to the faithful who worship them, can also turn into terribly dangerous entities at certain times of the year, threatening those who offend

---

55. According to Schlegel (1875), vol. 1: 529, the Three Terraces, or Three Eminences, are composed of three groups of stars corresponding to the "three legs of the Great Bear."

56. The names of the third star, Bixing 辟星, and the last one, Weixing 危星, seem, in fact, close to the names of two of the "twenty-eight lunar mansions" (*ershiba xiu* 二十八宿): respectively, the "Domicile of the Wall" (辟 for 壁?) and the " Domicile of the Peak" (Jiawu 架屋 or Weixu 危宿), of which the principal stars belong to the Pegasus constellation. See Schlegel (1875): 233, 845.

them or neglect to honor them.[57] The names given by the *Yisuan jing* to three of these Five Stars—"hate," "punishment," and "peril"—thus seem to indicate that their apotropaic properties are paired with their capacity to harm.

The *Yisuan jing* equally makes much of the seven (or nine) stars of the Dipper and their associates, the Three Terraces. These two constellations, widely venerated in numerous Chinese cults and rituals (and detailed in chapter 4), are assigned particular missions by practitioners of the *Yisuan jing*. The Three Terraces assure "protection for human life," while each of the stars of the Beidou fulfils a demonifuge function. Each of these seven stars is designated by its usual Taoist esoteric appellation. The first star, Greedy Wolf (Tanlang 貪狼) controls (*zhu* 主)[58] evil *qi* (*e'qi* 惡氣); the second, Great Gate (Jumen 巨門), ghosts (*feishi* 非屍); the third, Persistent Happiness (Lucun 祿存), demons (*baigui* 百鬼); the fourth, Civil Song (Wenqu 文曲), evil fate (*koushe* 口舌); the fifth, Pure Virtue (Lianzhen 廉貞), nightmares (*e'meng* 惡夢); the sixth, Military Song (Wuqu 武曲), administrative entanglements (*guanshi* 官事); and the seventh, Destroyer of Armies (Pojun 破軍), bankruptcies (*xuhao* 虛耗).[59] The eighth and ninth stars, the two minor stars of the constellation, namely Fuxing 輔星 and the invisible Bixing 弼星, have a less focused function. The eighth, Fuxing, which is the companion of the sixth star, safeguards human destiny, while the ninth, Bixing, located in the neighborhood of the Dipper's handle, pertains to the exorcism of demons.[60] We should note that these last two stars are omitted from the Buddhist sūtra, though it is unclear whether they were simply neglected or intentionally censored.

To keep evil and misery at a distance and to attract the auspicious influence of the Five Stars, the Three Terraces, and the Northern Dipper, the followers of the *Yisuan jing* in all likelihood had to recite their names, an exercise that may be discerned, once more, by the presence following each enumeration of the usual formula "in all haste, obey the Law!" (*jiji rulü ling*). We will see in chapter 4 that the recitation of the names of the seven stars of the Beidou was a basic practice for the adepts of its cult and that the talismans of the seven stars found in the "second" Taoist text (fig. 3.2)—the *Marvelous Scripture of the Divine Talismans to Increase the Account, Revealed by the Most High Lord Lao*—which are probably related to these astral invocations, figure in identical form in a late Taoist work related to the Northern Dipper.[61]

---

57. See Hou (1979).

58. Or "chases away" (*qu* 祛), according to Dz 672.

59. Dz 650. 4a; T. 2904, 1446a.

60. Dz 650. 4a. On the worship of these two stars, see Andersen (1989–1990): 34–35.

61. The *Winged Stanzas on the Golden Mystery of the Seven Principles of the Northern Dipper* (*Beidou qiyuan jinxuan yuzhang* 北斗七元金玄羽章, Dz 753). See fig. 4.7.

Finally, I should add that the decision by the authors of the Buddhist *Yisuan jing* to place their sūtra under the auspices of the seven (thousand) buddhas may also be clarified with reference to the complementarity between the *Yisuan jing* and the tradition of the Great Dipper. Though it is not made explicit in the text, the Seven Buddhas are certainly none other than the seven *tathāgatas* of Bhaiṣajyaguru, the Master of Medicine (Yaoshi 藥師), that were evoked in chapter 2 in relation with their anti-sorcery curative powers.[62] In the Buddhist *Beidou jing,* as will be seen below, each one of these seven *tathāgatas* is associated with one of the seven stars of the Dipper.

Talismans for Increasing the Life-Capital

The fifteen talismans that figure in the Taoist and Buddhist *Yisuan jing* no doubt constitute the core of its method for "increasing the account." The Buddhists preferred, in accord with their confessional requirements, to confer on them the generic label "talismans of the thousand buddhas," rather than to maintain the Taoist designation of "divine talismans of the Six *jia*," which, it should be noted, accentuates their affinity with the similarly titled invocation. Nevertheless, taken individually, each of the Buddhist *fu* (fig. 3.3) is graphically and nominally identical to its Taoist homologue (fig. 3.4).

The talismans are divided into two series, one of five prophylactic *fu* and the other of ten demonifuge *fu* (fig. 3.5). In accord with ancestral custom, they each bear titles revealing their specific functions. In the first series, one thus finds the following talismans:

1. "to open the heart" (*xinkai fu* 心開符)
2. "to increase the life-account" (*yisuan fu* 益算符)
3. "to protect life" (*jiuhu shengming fu* 護身命符)
4. "to regulate the Five Phases" (*jin mu shui huo tu bu xiangke fu* 金木水火土不相剋符)
5. "to govern human life [against] the murderous Aji demons and decrepitude" (*zhu shengren Aji sigui haoxu shenfu* 主生人阿姬死鬼耗虛神符)[63]

Connected most likely to the Five Stars, these five talismans serve as a shield to fend off the dangers that these astral conjunctions present during the course of each human life. As regulators of energies and protectors of life, they offer

---

62. The Seven Buddhas are Bhaiṣajyaguru and the six mythical buddhas who preceded the historical Buddha, Śākyamuni. See Kuo (1994a): 152–155, 163.

63. I have found no other reference to these "Aji" demons.

北斗破軍星君主誅虐耗

北斗左輔星君主人命算

北斗右弼星君主人身形

三台星君共增錄壽令無禍殃

第一惡星第二良星第三碎星第四熒惑星
第五危星是諸眾星尊神各為弟子某消災
度難辟除天下疫氣疾病姦媱妲妨害之
鬼各令速去千里萬里之外急急如

太上神符律令

老君曰吾今宣傳妙經廣說道法以符救人
佩帶之者當須精勤心常敬信無不安寧千
災萬禍俱時消化行藏動靜善瑞日臻所求
所願皆得遂心於是天師受得妙法而作頌
曰

神符神符　闓目太無　生天生地　與道卷舒

佩奉之者　厄難消除　得成真道　身昇玄都

天師說是頌畢與弟子趙昇王長稽首奉辭
而退

太上老君說益算神符妙經

Fɪɢ. 3.2. The talismans of the Great Dipper in the Taoist *Yisuan jing* (Dz 672).

二十道所護人身為除魔感甲申將軍尾文
長遣官一百二十人添弟子某文
道所護人身為除虛耗甲午將軍術上卿遣
官一百二十人為添弟子某福算萬二千道
所護人身為除橫害甲辰將軍孟非卿遣官
二十人永弟子某壽算萬二千道所護人身

一百二十人保弟子某財算萬二千道所護
人身令無衰損甲寅將軍明文章遣官一百
二十人永弟子某壽算萬二千道所護人身
令無夭折

老君曰六百甲子三元道泰君萬生益算君
大慈曜明等三千五百真人一時下降救護。

人身得延萬歲昇入正真
爾時諸天星宿大聖為絕冤讎

北斗貪狼星君主祛惡氣

北斗巨門星君主祛伏屍

北斗祿存星君主祛百鬼

北斗文曲星君主祛惡夢。

北斗廉貞星君主祛口舌

北斗武曲星君主祛官事

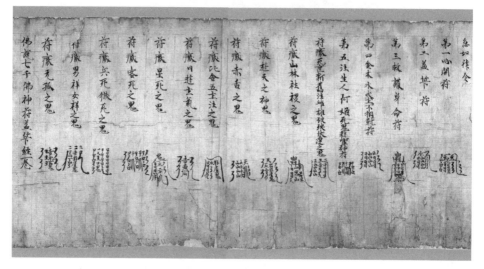

FIG. 3.3. The talismans of the Buddhist *Yisuan jing* from Dunhuang (P. 2558 R°). Courtesy of the Bibliothèque nationale de France.

the double advantage of acting not just on a cosmic scale but in terrestrial space as well, since they equally incorporate the virtues conferred upon them by the Generals of the Five Peaks—that is to say, the sacred mountains of China that are situated at the four cardinal points and the center.[64]

The ten talismans of the next series are possibly placed under the aegis of the ten stars of Ursa Major—that is to say, the pair formed by the Three Terraces and the seven stars of the Dipper. As indicated by their titles, each of these ten *fu* is specialized in the exorcism or "suppression" (*yan* 厭) of one particular species of demon:

1. "demons that travel in the light" (*youguang zhi gui* 遊光之鬼) (Buddhist: "demons that travel in the sky," *youtian zhi gui* 遊天之鬼)
2. "demons of mountains and forests" (*shanlin zhi gui* 山林之鬼)
3. "demons of the five regions" (*wutu zhi gui* 五土之鬼)
4. "wandering demons of the chthonic breaths" (*youzhi tuqi zhi gui* 遊止土氣之鬼)
5. "demons of deceased foreigners" (*gesi zhi gui* 客死之鬼)
6. "demons of those dead in prison" (*yusi zhi gui* 獄死之鬼)
7. "demons of innocent [victims]" (*wugu zhi gui* 無辜之鬼)
8. "demons induced by evil spells" (*chishe zhi gui* 赤舌之鬼)

---

64. Dz 650. 5a.

9. "male and female demons" (*cixiong zhi gui* 雌雄之鬼) (Buddhist: "demons of the past or recent dead, male and female, for three generations," *sishuai xinjiu zhu cixiong pofulian zhi gui sanshi* 死衰新舊注雌雄破伏連之鬼三世)

10. "demons of putrid cadavers" (*xingsi zhi gui* 腥死之鬼)

Above and beyond invulnerability, this collection of fifteen talismans is able to confer and to guarantee longevity. For those who receive them, the *Yisuan jing* promises a deposit of "nine billion units" in their personal life-capital, without doubt a considerable reprieve, as a span of 120 years is thereby acquired. This ability to preserve and to extend life depends, for the Taoist *Yisuan jing,* upon the energetic potential of these *fu.* They incorporate, it explains, innumerable "perfect breaths" (*zhenqi* 真氣) that nourish the Three Fields of Cinnabar (*dantian* 丹田), that is, the vital zones in the body.[65] According to conceptions still prevalent today, the energies projected into the graphs of the talisman by the diviner or the cleric, by means of the brush or fingers, are then absorbed by the patient to whom the *fu* is administered. Swallowed or "worn" (*pei* 佩), as in the case of the talismans of the *Yisuan jing,* it alleviates his organic or psychic deficiencies, restores his immunity and reinforces his health.

Did the devotee receive one or several of them? How were they chosen? The manner in which they were transmitted remains a mystery. The process whereby the *fu* were fabricated, though often noted among the prescriptions accompanying them, is also absent in this case. However, given the diversity and the apotropaic qualities of the talismans of the second series, we may imagine that they were prescribed on the basis of a diagnosis (perhaps through divination) establishing the demonic origin of the evil in question. The harmful spirits against which the exorcistic *fu* of the *Yisuan jing* are supposed to act belong in effect to the common demonology that was widespread during the medieval period, emphasizing the divinities of nature and the ghosts of persons who died violently or prematurely. The latter have always been much feared, owing to the tenacious and virulent rancor that they harbor for the living, and the terrible diseases they are able to inflict.[66]

A Litany for Personal Protection

The long incantation that accompanies the talismans of the *Yisuan jing* appears to be their oral complement. It is a litany entirely consecrated to personal pro-

---

65. Dz 650. 4b.
66. See Mollier (2006).

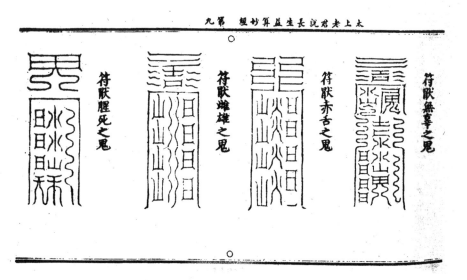

FIG. 3.4. The fifteen talismans of the Taoist *Yisuan jing* (Dz 650).

無轝柱殺人之鬼弟子本受
大道神符行流動靜四道開通寢不恐夢善
瑞旦綠所求所願皆得遂心千道萬法正真
之感如符所勅急急如
太上道君律令

第一開心符

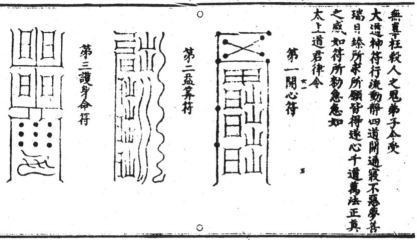

第二益算符

第三護身命符

第四金木水火土不相剋符

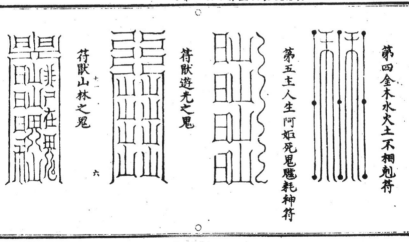

第五主人生阿姑死鬼魅耗神符

待猒遊光之鬼

待猒山林之鬼

符猒尸在巫

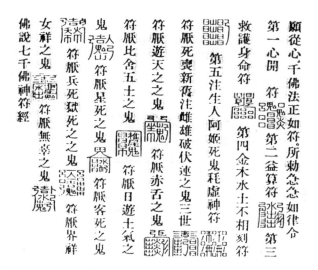

FIG. 3.5. *Reading from right to left:* The five prophylactic talismans
followed by the ten demonifuge talismans (T. 2904).

tection. Composed of 33 four- or five-character lines of verse, each of which
ends with "me" (*wo* 我), it lends itself naturally to recitation. Following is the
translation of its first verses, with the Taoist version of the text given on the left
and the Buddhist version on the right:

May all the immortals grant me life,	May the buddhas grant me life,
The sacred scriptures sustain me,	The sūtras sustain me,
The sun and the moon illuminate me,	The luminaries illuminate me,
The light of jade make me shine,	
The Yin and Yang make me grow,	The Yin and Yang make me grow,
The four seasons nourish me,	The four seasons nourish me,
The five fungi [of immortality][67] give me shade,	The five Heavens guide me,[68]
The five clouds shelter me,	The five clouds shelter me,
The five Perfected protect me,	The bodhisattvas protect me,

67. On the meaning of *zhi* 芝 as fungus or "mineral, vegetal or animal emanations," see
Campany (2002): 27.

68. Following P. 3022 R° and P. 2558 R°. Other versions, however, give the character *da*
大 instead of *tian* 天 (heaven).

The Six *jia* vivify me,	The six hundred *jiazi* blanket me,
The Five Emperors assist me,	The Five Emperors assist me,
The five sounds gladden me,	The five sounds gladden me,
The five weapons defend me,	The five weapons defend me,
Stars and planets blanket me . . .	Stars and planets blanket me . . .[69]

Heaven and earth, the stars, cosmic regulatory principles, natural elements, the deities of time and of space, and so on, down to humanity as a whole with its nobles and humble subjects, all are petitioned in turn to safeguard the initiate in accord with his honor and will. The text gives the immediate impression that, in chanting this litany, the practitioner stations himself, in the image of the emperor seated at the center of the universe, in the heart of the cosmic perimeter at the convergence of the effusions of all of the benevolent beings who are verbally summoned. In this aura of worthiness and prestige, he nourishes himself with the positive energies that reinforce him and guarantee his longevity. Immunized against demonic attack, he becomes all-powerful.

This litany is no more an original creation than is the invocation of the Generals of the Six *jia*. Its resemblance to the famous formula of the *Marvelous Scripture of the Celestial Youths of Utmost Purity, Protectors of Life* (*Taishang taiqing tiantong huming miaojing* 太上太清天童護命妙經) has been previously noted by Michel Strickmann.[70] Among the twenty-eight tetrameter verses of the latter, eleven are, despite some minor variants, effectively identical to those of the *Yisuan jing*. This is of interest particularly for historians of Taoism, as the formula that comprises the *Marvelous Scripture of the Celestial Youths, Protectors of Life* enjoyed great renown under the Song, when it reappeared in the wave of newly revealed apotropaic rituals at Maoshan 茅山, the holy mountain that was headquarters of the Shangqing lineage in Jiangsu. The formula was then claimed to have been revealed by Lord Lao in the year 1109 to an illiterate *daoshi* of Maoshan named Liang Guangying 梁光映 (alias Liang Wuzhen 梁悟真), who was a victim of leprosy.[71] If none of the several versions of the incantation, whether

---

69. Dz 650, 4b–5a, and T. 2904: 1446b.

70. Dz 632. 1a. See Strickmann (2002): 107–108, who gives a translation in extenso of the litany of the Buddhist *Yisuan jing* (one sentence is missing) but does not seem to have had knowledge of its Taoist counterpart.

71. A version of the formula is also found in the *Yunji qiqian*, 122/16a–18a. For another enlarged version with added phrases in pesudo-Sanskrit, see the twelfth-century *Immortal Scripture of the Celestial Lad Who Provokes Thunder, in the Secret Language of Brahman, Revealed to Lord Emperor Huanglao* (*Taishang taiqing huanglao dijun yunlei tiantong yinfan xianjing* 太上太清皇老帝君運雷天童隱梵仙經, Dz 633). See Boltz (1987): 134; and Shipper and Verellen (2004), vol. 2: 1050–1051.

abridged or expanded, preserved in the *Daozang* is undeniably prior to the Song, it remains nevertheless certain that, given its proximity to the litany of the *Yisuan jing,* a prototype of this incantation must have existed in a far earlier epoch, probably the Sui or even the Six Dynasties. Though nothing, to the best of my knowledge, allows us to trace its origins more precisely, it is important nevertheless to underscore its evident antiquity.

☙   ❧

IN SPITE OF whatever light we have been able to shed upon the ritual elements constituting the "system" of the *Yisuan jing,* its practical aspects remain mysterious. Which particular talismans were transmitted to the initiate? Under what circumstances was he to recite the invocation of the Six *jia,* the litany for personal protection, or the names of the stars and planets? When and where was the scripture to be worshipped? Such secrets, probably transmitted orally, will be forever impenetrable. It remains nevertheless sure that the tradition of the *Yisuan jing* was drawn from the vast astrohemerological, demonological. and soteriological inheritance of Six Dynasties Taoism—in particular, from the Way of the Heavenly Master—and that it can be classified among the panoply of Chinese techniques of personal salvation, transmitted from master to disciple through the engagement of the latter to respect and apply himself to it.

Responding to universal aspirations for security, health, and longevity, the salvific potential of the *Yisuan jing* could not be ignored by Chinese Buddhist clerics who were concerned with promoting the Dharma while assuaging ills and offering to everyone a better and longer life. If the means to which they resorted in order to fabricate this scripture were not entirely respectable, their intention to serve the public well-being remains nevertheless unquestionable. What these Buddhist authors could not have imagined, however, is the path that their sūtra would take during the centuries following its creation.

The Dunhuang materials further allow us to disclose that, some two or three hundred years after its adoption by Buddhism, the *Yisuan jing* resurfaced in a collection of heterogeneous mantic methods dating to the ninth century (P. 4667 V°).[72] One finds its talismans bundled in this manual and reprocessed to be used as "magical" implements to rid believers of the evils that are the common lot of humanity. It may appear that, for the Dunhuang diviner, author of this manuscript, the *Yisuan jing* was no more than a recipe, in the literal sense of the term, just like the other procedures that he gathered into his manual and that belong to the prevalent Chinese mantic traditions: topo-

---

72. P. 4667 V° (P. tib. 2207).

mancy, prognostication by means of the crow's cries, love potions, and amulets to ensure prosperity, protection for the house, and conjugal harmony. This, however, by no means suggests that he was ignorant of or sought to occlude the provenance of the *Yisuan jing* talismans. Not only did he faithfully calligraph each model of the fifteen talismans, but he also recopied a fragment of the Buddhist apocryphon under its abridged title: *Yisuan jing* in one *juan*. One might even conjecture that in this laudable effort to restore the text and put forward its noble Buddhist pedigree, he hoped to enhance the prestige of his willy-nilly composition in the eyes of his clientele.[73]

In this development, there is a peculiar irony. The talismans of the *Yisuan jing* probably derived, like many other ritual practices, from the fount of traditional religion. Thence, they passed from the hands of the Taoist masters to those of the *śramaṇas,* only to recover at Dunhuang, toward the end of the Tang, something resembling their original milieu. They now belonged once again to the diviner-technicians, who in former times had imagined them and given them form.

Did the Taoists and the Buddhists, for their part, continue the practice of the *Yisuan jing* in parallel with the ninth-century Dunhuang experts of divination? Though nothing permits us to decide, we do know that the *Yisuan jing*'s diffusion did not come to a halt at the gates of Dunhuang. It continued its westward journey, as is proven by a manuscript fragment of the sūtra that was discovered at Turfan. Thus, even in the distant desert regions of the Silk Road, there were some who continued to believe in the miraculous benefits accruing from the talismans of the *Sūtra to Increase the Account.*

As labyrinthine as its trajectory may appear, the *Yisuan jing* was not alone in its religiocultural and geographical vicissitudes. The Buddho-Taoist peregrinations of the Heavenly Kitchens and their later recuperation by Dunhuang Buddhist healers (chapter 1) are clearly comparable in this respect. Turning to the talismanic tradition of the Great Dipper, the next chapter will disclose an even more sinuous circuit traversing the medieval period down to the fourteenth century, from China to Central Asia, and from Taoist and Tantric astral meditation to Dunhuang magical medicine and calendar almanacs.

---

73. See Mollier (2003): 422–423.

CHAPTER 4

Under Stellar Protection

Who knows the names of the stars,
their comestible offerings and the manner
in which they are worshipped,
will live forever in happiness and success.

As is the case for the *Yisuan jing,* the principal objective of the talismanic tradition of the constellation of the Great Dipper, or Beidou 北斗, which is our concern in this chapter, is to assure the prolongation and preservation of the lives of the faithful. More complex in its formation than the *Yisuan jing,* the tradition of the Beidou is deeply embedded within the millennial fabric of Chinese culture and religion, in which the diverse threads of astrology and soteriology are intimately intertwined. Let us rapidly sketch out here some of the major lines.

Human beings, as integral constituents of the cosmos, are submitted to its regulating principles, conceived as universal natural laws. Beginning with one's birth, and even at the moment of conception, an individual's destiny is set within the cosmic chart configured by the stars and planets, the indicators of temporal cycles, the Five Agents, and the sexagesimal binomials.[1] One's personality is thus "formatted," the course of one's life laid out together with one's social and familial rank, as well as the potentialities and talents, inclinations and tastes, qualities and faults that predetermine a specific developmental pattern. Too, the evolution of each individual's physical condition and manner of aging, besides key events and the duration of his passage on earth, are conditioned by

---

Epigraph: *Secret Instructions for Prolonging Life from the Purple Court of the Seven Principles of the Northern Emperor* (*Beidi qiyuan ziwei yansheng mijue* 北帝七元紫微延生秘訣, Dz 1265. 1b).

1. The sexagesimal binomials are formed of four pairs of two character-numbers, each pair associating one of the ten celestial stems (*tiangan* 天干) with one of the ten terrestrial branches (*dizhi* 地支). Sixty cycles are required in order to realize all of the combinations of the signs of the two series. To the ten terrestrial branches are associated twelve animals that serve, in current usage, to mark each of the years of the cycle.

the implacable logic of that which the Chinese call personal destiny, or original destiny (*benming* 本命).

The interpretation of this cosmic identity card, as revealed in one's horoscope, is one of the points of emphasis among the divinatory arts that have developed since high antiquity and have never ceased to influence social and individual life. All had recourse to it, from the highest governmental dignitaries to the simple folk. Chinese religions, despite their often ambivalent relations with the occult arts and their experts, nevertheless borrowed certain fundamental tenets and beliefs from sophisticated horoscopic science, within which astrology occupied an outstanding place. The idea, which is as ancient as the earliest Chinese writings, that the heavens are in constant interaction with the human world, upon which they exercise punitive or favorable effects, has forever remained central, bringing in its train the conviction that the heavenly bodies, the twenty-eight lunar mansions,[2] the planets and stars, variously help or hinder our endeavors.[3]

The Great Dipper, which precisely interests us here, occupies a position of the highest order in Chinese astrological theories. Seen as a cosmic pivot, governing time and space and regulating the natural rhythms and astronomical events, the Beidou stands also as the superintendent of human destiny. Cleaving to these secular Chinese astrological conceptions, Taoism held the constellation to be the abode of the One supreme, the Dao, the site of origination and return, as well as the arbiter of good and evil. The Great Dipper represents the north, seat of the Great Yin—Yin at its apogee—which engenders the Yang that is life. As the cosmic matrix, it presides over the nine transformations, the complete cycle of gestation. For, as noted in chapter 3, the constellation is composed of nine stars. To the seven, universally known stars forming the bowl and handle of the Dipper, two minor stars are attached: the eighth star, Fuxing 輔星, is the companion of the sixth star; and the ninth star, Bixing 弼星, is situated in the neighborhood of the constellation's handle. Though the latter is entirely invisible, Fuxing is discernible at certain times. The belief is widespread among Taoist adepts that those who have the ability to see it with the naked eye draw from it great benefits and supernormal powers, extraordinary longevity above all.[4]

We have seen in the preceding chapter that the seven stars of the Dipper are also held to be the awakeners of prenatal life. They attend to the opening of the

---

2. The twenty-eight lunar mansions are the constellations through which the moon passes in the course of its rotation in the heavens. They are divided into four groups, corresponding to the seasons.

3. See Hou (1979).

4. Schafer (1977): 49–51, translates their names as "Sustainer" and "Straightener." On the cults relative to these two stars, see Andersen (1989–1990): 34–35.

embryo's seven orifices and insufflate it with its seven celestial souls (*hun* 魂). The circumstances of this vital and delicate intrauterine operation are meticulously described in the *Lingbao Scripture of Karmic Retribution*. Under the influence of the cosmic cycles, the text explains, the embryo is invested in the course of its development with the different *qi* and the numerous divinities that fashion its psychogenetic identity. In the seventh month of gestation, the essences (*jing* 精) of the Beidou, in the form of seven divine boys (*qi shentongzi* 七神童子), descend into the womb, penetrating the fetus, and piercing it so as to open its corporal orifices. During this decisive phase, the new human being that is thus fully constituted is entered into the celestial registers. His destiny is henceforth consigned to the permanent protection and control of the constellation, with its cohort of subaltern divinities who inhabit the body.[5] For, as producers of life, the stars of the Great Dipper serve also as managers and censors, with the same entitlements as all of the Directors of Destiny (Siming), who survey everyone's conduct and keep track of good and bad actions.

These few considerations allow us to take measure of the importance of the Great Dipper in Taoist eyes. The practices and rituals placed under its governance are legion. Medieval Shangqing adepts, in particular, devoted numerous techniques of self-perfection to it. Much later, during the Song period, Taoists made of their *Supreme Scripture of the Great Dipper of Mysterious Power* [*Guiding*] *Destiny and Prolonging Life* (*Taishang xuanling beidou benming yansheng zhenjing* 太上玄靈北斗本命延生真經, Dz 622) one of the most revered devotional texts in all of Chinese history. The great popularity of this work, which may be counted among the most widely printed and distributed books under the Yuan (1279–1368) and Ming (1368–1644) dynasties, has endured down to the present day.

Despite all this, the text concerning the Beidou that has caused by far the most ink to flow among Occidental scholars is to be found not in the Taoist corpus but in that of Buddhism. For almost a century, historians of East Asian religions, as well as specialists of Central Asia, have been puzzled by the enigmatic *Sūtra on Prolonging Life through Worship of the Seven Stars of the Northern Dipper, Preached by the Buddha* (*Foshuo beidou qixing yanming jing* 佛說北斗七星延命經)—edited in the *Taishō shinshū daizōkyō* (T. 1307) and best known by its abridged title as the *Great Bear Sūtra*, or *Great Dipper Sūtra* (*Beidou jing* 北斗經)—a modest work whose destiny has been altogether exceptional. Besides its Chinese version, which was exported to Korea and Japan, it is also found in Uighur, Mongolian, and Tibetan recensions.[6]

---

5. Dz 336, "Birth of the Spirit" (*Shengshen pin* 生神品), 8/7a–b.
6. See Franke (1990). The Korean edition dates to the seventeenth century. See Sørensen (1995).

The Chinese text, which presents itself as a sūtra transmitted anonymously under the Tang by an "Indian monk" (*poluomen seng* 婆羅門僧),[7] was early on suspected by the Western pioneers of Buddhist studies to be a work of doubtful provenance. Nevertheless, it was only with the publication in 1990 of an article by Herbert Franke that a corner of the curtain hiding the real face of the *Sūtra of the Great Dipper* was at last raised. Franke established that the work was in effect a "pseudo-sūtra," a Buddhist apocryphon, redacted in China during the late thirteenth or early fourteenth century on the basis of a Taoist prototype two or three centuries older.[8] The late and humble derivation of this apocryphal sūtra did not preclude its winning uncommon renown. For not long after its diffusion in China under the Yuan, it was translated into the aforementioned Central Asian languages. So it was that the Taoist Beidou tradition, once it had been appropriated within the milieu of sinicized Buddhism, came to be rapidly absorbed into entirely foreign sociocultural and linguistic contexts. The best witness to its broad distribution in Central Asia is found in the fourteenth-century Uighur manuscripts discovered at Turfan, which include the Taoist talismans of the constellation.[9] The *Sūtra of the Great Dipper*'s remarkable career is primarily explained by the decisive role that it played in the consolidation of Yuan imperial ideology. On the one hand, it no doubt favored the entry of the worship of the Dipper, eternal symbol of Chinese sovereignty, into court Buddhism. On the other, its Uighur, Tibetan, and Mongolian diffusion would have reinforced the multiethnic policies promoted by the Yuan rulers.[10]

If the historical and international dimensions of the *Sūtra of the Great Dipper* were thus magisterially set forth, thanks to Franke, the work nonetheless continues to intrigue researchers, who have added further pieces to the vast cultural and religious puzzle that it represents. Henrik Sørensen, notably, in a study concerning the spread of the sūtra in Korea during the Chosŏn 朝鮮 dynasty (1392–1912), has questioned its supposedly late origins. Referring to citations of the sūtra in Japanese liturgical manuals of the Shingon school and iconographic encyclopedias of the twelfth and thirteenth centuries, he argues that "it is quite plausible that a Buddhist version of the *Beidou jing* could have been in circulation in the middle of the eighth century, or perhaps slightly

---

7. Given in the column directly following the title of the work, which indicates, according to custom, its provenance. No name is specified, and this anonymous attribution must thus remain subject to caution.

8. Franke (1990).

9. Berlin manuscripts Ch/U6785, Ch/U6786, and Ch/U6944 (T.II Y61); see the reproductions in Niu (1997). See also Nishiwaki (1999): 52 and reproductions on 66.

10. Franke (1990): 110–111.

later."[11] As will be seen in relation to the sources introduced below, I concur with this hypothesis.

In all events, the dossier on the *Sūtra of the Great Dipper* is by no means closed. Areas of obscurity remain, principally in connection with the tradition from which it issued. Although some of the relevant Buddhist literature has already been thoroughly examined, Tantric sources have still not received the attention they merit. Additionally, the medieval Taoist sources that inspired this apocryphon,[12] as well as materials from Dunhuang testifying to the Beidou cult, have been entirely neglected.[13] These are the three dimensions that I propose to treat here, in order to trace out the early development of the Chinese Great Dipper tradition.

The Buddhist Cult of the Beidou

The ideal point of embarkation for our investigation remains the Yuan *Sūtra of the Great Dipper*. It will not be necessary here to rewrite the history of the text, a task already achieved by Franke, but rather the main ritual elements that characterize it will be emphasized. Let us recall that the work presents itself as a sūtra preached by the Buddha to Mañjuśrī. Its cult, the Buddha explains, provides the opportunity for all faithful practitioners—monks and laymen, rich and poor—to cleanse their faults and obtain good fortune, a happy rebirth, and freedom from all the many torments of daily life, among which one cannot help but recognize some distinctly Chinese worries: demons and nightmares, obstacles to an administrative career, illness and financial problems, unproductive silkworms, sterility of domestic animals, and difficult childbirth. The apotropaic and curative virtues of the sūtra are addressed primarily to the living, but the dead are not forgotten: the scripture offers them the prospect of escaping the hells to reach Sukhāvatī, the pure land of the buddha Amitābha.[14]

With reference to practice, which is our central concern here, the *Sūtra of the Great Dipper* encourages its devotees to render a cult conforming to established convention: one must worship the scripture while reciting it incessantly, burning incense, and making offerings to it in a pure room. Nothing out of the ordinary in this. By contrast, the ritual trademark of the *Beidou jing*

---

11. Sørensen (1995): 75–78.

12. Besides adducing their determining role, Franke (1990): 96–101, who provides a list of some of these texts, did not venture into their exploration.

13. Franke (1990): 94, mentions works relative to the Beidou cult that are edited in the *Taishō shinshū daizōkyō*, but he does not consider them in detail. Some of these texts are translated, without further analysis, by Orzech and Sanford (2000).

14. A translation of the sūtra is given in Orzech and Sanford (2000): 389–392.

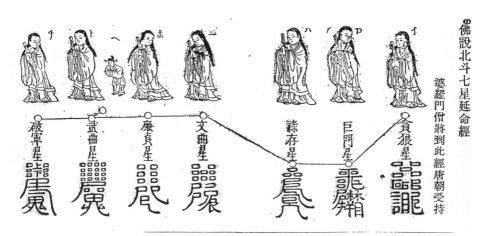

F<small>IG</small>. 4.1. Diagram of the Great Dipper (T. 1307).

is found in its talismans of the seven stars together with their horoscopic functions and the characteristic offerings of grains and cereals to them that it recommends. A close look at the illustration placed at the head of the *Taishō shinshū daizōkyō* edition of the *Sūtra of the Great Dipper* suffices to exhibit the essentials of the Beidou ritual (fig. 4.1).[15] This didactic image depicts a diagram of the seven stars with their divine Taoist names, together with their anthropomorphic forms, and the corresponding talismans. The *kana* placed above the deities are, to be sure, additions due to the early nineteenth-century Japanese editors. As for the iconography of the stars, we shall see that this conforms in all respects to descriptions derived from medieval Taoism, and that it continued to prevail in the ritual paintings of the fifteenth century that can still be admired today.

The text following the illustration begins with a list of the traditional Chinese calendrical markers corresponding to each of the seven stars,[16] specifying also the food offerings that each practitioner must provide according to his year of birth. The formula applied to the first star of the Beidou, Tanlang 貪狼 (Greedy Wolf), for instance, is articulated as follows:

> Persons born under the sign *zi* 子 [the first of the twelve terrestrial branches of the calendrical system], are placed under this star. Their wages (*lushi* 祿食) are husked

---

15. The Japanese edition dates from 1802. The colophon at the end of the text mentions that it is derived from the edition of the monk Kaidō 快道 (1751–1810). Refer to Franke (1990): 91–92.

16. That is to say, the twelve branches. A single branch is associated with the first and seventh stars. To the other five stars, two branches each are assigned.

[glutinous] millet. If in danger, they should worship this sūtra and wear the talisman corresponding to this natal star. Great happiness.

The six other stars are associated, in the same way, with grain offerings, with a talisman that the adept must wear, and with one or two of the twelve terrestrial branches: the second star, Jumen 巨門 (Great Gate), corresponds to the signs *chou* 丑 or *hai* 亥 (second and twelfth branches) and to millet; the third, Lucun 祿存 (Persistent Happiness), to the signs *yin* 寅 and *xu* 戌 (third and eleventh) and to rice; the fourth, Wenqu 文曲 (Civil Song), to the signs *mao* 卯 and *you* 酉 (fourth and tenth) and to peas (or wheat); the fifth, Lianzhen 廉貞 (Pure Virtue), to the signs *chen* 辰 and *shen* 申 (fifth and ninth) and to hemp seed; the sixth, Wuqu 武曲 (Military Song), to the signs *si* 巳 and *wei* 未 (sixth and eighth) and to soybeans; and the seventh star, Pojun 破軍 (Destroyer of Armies), to the sign *wu* 午 (seventh) and to peas.[17]

In order to lend a Buddhist aspect to this manifestly Taoist configuration, the author of the apocryphon has assigned to the seven stars seven *tathāgata*-buddhas (*rulai* 如來). As we have seen in chapter 3, these seven *tathāgata*s are the seven hypostases of the buddha Bhaiṣajyaguru, Master of Medicine (Yaoshi 藥師).[18] Here, in the *Beidou jing,* the practitioner has to pay homage (*nanwu* 南無, Skt. *namas*) by invoking their names:

> Yunyi tongzheng rulai 運意通證如來
> Guangyin zizai rulai 光音自在如來
> Jinse chengjiu rulai 金色成就如來
> Zuisheng jixiang rulai 最勝吉祥如來
> Guangda zhibian rulai 廣達智辨如來
> Fahai youxi rulai 法海遊戲如來
> Yaoshi liuli guang rulai 藥師琉璃光如來 (Bhaiṣajyaguru-vaiḍūryaprabhāsa)

No doubt the association of the seven stars with this group of Buddhas was in itself sufficiently compelling in the eyes of the Chinese faithful to supply the *Sūtra of the Great Dipper* with its indisputable Buddhist certificate of authenticity. But to satisfy the curiosity of the contemporary historian of Chinese religions, an investigation into earlier related materials will be required to disclose the manifold development of the Great Dipper cult throughout the medieval period.

---

17. For a complete translation of this passage, see Orzech and Sanford (2000): 389–390.

18. On the Seven Buddhas and the Tathāgata Tejaḥprabha, see Sørensen (1995): 78. On the association of the seven stars and the bodhisattvas (notably Guanyin) in Tang Tantrism, see Xiao (1993): 151–154.

Ge Xuan's Method for Honoring the Great Dipper

To seek our sources in the medieval Buddhist bibliographical catalogues proves to be a dead end. They contain no reference whatsoever to the *Beidou jing* or to any apocryphal sūtra that might have been its prototype or even approximately related to it. Nevertheless, as Paul Pelliot rightly commented, "the silence of the [Buddhist] catalogues after A.D. 800 does not imply that the production of apocrypha was interrupted."[19] Moreover, it is a curious fact that even the mention of the term "Beidou" is to all appearances totally absent. This observation is sharpened when one turns to the medieval manuscript collections from Dunhuang and Turfan, invaluable stores of writings otherwise lost or unpublished. For here, too, it must be admitted, there remains not the slightest fragment of any Buddhist text directly connected to the *Sūtra of the Great Dipper*.[20] Does such an absence suggest that medieval Chinese Buddhism was ignorant of the Beidou cult and that only much later, under the Yuan dynasty, a decision was made to integrate it into Buddhist liturgy?

In considering the preeminent role of the constellation in Chinese culture, this would seem inconceivable. In reality, the cult of the Dipper is well attested in the works of renowned masters of Tang esoteric Buddhism. Specialists, however, have so far accorded little attention to the relevance of these texts for the study of the Yuan *sūtra,* whether this be due to the suspicion that the relative lateness of their available recensions renders them unreliable, or to simple lack of inquiry in the context of plain translation.[21]

It is the famous monk Yixing (一行 683–727), the disciple of Śubhākarasiṃha (Shanwuwei 善無畏 637–735), who provides the most substantial expression of the Beidou cult in the context of medieval Buddhism. In his outstanding astrological treatise—the *Fantian huolu jiuyao* 梵天火羅九曜, a synthesis of Chinese and Indian traditions[22]—this *śramaṇa*-scientist advocates a Method of Sir Immortal Ge for Honoring the Great Dipper (Ge Xiangong li beidou fa 葛仙公禮北斗法), of which the detailed ritual modalities closely

---

19. Pelliot (1911).

20. A fragment of a printed Yuan edition of a Taoist version of the *Beidou jing* was, however, discovered by Aurel Stein in Khara-khoto. See Franke (1990): 101–102.

21. As indicated in Franke (1990): 91–92, the editions of these texts in the *Taishō daizōkyō* are in effect founded upon Japanese manuscripts and prints that, according to their colophons, are not earlier than the twelfth century. See also Sørensen (1995) and the translations of Orzech and Sanford (2000).

22. The Chinese astrological conceptions related to destiny are combined here with the Indian system according to which human beings are successively placed, during the course of their lives, under the influence of the "nine heavenly bodies" (*jiuyao*), that is the sun, the moon, the Five Planets, and the lunar nodes Rāhu and Ketu.

resemble those of the Yuan-period sūtra. As in the latter, the Method consists
in a domestic cult in honor of the constellation that includes the veneration of
stellar images, offerings of grains and cereals for each of the stars, and the recitation of a mantra (*zhenyan* 真言) in pseudo-Sanskrit.[23] Here is a tentative
translation of Yixing's Method of Sir Immortal Ge for Honoring the Great
Dipper:

> From the sovereign down to the common man, all alike depend upon one of the
> seven stars of the Northern Dipper. By venerating them constantly, one encounters
> neither misfortune nor evil, because they universally save beings from decrepitude
> and critical circumstances and permit them to "prolong their lives by augmenting
> their accounts" (*yannian yi suan* 延年益算), while dispelling all adversity. In wor-
> shipping the Original Spirit of Personal Destiny (*benming yuanshen* 本命元神) and
> offering to him with a sincere heart, one fulfils one's vows [to obtain] longevity and
> profit. Calamities, ills, and failures are due only to inattention to the cult of the stel-
> lar images. To be unaware that one can offend them is to move forward in darkness
> and thus to provoke disasters and difficulties. By counterattacking [by means of the
> cult], one will obtain great happiness.
>
> The days for making offerings to the Original Spirit of Personal Destiny are six
> each year. One should render the cult before an image of the Beidou by offering a pure
> mat, paper, a scribe's knife, sacrificial money, tea, and fruits in three piles, as well as in-
> cense, and to address to it the following prayer: "I, an insignificant person dwelling in
> this world, cherish the Dao and am seeking transcendental [support]. I have often been
> able to see your divine presence. On this day of my personal destiny, I respectfully
> offer silver coins and the fruits of immortals to the Northern Dipper and to the image
> of the Spirit of Personal Destiny (*gongyang yu beidou chenxing bai benming shenxing* 供養
> 於北斗辰星拜本命神形). I wish to obtain an increase of longevity, [the expulsion] of
> all calamity, serenity of spirit and souls, the perdurance of my Original Spirits, sup-
> pression of decrepitude, and the removal of critical lunar phases." One prostrates once
> again, burns the sacrificial money, and salutes with joined hands.[24]

These ritual prescriptions are followed by a diagram of the Beidou with the
Taoist names of the seven stars and the corresponding twelve branches. Yi-
xing then gives a citation from the *Book of Destiny,* or, more precisely, the
Book of Wages and Fate (*Luming shu* 祿命書), where there figures a list of the

---

23. T. 1311, vol. 21: 462. On this passage, see Soymié (1972–1973): 703–704; and Hou
(1975): 109–110. Franke (1990): 94, mentions it in passing. As Franke (1990): 93 also underscores, the hypothesis of Needham et al. (1959, vol. 3: 283n), according to which the *Sūtra of
the Great Dipper* may be attributed to Yixing, is not plausible.

24. T. 1311, vol. 21: 462. See the French translation of Hou (1975): 109–110.

seven stars, with life expectancy calculated according to each birth star and the twelve branches. Though the cereals are not mentioned here, the exact measures are specified:

First star = 2 *sheng* 升 (= about two liters) = 65 years
Second star = 8 *sheng* = 80 years
Third star = 5 *sheng* = 80 years
Fourth star = 4 *sheng* = 90 years
Fifth star = 1 *sheng* = 80 years
Sixth star = 1 *sheng* = 85 years
Seventh star = 1 *sheng* = 80 years

Unfortunately, we know little of this *Book of Wages and Fate* from which Yixing claims to have drawn his information. The biography of Lü Cai 呂才, the reformer of the arts of Yin and Yang at the beginning of the Tang, suggests that the *luming* procedure, through which one could calculate longevity and fate, reached back to antiquity and that it was the ancestor of the calendrical horoscope systems based on the birth binomials.[25] Moreover, Yixing is not the only Buddhist to refer to the *Book of Wages and Fate* and to underscore its connection to the cult of the Great Dipper. A Buddhist rite of fire of uncertain origin, similarly placed under the aegis of the constellation and entitled *Secret Essentials for Performing Homa to the Seven Stars of the Northern Dipper* (*Beidou qixing humo biyao yigui* 北斗七星護摩秘要儀軌), also refers to it:[26]

The *Book of Wages and Fate* says: "In this world are the divinities [who are] the Comptrollers of Fate (*zhuming shen* 司命神), who, on each *gengshen* 庚申 day (the fifty-seventh day of the sexagesimal cycle) go up to the Celestial Emperor to report the sins and evils that people do. Those who commit serious offenses will see a *suan* 算 deducted [from their life-account]. Those who commit lighter offenses lose a *ji* 紀.[27]

---

25. *Jiu Tang shu, juan* 79, Zhonghua shuju ed.: 2719–2723. Hou (1975): 99; Kalinowski (2003): 243–245.

26. T. 1306, vol. 21: 424–425. See Yoshioka (1970), vol. 2: 193; and Xiao (1993): 108. The text was conserved in many monasteries in Japan, notably at Kōyasan 高野山. In the *Taishō daizōkyō* edition, the work is attributed to a certain monk named Guanding 灌頂 of the monastery of Daxingshan 大興善寺 in Chang'an. It is improbable that this refers to the monk Guanding (561–632) of the Tiantai 天台 sect. Given that the term *guanding* signifies "consecration" (*abhiṣeka*), it is more likely that this refers to a title: "Master of *abhiṣeka*." This point is also raised by Sørensen (1995): 76n20.

27. T. 1306, vol. 21: 425. My translation differs somewhat from that of Orzech and Sanford (2000): 394. The passage is also translated in Japanese by Yoshioka (1970), vol. 2: 193.

We have seen in chapter 3 that the *Baopuzi neipian* uses the same technical terminology and the same *suan* and *ji* units for the evaluation of life-allocations by
the Directors of Destiny.[28]

Was the *Book of Wages and Fate* mentioned by Yixing and in this *homa*-ritual
the real source of inspiration of the Buddhist cult of the Dipper? No certain response is possible. In all events, these citations manifestly indicate the degree to
which Taoist concepts were integrated into early-Tang esoteric Buddhism. The
role in the management of life that the author of the *Secret Essentials for Performing Homa to the Seven Stars* credited to the Beidou, the allusions that he also made
to the registers of life and death (*shengji* 生籍, *siji* 死籍), and his references to
such technical notions as the units of accounting (*suan* and *ji*) and the *gengshen*
days are entirely eloquent in this regard.[29] Even more striking is that Yixing
chose unambiguously to label as Taoist the cult of the Great Dipper that he exposed. The very title that he gives, Method of Sir Immortal Ge for Honoring
the Great Dipper, speaks in and of itself to any Taoist scholar, for Sir Ge is none
other than the renowned master of the occult arts, Ge Xuan 葛玄, who was the
grand-uncle of the famous fourth-century alchemist Ge Hong. Ge Xuan is said
to have been introduced to the court of the first emperor of the southeastern
Wu 吳 dynasty during the period of the Three Kingdoms (220–265) and to
have been the recipient of a majority of the founding texts of the Lingbao canon,
one of the three great scriptural corpora of medieval Taoism.[30]

What may have impelled Yixing to include this Beidou ritual, certified
as 100 percent Taoist, in his great work on Buddhist astrology? Though it
may seem merely indicative of the syncretic character of the *Fantian huolu jiuyao,* a more convincing explanation is suggested by the biography of our eminent exponent of Tantrism, where one learns that, before becoming a
Buddhist monk, and parallel to his learned investigations of astrology, divination, and mathematics, Yixing studied with a Taoist master named Yin-
chong 尹崇. Indeed, Yixing himself appears to have authored several treatises
on Taoist practices.[31] One can therefore speculate that the Buddhist monk,

---

28. The sole difference is that in T. 1306 the *suan* and *ji* units are inverted.

29. The *gengshen* days are considered critical because they are points in the calendar when the
divine censors, particularly the Three Worms and the god of the furnace, leave the human body
and report to the Directors of Destiny the sins that one has committed. These days were therefore
devoted to fasting and rituals, a tradition that has been perpetuated in Japan. See Kubo (1981).

30. The relevant information belongs more to legend than to history. Ge Xuan probably
lived during the years 164–244 C.E. See his biography in the *Shenxian zhuan* 神仙傳 (Traditions of divine authorities) of Ge Hong, trans. Campany (2002): 152–159. On the question of
the transmission of the Lingbao scriptures, see Bokenkamp (1997): 377–379.

31. *Jiu Tang shu,* chap. 141, Zhonghua shuju ed.: 5111–5113. Refer to Weinstein (1987):
55–56, 169n36.

faithful to his past, judged the Taoist cult of the Beidou worthy to be transmitted in its authentic form and under its original designation.

Less personal considerations may have also encouraged Yixing to edit the Method of Sir Immortal Ge for Honoring the Great Dipper (hereafter, the Method of Ge Xuan). In assuring the promotion of the Great Dipper cult and embracing it in the Buddhist fold during an epoch when the "foreign" religion had regained an aura of sanctity in court circles, he perhaps intended to use it as an instrument of ideological propaganda. Just as the *Sūtra of the Great Dipper* would later serve the mandate of the Yuan ruling house, the worship of the constellation, as an established emblem of rulership, would have reinforced the political aura of the emperor Tang Xuanzong 玄宗 (r. 712–756), Yixing's protector. After a period of repressive measures and successive edicts aimed at bringing a halt to the development of Buddhism and propping up the state religion, Xuanzong demonstrated later in his reign a lively taste for esotericism, whether Taoist or Tantric. It was at this time, in 721—in the midst of the Kaiyuan 開元 era (713–741)—that, having fallen under Yixing's charms, the emperor called him to court and granted him a distinguished appointment, charging him with the composition of the official calendar, the *Dayan li* 大衍曆.[32] The biography that the *Song gaoseng zhuan* 宋高僧傳 (*Biographies of Eminent Monks Compiled in the Song*) devotes to Yixing succinctly mentions the séances of divination by the seven stars of the Great Dipper that he personally performed in the context of his functions at the imperial court.[33] There are also other important traces of his attachment to the Great Dipper: among the Tantric fire rituals he left to posterity, one finds a *Homa Ritual to the Seven Stars of the Great Dipper* (*Beidou qixing humo fa* 北斗七星護摩法), where he describes how the seven stars, by a series of *mudrā*s, mantras, evocations, and visualizations, may be brought forth from the altar flames in order to expel evils, counterbalance the malefic effects of the Five Planets, and erase the names of the faithful from the registers of death, thereby ensuring their longevity.[34]

Tang-period Tantrism, well furnished with proficient means for absorbing and remodelling native pantheons and religious practices in the lands of its adoption, thus successfully integrated the Chinese cult of the Beidou into its liturgy. Yixing was by no means the only artisan at work. His contemporary, the equally celebrated Vajrabodhi (Jingangzhi 金剛智, 669–741), also contributed

---

32. See the comprehensive study of Yixing by Osabe (1963). See also Faure (1988): 89–90; and Needham et al. (1959), vol. 3: 282–283.

33. *Song gaoseng zhuan,* chap. 5, Zhonghua shuju ed. (1987), vol. 1: 93.

34. T. 1310, vol. 21: 457–459, after an 1802 Japanese edition of the monk Kaidō. On Yixing and the development of the *homa* rite with reference to the *Mahāvairocanasūtra,* see Strickmann (1983): 436–446.

to the promotion of the Tantric practice of the Great Dipper. In his *Ritual Procedures for Invoking the Seven Stars of the Great Dipper* (*Beidou qixing niansong yigui* 北斗七星念誦儀軌), he advocates this not only as an individual discipline, involving the recitation of mantras endowed with demonifuge, redemptive, and vitalizing powers, but also as a collective ceremony, organized at the initiative of sovereigns and high functionaries and requiring the fabrication of a *maṇḍala* together with the performance of the *homa* ritual of the seven stars. By means of this official ritual, the government sought to employ the Great Dipper cult to guarantee the peace and well-being of the nation.[35]

It may be also noticed that a "liturgy of the Seven Buddhas of Bhaiṣajyaguru" (*Qifo yaoshi fa* 七佛藥師法), bearing the signatures of the most noted masters—Yixing, Vajrabodhi, and Amoghavajra—was similarly introduced onto the Tang imperial stage in the context of Tantric orthopraxis.[36] It is plausible that these Seven Buddha "longevity rituals" (延命法), performed with lamps and *homa* offerings, were sometimes conjoined with the rites of the Great Dipper, whose stars were, as seen above, related to the seven *tathāgata*s of Bhaiṣajyaguru. Nevertheless, in the absence of further data this must remain a tentative speculation.

Although the information given in seventh- and eighth-century Tantric sources does not allow us to establish the existence of a genuine Buddhist prototype of the Yuan *Sūtra of the Great Dipper,* it nonetheless underscores that a Buddhist cult of the Great Dipper was already current under the Tang. The ritual modalities of the individual cult of the Method of Ge Xuan, moreover, are strikingly close to those put forward in the Yuan apocryphal *sūtra.* As we shall see shortly, during the intervening period, that is to say, between the end of the Tang and beginning of the Northern Song (960–1127), this same cult is also attested in various documents from Dunhuang.

The Beidou at Dunhuang

The Dunhuang manuscripts include irrefutable proof that the Method of Ge Xuan still circulated at the frontiers of the empire roughly a century and half after its transmission by Yixing. Far from closed, esoteric religious circles, it had taken there a much more pragmatic path, that of parareligious medicine. The oldest manuscript bearing witness to this is an important manual of iatromancy,

---

35. T. 1305, vol. 21: 423–424. See the translation by Orzech and Sanford (2000): 392–393.

36. It was celebrated in the year 756, in the presence and honor of the newly enthroned emperor Suzong 肅宗 (r. 756–762). The ritual of Bhaiṣajyaguru was much in vogue, during the same period, in the Japanese court, where it was organized on several occasions. Refer to Kuo Li-ying (1994a): 149–167.

or medical divination—P. 2675 V°, which includes a colophon dating to 862 and signed by two copyists, both functionaries in Dunhuang. One of them, Fan Jingxun 氾景詢, was a known expert in the arts of Yin and Yang at the prefectoral school.[37] The treatise, whose central theme is the localization of the "human spirit" (renshen 人神) within the body, includes a ritual prescription entitled the Method for Correlating Personal Destiny and the Seven Stars [of the Great Dipper] (Qixing renming shu fa 七星人命屬法).[38]

Although the name of Ge Xuan is not given in this treatise, there can be no doubt that it involves the method that is attributed to him. The manuscript is damaged with many lacunae, but it is possible to deduce the structure of the text. The twelve calendrical branches of the horoscope are associated with the seven stars of the Beidou, with precise measures of cereals and grains, and with given life expectancies—from eighty-three to ninety-five years, depending upon the stars—and talismans.[39]

Another Dunhuang document, undated and even more fragmentary—a portion of a page from a medical manual for the diagnosis of illness—also bears a trace of our Method (P. 3064 R°).[40] Among the three drawings of constellations that appear here, one finds a diagram of the Great Dipper accompanied by the names of the seven stars and the corresponding twelve branches, followed by a medical prognostication ascribed to a certain Weng 翁 (fig. 4.2). As "Weng" is one of the appellations of Ge Xuan, there is strong reason to hold that what we have here is an extract of his method that is intended for therapeutic use.[41] A third Dunhuang iatromantic manual (P. 3081 V°) may have also emanated from the same tradition. It mentions the Talismans of the Spirits of Personal Destiny (Benming shenfu 本命神符) for counteracting the harm caused by bad astral conjunctions that occur during the course of the year.[42]

One point deserves to be underlined concerning these medical documents. However bizarre they may appear to modern readers, these manuals were held in great seriousness by the society in which they circulated. The diviner-healers

---

37. The other, Fan Ziying 范子盈, was a functionary responsible for communications. See Harper (2003): 475.

38. See Mollier (2003): 410. Another version of the text is found in P. 2675 bis R°, which is probably a copy of P. 2675 V°. Refer to Harper (2003): 495–498.

39. The estimations of life expectancy are given in the following order: 95 years for the seventh star, 87 for the sixth, 83 for the fifth, 95 for the fourth, and 85 for the third (the two first stars are missing). These differ therefore slightly from those one finds in the Buddhist Beidou jing (see above). In the manuscript P. 2675 V°, cols. 36–41, only two talismans survive (one for the star Pojun, the other for Luming). There are no talismans in P. 2675 bis R°, cols. 29–34.

40. See Kalinowski (2003): 258–259.

41. See Mollier (2003): 411.

42. See Harper (2003): 502.

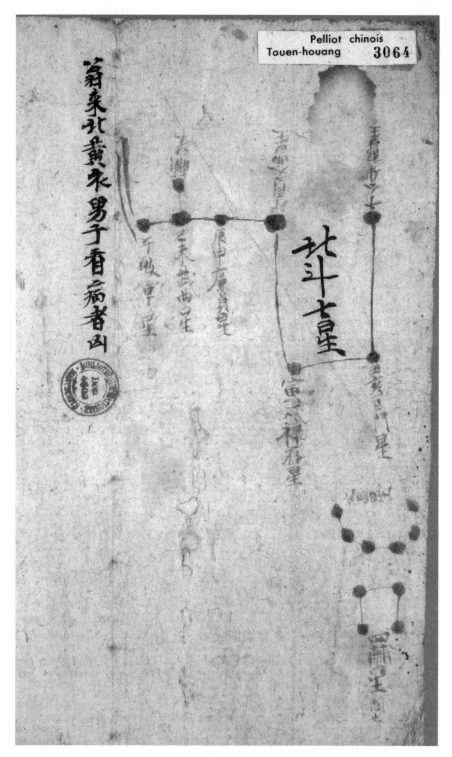

FIG. 4.2. Medical prognostication related to the seven stars of the Beidou (P. 3064 R°).
Courtesy of the Bibliothèque nationale de France.

who composed them were by no means anonymous charlatans; rather, they were noteworthy experts who served as functionaries in the Dunhuang administration. As did Fan Jingxun, one of the authors of the medical manuscript copied in 862, astrologer-physicians often occupied institutional positions and were teaching at the prefectoral school (*zhouxue* 州學) of Dunhuang while maintaining a clinical practice. This afforded them the means to put their methods to work so as to respond to their patients' demands for health and longevity.[43]

To continue to trace the itinerary of the Method of Ge Xuan at Dunhuang, we must leave behind the world of medical "magic" and penetrate another arcane domain, that of almanacs and calendars, the media whereby the cult of the Beidou was diffused on behalf of the general public. The Stein Collection conserves a calendar (S. 2404) dating to the year 924 that includes a detailed and, what is more, illustrated version of the Method of Ge Xuan (fig. 4.3).[44] Its title as recorded there is identical to that given by Yixing, *Ge Xiangong li beidou fa*, and it is presented in the form of two vignettes, each accompanied by a drawing and preceded by an introduction celebrating the cult of the Beidou:

> According to the *Book of Immortals* (*Xianjing* 仙經), it is said that if a person whose heart is set does homage each night to the Great Dipper, he will obtain long life, avoid calamity, and attract benefits.

In the first vignette we see a kneeling devotee, to all evidence worshipping the Dipper. Before him stands a divinity in courtly robes, accompanied by a female servant or partner. To the side, smoke rises from an incense burner placed upon an altar situated beneath a prominent stellar diagram. The inscription, given below the drawing, specifies the origins of this cult of the Beidou:

> Method of Ge Xuan for honoring the Great Dipper. In former times, Xiangong offered homage to the Great Dipper each night with his heart set, which yielded for him prolongation of life and an augmentation of his account (*suan* 算). Sir Zheng 鄭 rendered a cult to the functionaries of the Northern [Dipper] 北官. In this way he obtained longevity and avoided becoming the victim of the knives and blades to which he was predestined.

The second vignette deals with the cult of the Original Spirit (*yuanshen* 元神) of the current year (*xingnian* 行年), the monkey deity corresponding to a *shen*

---

43. See Kalinowski (2003): 23–27.
44. See Hou (1975): 115–116; Deng Wenkuan (2002): 374–386; and Arrault and Martzloff (2003): 96–97, 190–193.

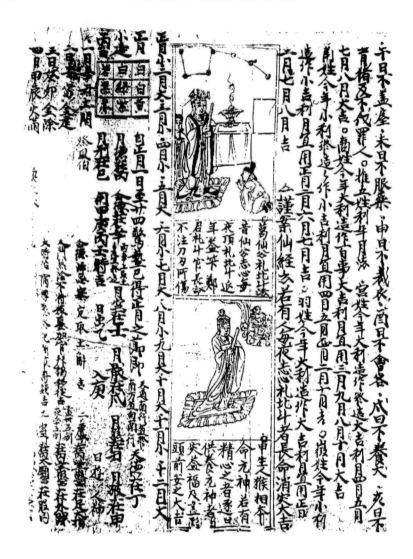

FIG. 4.3. The Method of Ge Xuan for Honoring the Great Dipper (S. 2404). Courtesy of the British Library.

申 year (924). The illustration displays a figure above whom floats a monkey in the clouds. Dressed in official garments, he carries a court tablet and, on his crown, an image of a monkey. The text accompanying this design runs as follows:

> An individual born in a *shen* year depends upon the Original Spirit of Personal Destiny of the monkey sign. If, with a pure heart, he makes offerings to the Original

Spirit of Personal Destiny on opportune days calamities will disappear and his happiness increase. It is of very good augur to place an image of this divinity [on the altar?] before him.

These two cults—of the Beidou and the Original Spirit—are of course complementary. The ritual procedures explained and pictured here are completely in conformity with those described by Yixing, who equally envisioned a daily cult to the image of the Dipper and a rite observed six times each year in honor of the Original Spirit of Personal Destiny. The basis for this cultic duet is perfectly clear, for, while the Dipper regulates our everyday existence, the Original Spirit corresponding to our birth date and marking our destiny, manifests itself in a repeating cycle of sixty days.

As did Yixing, the author of the Dunhuang calendar conspicuously asserts the Taoist pedigree of the Method for Honoring the Great Dipper. Not only does he attribute its paternity to Ge Xuan, but he associates it with another Taoist devotee, a certain Sir Zheng. We have reason to suppose that the individual in question is Zheng Yin 鄭隱, or Zheng Siyuan 鄭思遠, Ge Xuan's disciple. Zheng played a cardinal role in the history of early Taoism, as it was from him that Ge Hong inherited the famous library of esoteric and alchemical works among which some stood at the origin of the first Taoist canons.[45] Ge Hong recounts in his *Baopuzi neipian,* as we find too in the text accompanying the second vignette of the Dunhuang calendar, that Sir Zheng, thanks to his devotion to the Beidou, was able to make himself invulnerable to bared weapons:

> By writing in red the words "Great Dipper" and "Sun" and "Moon," it was claimed, one need have no fear of bare blades. . . . Lord Zheng said that the same results could also be obtained by reciting the names of the five different weapons [each corresponding to a planet or a star].[46]

The presence of the Method of Ge Xuan in this tenth-century manuscript calendar apparently owes nothing to the medical uses to which it had already been put in Dunhuang by the end of the Tang. Its goal, rather, is to assure the promotion of the Method in its religious form and to make the Beidou cult available to all. Necessary for regulating the official year as well as for guiding agricultural activities and everyday life, calendrical almanacs were, no less than the printed almanacs (*tongshu* 通書) still published today, destined for large-scale distribution. Families could draw on them for varied recipes, prognostications,

---

45. See Robinet (1984): 10.
46. *Baopuzi neipian,* chap. 15, Wang Ming, ed.: 269–270.

interdictions, and prescriptions, supposed to aid or to orient them throughout the annual cycle in various domains such as domestic and construction work, traditional religious rituals and festivals, hemerological procedures, hygiene and medical care, farming and commercial activity, voyages and official affairs, marriages, and funerals, The illustrations sometimes adorning these calendars generally have a pedagogical character. They offered concrete, explicit, and accessible guidance to all who wish to engage in the practice depicted, whether literati or uneducated. Likewise, the images of the Method of Ge Xuan in the Dunhuang calendar made it easy to apprehend its ritual modalities and the appropriate altar arrangements.

Given the visual and didactic publicity that such calendars afforded the cult of the Dipper, it may be supposed that, toward the beginning of the tenth century, it had become an integral part of the cultural patrimony of Dunhuang. This, in all events, does not imply that it should be relegated to the capacious storeroom of "popular" folklore. Far from being the base product of vulgarization, the calendar of 924 is an official document bearing the signature of a high-status dignitary in Dunhuang, Zhai Fengda 翟奉達 (883–961?), whom we met in chapter 2 in connection with the commission of sūtra copies for his deceased spouse. A diviner with excellent technical competences as well as an accomplished scholar and a fervent Buddhist, Zhai was also the principal at the Dunhuang prefectoral school. His distinguished career as a calendrical expert in the service of the Cao 曹 family unfolded during the period of the "army of the return to allegiance" (Guiyijun 歸義軍, 848–1036), and above all under the reign of the "King of Dunhuang," the military governor Cao Yuanzhong 曹元忠, who succeeded in maintaining an independent city-state at Dunhuang during his rule (944–974).[47]

The calendar of 924 was just one of many that Zhai produced for the Dunhuang administration, of which just five, including that which interests us here, have come down to us.[48] The question of the legacy of these Dunhuang calendars is pertinent here: how could this regional production have been recognized as official, given that the imperial Chinese government formally prohibited the creation and diffusion of calendars by local administrations and private agents? Calendars belonged exclusively to the imperial court astronomers' sphere of authority. Despite this, the independence of the Dunhuang region, together with difficulties in communication with the distant capital during Zhai Fengda's

---

47. On Zhai Fengda, see Teiser (1994): 117–121, 242–243. See also Fujieda (1973): 434–439; Deng (2002): 469–505; Kalinowski (2003), 21, 54; Arrault and Martzloff (2003): 90–91; and Rong (2004): 58–59.

48. The others are the calendars for the years 926 (P. 3247 V°), 928 (Beijing 836 V°), 956 (S. 95 R°), and 956 (P. 2623 R°). See Teiser (1994): 242–243; and Arrault and Martzloff (2003).

time, left the local functionaries with no alternative but to contravene the law and arrogate to themselves the right to fabricate their own calendars, indispensable tools for the development and management of society.[49]

Was it then Zhai himself who introduced the Method of Ge Xuan into the 924 calendar, or had it become current earlier in Dunhuang or in central China? The Method, in this case adapted to the current year of the monkey, might be supposed to have been periodically reedited to reflect the variations necessitated by the cycle of animals. Nevertheless, it is a curious fact that neither the extant Dunhuang calendars anterior to those of Zhai Fengda, nor the four other calendars that he is known to have composed later on and that have come down to us in their entirety, repeat Ge Xuan's cult of the Beidou. Perhaps Zhai's inclusion of it is but one more instance of mantic recipes or rituals making furtive appearances in the calendars. This, however, was not quite the case with the Beidou cult. Fifty-four years after its publication in Zhai's calendar, it made a resurgence in another almanac discovered at Dunhuang (S. 612 R°), but one whose provenance lay elsewhere (fig. 4.4).

In this case, it is significant that we are no longer considering a regional work, produced by the frontier administration of Dunhuang, but rather a publication representing the central government chancery and emanating from the imperial capital. The almanac in question is a "large-format calendar established according to the official version of the Bureau of Celestial Affairs" (*qing sitiantai guanben kanding daben rili* 請司天臺官本勘定大本曆日) for the "Empire of the Great Song" (*da Song guo* 大宋國) and dates to the year 978. Its surviving fragment consists of an illustration depicting the year-planet Jupiter (Taisui 太歲) surrounded by the anthropomorphic figures of the "true forms" (*zhenxing* 真形) of the twelve Original Spirits (*yuanshen*). As in the case of the Original Spirit of the monkey in the calendar of Zhai Fengda, these temporal deities are represented in the form of young officials holding court tablets and wearing caps adorned with the effigies of the twelve cyclical animals (rat, buffalo, tiger, hare, dragon, serpent, horse, sheep, monkey, cock, dog, pig), which they incarnate.[50] The cartouches in which their names were to be inscribed have remained empty, but there can be no doubt in regard to their identity, for the ritual prescription inscribed in a column to the left of the drawings confirms that the cult of the Original Spirit is at issue. Just as in the calendar of Zhai Fengda and, earlier, Yixing's astrological treatise, the text indicates that, on the day of one's personal destiny (*benming*), the practitioner must change into clean clothes before

---

49. S. Whitfield (1988): 4–22; Rong (2004): 58–59.
50. See Fujieda (1973): 426; Deng (2002): 513–519; Arrault and Martzloff (2003): 96, 182–184; and S. Whitfield (2004): 234.

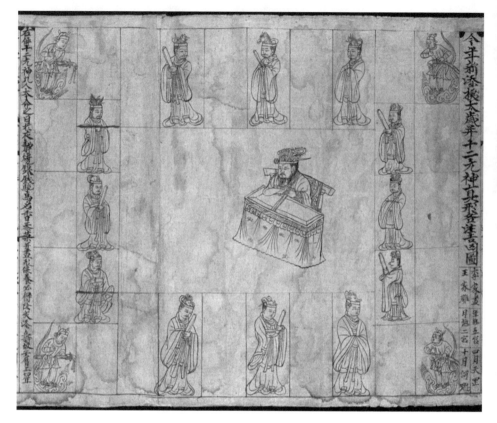

Fig. 4.4. The true forms of the twelve Original Spirits (S. 612 R°). Courtesy of the British Library.

rendering homage to the image of his Original Spirit while burning sacrificial money, paper camels, and high-quality incense and making offerings of tea and fruits. By performing this cult, the text adds, he can expel sorrows and assure his longevity.

Although in Zhai's calendar the cult is dedicated to the animal of the current year, the monkey, S. 612 R° does not highlight the tiger divinity corresponding to its year of publication, 978. It offers, by contrast, a global system of the twelve animals. Because the upper segment of the document has been cut off, it is impossible to know whether, as in the calendar of Zhai Fengda, a second illustration relative to the Beidou cult itself was included and whether the title "Method of Ge Xuan" was applied to designate the whole, though this was likely the case. The almanac as drawn here, moreover, is a draft for a printed version intended for national diffusion. This strongly suggests that the method was officially approved by the administration of the emperor Taizong 太宗 of the Northern Song toward the beginning of his reign (976–997).

THE BODY OF MATERIALS from Dunhuang that we have examined, whether medical texts or calendars, demonstrates that the worship of the Beidou and of the Original Spirits was current during the ninth and tenth centuries in this remote region of Gansu as well as in central China. The information provided in the prescriptions and illustrations of these Dunhuang documents taken together is consistent with the instructions expounded earlier by Yixing in the Method of Sir Immortal Ge for Honoring the Great Dipper. There can be no question but that they stem from the same tradition. In sum, we find the elements here of a nightly domestic cult of the seven stars of the Dipper, punctuated by six major points in the year during which one worships one's Original Spirit of Personal Destiny. The adept must wear one of the seven talismans associated with his protective star. The cult is to be performed in the household oratory, facing the incense burner of the altar, above which a diagram of the constellation (*xingxiang* 星像) and/or an image of one of the twelve Original Spirits must be suspended. The practitioner prays and presents diverse offerings, most significantly the metaphorical sacrificial money that he has to burn, as well as comestible offerings consisting of cereals and grains, in exact quantities, corresponding to his natal star.

Taoism and the Great Dipper

Neither the *Book of Wages and Fate* to which Yixing makes allusion, nor the *Book of Immortals* cited by Zhai Fengda has come down to us.[51] The little we know of Ge Xuan, the supposed promoter of the cult of the Great Dipper, does not contribute in any event to the clarification of its origin. Though several Taoist works have been attributed to this great "master of esoterica," in most cases such attribution served just to seal them with his long-standing fame. Was the Method for Honoring the Great Dipper similarly placed under his patronage for promotional ends? To what extent, under these circumstances, can we credit the assertions of Yixing and of Zhai Fengda concerning its Taoist antecedents?

---

51. The only reference to a *Xianren jing* 仙人經 is that found in the list of works pertaining to the ordination of the Taoist clergy according to the *Lingbao Scripture of the Symbolic Names for Augmenting Merits and Eliminating Sins* (*Taishang lingbao hongfu miezui xiangming jing* 太上靈寶洪福滅罪像名經, Dz 377. 11b), probably of the Song period.

Specialists have not previously delved into these questions. The only Taoist works so far examined in attempting to reach back to the sources of the Yuan *Sūtra of the Great Dipper* have been limited, as noted earlier, to the popular Song-dynasty *Supreme Scripture of the Great Dipper of Mysterious Power [Guiding] Destiny and Prolonging Life (Taishang xuanling beidou benming yansheng zhenjing)* and its commentaries.[52] This is the "standard" Taoist *Scripture of the Great Dipper,* and like its Buddhist counterpart, it proclaims its capacity to save the living from all ills and to extract the damned from the infernal dungeons to which their bad karma has condemned them. It insists principally upon its own worship and the recitation of the incantations and formulaic vows that constitute the core of its teaching:

> If a family possesses the *Scripture of the Great Dipper,*
> Its destiny will be blessed.
> If a family possesses the *Scripture of the Great Dipper,*
> Its house will enjoy peace.[53]

That said, the work also sets forth the ritual elements of the cult of the Beidou with which we are familiar. It mentions the rites of "original destiny" (*benming*) to be performed six times per year and stresses the correspondences between the duodecennial signs and the individual's natal star.[54] Although the basic text includes no reference to the cereals or talismans of the Great Dipper,[55] three of its commentaries, which were presumably redacted during the late Southern Song (1127–1279) or the beginning of the Yuan, present one and the same series of *fu* in relation to the seven (or nine) stars of the constellation.[56] One of these commentaries, the *Taishang xuanling beidou benming yansheng zhenjing zhujie* 註解, in addition associates these talismans with icons of the stellar divinities of the Beidou. As one sees in the accompanying illustration (fig. 4.5), they closely resemble those given in the Buddhist apocryphal *Beidou jing.*[57]

A second series of talismans of the seven stars figures also in an appendix to another of these three late commentaries, the *Winged Stanzas on the Golden Mys-*

---

52. See the list given by Franke (1990): 97–98.

53. Dz 622. 8b.

54. Dz 622. 4b–5a. The rites of original destiny form the object of a domestic cult (*zhai-jiao* 齋醮), celebrated on six days annually according to the horoscope of the practitioner.

55. In the Dz 622, the offering is limited to flowers and fruits (2a).

56. *Taishang xuanling beidou benming yansheng zhenjing zhu* (Dz 750. 5/4a–6a) with a post-face dated 1334. *Taishang xuanling beidou benming yansheng zhenjing zhujie* 註解 (Dz 751. 2/11b–14a) and *Taishang xuanling beidou benming yansheng jing zhu* (Dz 752. 2/9a–15a) dated probably to the thirteenth century.

57. Dz 751. 2/11b–14a.

Fig. 4.5. The talismans of the seven stars and icons of the nine stars of the Great Dipper (Dz 751).

tery of the Seven Principles of the Northern Dipper (*Beidou qiyuan jinxuan yuzhang* 北斗七元金玄羽章), likely dating from the end of the twelfth century (fig. 4. 6).[58]

The talismans that we find in these sources interestingly resemble those of the Yuan Buddhist *Beidou jing* and are identical with those given in the "second" Taoist *Yisuan jing* that was dealt with in chapter 3. The types of cereals with which the text associates them also correspond to those of the Method of Ge Xuan and to those of the Buddhist *Beidou jing.* The sole singularity that the *Winged Stanzas on the Golden Mystery of the Seven Principles of the Northern Dipper* introduces into its system of correspondences involves the essences of various trees supposedly growing on Mount Tai 泰山, located in Shandong Province and one of China's five famous sacred peaks, traditionally considered to be the seat of the divine administration presiding over human destiny and afterlife. For the *Winged Stanzas on the Golden Mystery of the Seven Principles of the Northern Dipper,* each person, according to his birth year, is re-

---

58. Dz 753. 2a–4b. These same talismans figure also in the second part of the *Established Order of Taoism* (*Daomen dingzhi* 道門定制, Dz 1224. 8/17b–21a), compiled in 1188 by Lü Yuansu 呂元素. See Schipper and Verellen (2004), vol. 2: 1010–1012.

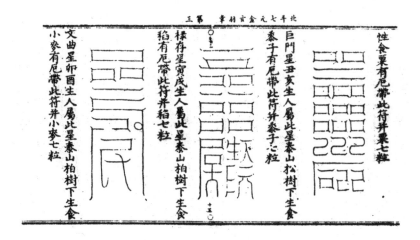

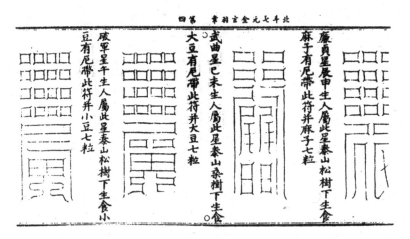

FIG. 4.6. The talismans of the Great Dipper in the *Winged Stanzas on the Golden Mystery of the Seven Principles of the Northern Dipper* (Dz 753).

lated to a cereal and a tree on Mount Tai. The first star, Tanlang, is associated with pine, cypress, and millet; the second star, Jumen, with pine and rye; the third star, Lucun, with cypress and rice; the fourth star, Wenqu, with cypress and wheat; the fifth star, Lianzhen, with pine and hemp seeds; the sixth star, Wuqu, with mulberry and soybeans; and the seventh star, Pojun, with pine and peas.

Is there a relationship to be established between these elements and the sticks of wood and grains offered into the flames during the Tantric fire ritual?

The answer remains uncertain.[59] What is patent, however, is the correlation between the cereals and destiny in the eyes of medieval Taoists. We have seen in chapter 3 that the life-account (*suan*) was conceived as a store of celestial grain, metaphorically assuring the subsistence of each human being during his earthly sojourn. In accord with the divine account, the exhaustion of this personal alimentary bank coincides with death. The offering of cereals was thus intimately tied to the management of each one's individual existence.

If the direct link between the standard Song-dynasty Taoist *Beidou jing* and the Yuan-dynasty Buddhist *Beidou jing* remains difficult to establish, the additional information gleaned from the later Taoist commentaries surely permits us to detect a genetic connection uniting the two traditions. But none of these Taoist texts, we must note, makes the slightest allusion to Ge Xuan. The Taoist *Beidou jing* is supposed to owe its existence not to the illustrious alchemist but to Laojun, the supreme deity who is said to have revealed it to his vicar, the first Heavenly Master, Zhang Daoling, during the first year of the Yongshou era 永壽 (155 C.E.) in Shudu 蜀都 (modern Chengdu).[60] This fictitious attribution need not surprise us if we take into account the scripture's historical provenance. Like the series of works respectively related to the Dippers of each of the four other directions, with which it is cognate, the Taoist *Beidou jing* was very likely redacted during the Song period under the aegis of the Heavenly Masters of the powerful, officially recognized, neo-Zhengyi institution of Mount Longhu 龍虎山 (Jiangxi Province). As an expression of the renewal of the astral cults, a priority for these Zhengyi experts in exorcism, this modern corpus of the Great Dipper would have logically been placed under the authority of their patriarch, Zhang Daoling, the mystical recluse of the second-century C.E. Taoist church, who by that time was venerated as an almighty exorcist.[61] The attribution of the Taoist *Beidou jing* to Zhang Daoling would remain unquestioned by the Taoist commentators of the twelfth through fourteenth centuries, such as the otherwise unknown Fu Dongzhen 傅洞真. In the aforementioned *Winged Stanzas on the Golden Mystery of the Seven Principles of the Northern Dipper,* Fu Dongzhen insists on Zhang Daoling's legacy and denounces the detractors of the Taoist *Beidou jing* who maintain that it was written by the Heavenly Master Du 杜天師, that is, the Tang and Five Dynasties court Taoist Du Guangting.[62]

---

59. We do know, however, that certain esoteric Buddhist rites also recommended that grains be buried to "anchor" or "fix" a given site. See Mochizuki (1936–1963), vol. 4: 3606 b–c; and Campany (2002): 311n111.

60. Dz 623–627 are considered to form a single group of texts. They correspond to the Dippers of the five directions.

61. See Schipper and Verellen (2004), vol. 2: 949–950.

62. The revelation of the *Beidou jing* to Zhang Daoling is mentioned by Xu Daoling 徐道

To return to Ge Xuan and his Beidou cult, and so to advance our inquiry, we must examine a more ancient Taoist source, the *Secret Instructions for Prolonging Life from the Purple Court of the Seven Principles of the Northern Emperor* (*Beidi qiyuan ziting yansheng bijue* 北帝七元紫庭延生祕訣; hereafter *Secret Instructions of the Seven Principles*). This work, a compendium of diverse rites of the Great Dipper, claims its historical origin in the second year of the "red crow" Chiwu 赤烏, that is to say, 239. It was then revealed by the Most High Lord Lao to Ge Xianweng 葛仙翁, another name for Ge Xuan.[63] No indication permits us to establish its real dating, but there is no doubt that it was compiled prior to 1025, as it is reproduced in extenso in the *Yunji qiqian*.[64] Besides its attribution to Ge Xuan, the text has much in common with the Tang-period method for honoring the Great Dipper, above all the cereal offerings, the burning of sacrificial paper money, the nightly cult of the stars of the Dipper, and the rite for the *benming*. It is possible therefore that it was similarly composed during the Tang and that it issued from the Heavenly Master organization, whose liturgy was by that time officially integrated into the unified Taoist system.[65] But the *Secret Instructions of the Seven Principles* also contains supplementary information that, though delivered in a tangled manner, offers us the opportunity to refine our understanding of several aspects of the Beidou cult and to relate it to earlier Taoist practices, in particular to medieval Shangqing techniques of meditation on the Dipper.

According to the *Secret Instructions of the Seven Principles*, when an adept wishes to apply himself to the cult of the constellation, a written petition is initially sent to the divinities of the Dipper, informing them of the identity and birth date of the candidate. This type of bureaucratic formality, it may be recalled, was current practice in the liturgy of the Way of the Heavenly Master. In exchange for this registration in good and due form by the astral administration, the initiate qualified himself through the provision of a quantity of symbolic objects and foodstuffs: substitutional effigies (*dairen* 代人), clothing, gold and jade rings, cash, a drum, white rice, incense, paper, a brush and ink, raw silk of five colors in precise dimensions, and a variety of fruits (chestnuts, plums,

---

齡 in his postface dated 1334 (Dz 750. postface 1a) and by Fu Dongzhen (Dz 751. preface 1a). Another unknown commentator, the Perfected Xuanyuan from Kongtong 崆峒玄元真人, attempts to provide the text with additional prestigious certifications by attributing to it a preface by the celebrated poet Li Bo 李白 (701–762), claiming that he was a practitioner of the *Beidou jing*, and a postface by the equally renowned savant Su Shi 蘇軾 (1034–1101) (Dz 751. preface 1a). See Franke (1990): 99–100; and Schipper and Verellen (2004), vol. 2: 950.

63. Dz 1265. 1a. The work is supposed to have been then transmitted under the Wei (220–265) to a certain Sir Ye 葉先生. The text is mentioned by Soymié (1972–1973) and Franke (1990): 105.

64. Dz 1032. 25/1a–10b.

65. See Schipper and Verellen (2004), vol. 1: 449–450, 485–486.

FIG. 4.7. An altar with lamps for the Beidou at the Laojun temple 老君廟, Xinjin 新津 (Sichuan). Photograph by the author, 2001.

peaches, jujubes, apricots, and walnuts).[66] In return, he received the talisman(s) of the seven stars to be worn on his belt.[67] The rite of "personal destiny" described in the *Secret Instructions of the Seven Principles*, we may note, is none other than the lamp ritual that has been practiced by Taoists since early medieval times and that remains common today (fig. 4.7).

The practitioner of this rite of personal destiny, after bathing himself and cleansing the place of performance, arranges the lamps of the seven stars (cups filled with oil), which also serve as a vehicle of divination, the manner in which they burn down being interpreted as prognosticating his future.[68] He then sets out wine, fruits, incense, cakes, and sacrificial paper money upon the altar. With the exception of the wine, these offerings—notably sacrificial money, which will be burned—are the same as those specified in Yixing's Method of Ge Xuan, as well as in the rite of the Original Spirits found in the

---

66. Dz 1265. 4a–5b.

67. Dz 1265. 9a–end. The talismans presented in the version of the *Yunji qiqian* are slightly different (Dz 1032. 25/9a–10b).

68. Dz 1265. 1a.

Dunhuang 978 C.E. almanac. Turning in the direction of his natal star, the adept calls it three times and prays for the realization of his vows.[69] Two sets of names are given for the stars, one in the Tanlang series (listed in chapter 3) and the second in the Yangming series, which was also frequently used in medieval Taoism: Yangming 陽明, Yinjing 陰精, Zhenren 真人, Xuanming 玄冥, Danyuan 丹元, Beiji 北極, and Tianguan 天關. The *Secret Instructions of the Seven Principles* stipulates that these latter are the stars' secret or taboo appellations (*hui* 諱).[70] The adept is additionally encouraged to perform three times each month—on the first, third, and twenty-seventh nights—an exercise that is held to be immensely profitable in terms of life expectancy: the observation of the two "minor" stars of the Dipper, the eighth (Fuxing) and the ninth (Bixing). Those who manage to glimpse these two stars are rewarded with a prolongation of three hundred years of life for the eighth and six hundred years for the hidden ninth star.[71] Greatly beneficial, too, is the homage rendered to the Santai stars, the Three Eminences, which bring success in an administrative career, as well as in the search for a wife or concubine.[72] The text further provides several incantations for pacifying the spirits (*anshen* 安神), to be recited on going to bed and on rising.[73] One among them, entitled the Divine Incantation of the Beidou to Prolong Life (Beidou yansheng shenzhou 北斗延生神咒), was taken up in the late Taoist *Beidou jing* commentary signed by Fu Dongzhen.[74]

It may be stressed, too, that the list of cereals and peas given by the *Secret Instructions of the Seven Principles* is identical to that of the Yuan Buddhist *Beidou jing*.[75] In all events, our Taoist text specifies that this comestible offering is in fact a rite of substitution, an alternative for those who have not mastered the esoteric practice of "pacing the seven stars' network" (*bu qixing gang* 步七星綱), also called the "rite of offering by pacing" (*bujiao zhi fa* 步醮之法).[76] Imitating the limping steps of Yu the Great (Yubu 禹步), the mythical arranger of the universe, and symbolizing ascension into the heavens, this stellar choreography, with its long, historical background, was mostly favored by

---

69. Dz 1265. 1b–2a.

70. Dz 1265. 8b.

71. Dz 1265. 2b; *Yunji qiqian*, 25. 2/25a.

72. Dz 1265. 3a.

73. Dz 1265. 7b.

74. Dz 1265. 7b–8a; Dz 752, 3.15a–b. See also Poul Andersen in Schipper and Verellen (2004), vol. 1: 485–486.

75. Dz 1265. 3a–4a. Franke (1990): 106, notes that the Buddhist text has *gengmi* 粳米 (nonglutinous rice) instead of *nuomi* 糯米 (glutinous rice) in the Taoist version (a misreading by the Buddhist copyist?).

76. Dz 1265. 3b–4a.

the Taoists of the early Shangqing lineage, who have left us varied poetic descriptions of it.[77]

A method of "lying down in the Dipper," also inspired by an ancient Shangqing practice, is equally recommended by the *Secret Instructions of the Seven Principles*. In a passage entitled Divine Incantations of the Great Dipper for Prolonging Life, Recited for Pacifying the Spirit and for Longevity (Beidou yansheng shenzhou nian zhi anshen yanshou 北斗延生神咒念之安神延壽), the scripture explains how the adept must stretch out on a map of the constellation, visualizing the stars around him, after invoking the four heraldic creatures (green dragon to the left, white tiger to the right, red bird in front, and dark warrior behind) and pronouncing an "incantation of reclining" (*wozhou* 臥咒), composed of the names of the stars. The aim, says the scripture, is to avert calamity, remove one's name from the registers of death, and obtain blessings.[78]

Several of the original Shangqing writings that were revealed to the visionary Yang Xi during the years 364–370 C.E. introduce an analogous rite of lying down in the Dipper, performed at night in order to benefit from the Great Dipper's therapeutic and salvific influxes. The *Shangqing Golden Scripture with Jade Characters* (*Shangqing jinshu yuzi shangjing* 上清金書玉字上經, Dz 879), for example, provides a detailed description of the bodily posture that the practitioner must adopt when reclining on the diagram of the constellation designed on his mat: the head is placed on the axis of the third star), with the feet on the eighth and ninth stars (Fuxing and Bixing), the left hand touching the second star and the right hand, the fourth (fig. 4.8). Lying in total tranquility, his arms forming a crossbar, the adept must grind his teeth, then recite a secret formula, concentrating himself on the Dongfang 洞房 Palace situated within his brain. He thus comes to see the essence of the nine stars fusing and transforming into a divinity, sitting in a chariot, who comes to visit him and to illuminate entirely the interior of his body. Nine years of such practice, says the Shangqing text, enable one to escape death; eighteen, to reach immortality.[79]

Complementary instructions are expounded in the Method of Lying Down with the Seven Lads of the Dipper (Qitong wobei fa 七童臥斗法), found in another work similarly revealed to Yangxi, the *Shangqing Scripture on Following the Three Paths and [Absorbing] the Yellow Breath and the Yang Essence* (*Shangqing huangqi yangjing sandao shunxing jing* 上清黃氣陽精三道順行經). Here, the practitioner isolates himself at night in a quiet room, burns incense, and then reclines, facing the north under the "canopy" (*gai* 蓋) of the seven stars of the Beidou. He visu-

---

77. On the *bugang,* see Robinet (1979): 308–328; and Andersen (1989–1990): 18.
78. Dz 1265. 8a–b.
79. Dz 879. 1a–2b, 5b–6b. A version of the text figures also in the *Yunji qiqian,* 25. 16b–18b. See Robinet (1979): 307.

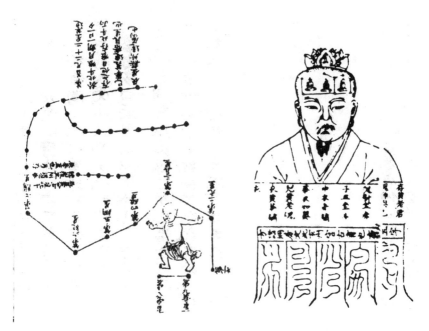

FIG. 4.8. The Method of lying down in the Dipper and meditating on the seven stars (Dz 879).

alizes the seven stellar lads, and calls them by their secret names, so that they emit a light that encircles him, concentrates into *qi,* and enters his body. The adept grinds his teeth and swallows saliva, gets up to roll himself in rice powder, and then lies down again. The text promises him that, after seven years of assiduous discipline, his body will glow with the splendor of the seven jewels, a purple aura will emanate from his head, and he will attain immortality.[80] This type of astral visualization and the circulation of light inside the body were also considered by the Shangqing adepts to be efficacious means of contrition. To expel their sins and those of seven generations of ancestors, they invoked the nine stars of the Dipper so that the stellar light entered their mouths and was then circulated within the bodily organs.[81] It may be stressed that a similar technique of meditation on the Dipper was already advocated in the *Baopuzi neipian,* but here the effulgence encircling the practitioner is produced from within:

> Visualize the seven stars of the Great Dipper with the chariot covering your head
> and the handle pointed forward. Meditate then on the energies of the five bodily or-

---

80. Dz 33. 25b–27b; also edited in *Yunji qiqian,* 25. 10a–12b.

81. *Shangqing zijing jun huangchu ziling daojun dongfang shangjing* 上清紫精君皇初紫靈道君洞房上經, Dz 405. 12b–end. Also edited in *Yunji qiqian,* 25/12b–14a.

gans [from which the light] flows out through the two eyes to form a halo around the body. . . . You will then be able to sleep [without apprehension] even with those who are sick with the plague![82]

The Lords of the Dipper

Whether used for reclining or installed as a shelter-canopy above the practitioner, whether they served as choreographic patterns for pacing the stellar network or as visual supports for meditation, maps and diagrams were indispensable for the early Shangqing practices relating to the Dipper cult. By the Tang period, visual representations of the constellation continued to play a central role, and iconographic depictions of the anthropomorphic stellar deities seem to have been standardized as well. We remember how Yixing insists on the necessity—as part of the practice of the Method of Ge Xuan—of venerating the stellar images of both the Beidou and the Spirits of Personal Destiny. Such icons were probably very close to the ones found in the illustrations of Zhai Fengda's calendar.

Further clarifications on the material aspects of the maps of the Beidou and the iconographic features of its stellar deities may be found, once again, in the Taoist literature. A short description of the Dipper map is given, for instance, in the *Secret Instructions of the Seven Principles*. Designed to be hung above the altar, this "chart of the seven principles" (*qiyuan tu* 七元圖) must be drawn on two panels of blue-black raw silk measuring nine feet in length and hung above the altar.[83] Considering the size of this map, there is a distinct possibility that a similar model was used to cover the bed of the adept reclining upon the Dipper.

Other descriptions of these maps of the Great Dipper, notably concerning their iconographic details, are found in the late Shangqing literature. Among the esoteric writs that were transmitted to the adepts of the movement during the Tang period, there figures a "Register of the Nine Stars of the River Chart" (Hetu jiuxing lu 河圖九星錄), corresponding to the highest degree of Shangqing initiation.[84]

Several versions of this "Register of the River Chart" have been preserved

82. *Baopuzi neipian,* chap. 15, Wang Ming ed.: 275.
83. Dz 1265. 4b; *Yunji qiqian,* 25/5a.
84. *Chronicle of Maoshan (Maoshan zhi* 茅山志, Dz 304. 2/9a). This highly valued chart of the Great Dipper was bestowed upon the emperor Tang Xuanzong, who received it in 748 C.E. from the hands of the thirteenth patriarch of the Shangqing lineage, Li Hanguang 李含光 (683–769), disciple and successor of the famous Sima Chengzhen 司馬承禎 (647–735). Shortly afterwards, in 754, at the emperor's request, Li celebrated a River Chart Great Retreat (Hetu dazhai 河圖大齋) on Maoshan 茅山, the headquarters of the Shangqing lineage. Refer to Schipper and Verellen (2004), vol. 1: 595. For Li Hanguang's biography, see Chen Guofu 1963: 59–62; Schafer (1980): 46–47; and Barrett (1996): 69–71.

in the Taoist Canon, one of them including instructions for its manufacture: the stellar diagram must be designed in blue on raw silk fabric measuring one foot, two inches in length and a foot in width, with the divinities, the Sovereign Lords of the Nine Stars (*jiu huangjun* 九皇君) and their Ladies (*jiu furen* 九夫人), represented in black.[85] Much smaller than the altar map of the *Secret Instructions of the Seven Principles,* this chart was intended to be carried on the adept's person.[86]

Another Shangqing version of the "Register of the River Chart" preserves a diagram of the Great Dipper with conspicuous representations of the constellation and its anthropomorphic divinities.[87] This diagram and its talismans (fig. 4.9) closely resemble those reproduced at the beginning of the Buddhist *Beidou jing* edited in the *Taishō daizōkyō.*[88] In contradistinction to the latter, the icons of the stars have not been included in this stellar chart, but they are given independently in a series of nine medallions, together with nine further medallions illustrating their palaces (fig. 4.10).[89] Such designs of the nine stars and their residences seem to have become the norm under the Tang. Other examples may be found in a third Shangqing edition of the same document, the "Precious Register of the River Chart" (Hetu baolu 河圖寶錄) (fig. 4.11),[90] as well as in a version stemming from the Heavenly Masters and called the "Precious Register of the River Chart of the Nine and the One from the Most High" (Taishang jiuyi hetu baolu 太上九一河圖寶錄).[91]

The affinity of these anthropomorphic images of the Great Dipper's divini-

---

85. The *Esoteric and Mysterious Scripture of the Shangqing River Chart* (*Shangqing hetu neixuan jing* 上清河圖內玄經, Dz 1367. 1/4a–b). The work does not supply images of the nine stars but does supply images of their female companions, the Nine Ladies, *jiufu* 九夫 (1/4b–5a).

86. Dz 1265. 9a. Similarly, the talismanic diagram entitled the Chart of the True Forms of the Seven Principles (*qiyuan zhenxing tu* 七元真形圖), of which the *Secret Instructions of the Seven Principles* provides the model, had to be attached to the initiate's belt.

87. This is in a collection of Shangqing registers compiled during the Tang period and entitled the *Shangqing Register for the Instructions on the Emanations from the Labyrinth* (*Shangqing qusu jueci lu* 上清曲索訣辭錄, Dz 1392. 18b–24a). See Robinet (1984), vol. 2: 436–437; Schipper and Verellen (2004), vol. 1: 607–609.

88. Dz 1392. 23a–24a. These talismanic scripts, the text stipulates, are the secret names of the stars. They must be written in vermilion. The talismans are followed by an invocation of the nine stars, the Nine Sovereign Lords (*jiuhuang jun* 九皇君), to be recited nine times consecutively, before sunrise and sunset, after clenching the teeth. The procedure permits one to acquire the faculty of flying through the air.

89. Dz 1392. 18b–20b.

90. Dz 1396. 1a–b. It is followed by a series of nine talismans also written in vermilion. See also note 86 above.

91. *Complete Division of the Liturgical Registers of the One and Orthodox Covenant of the Most High* (*Taishang zhengyi mengwei falu yibu* 太上正一盟威法錄一部, Dz 1209. 34b–38b). This register is classed as thirteenth among the fourteen initiatory documents punctuating the spiritual ascent of the Zhengyi devotees. See also the *Registers of the One and Orthodox Covenant of the Three and the Five of the Most High* (*Taishang sanwu zhengyi mengwei lu* 太上三五正一盟威錄, Dz 1208),

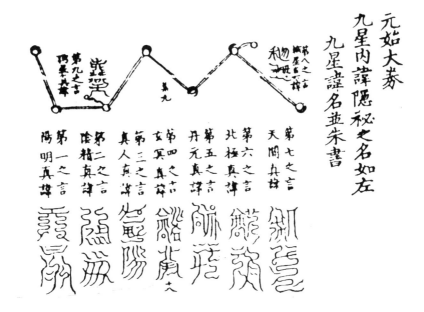

FIG. 4.9. The talismanic names of the nine stars of the Great Dipper (Dz 1392).

ties as they appear in these Taoist registers with their depictions in the tenth-century Dunhuang calendars and the late Buddhist and Taoist editions of the *Beidou jing* is striking. The same iconographic characteristics remain prevalent, moreover, in the fifteenth-century ritual paintings found in the Gongzhu 公主寺 and Baoning 寶寧寺 temples in Shanxi (fig. 4.12). In all these instances, the seven stars are young men with long hair, often worn loose, who are dressed in official garments and holding court tablets. The Taoist sources refer to them in fact as the "seven lads of the Beidou" or as young dignitaries or "lords" (*jun* 君). For the *Lingbao Scripture of Karmic Retribution,* for example, they wear five-colored brocade and course through the clouds in a chariot of seven lights.[92] In the *Secret Instructions of the Seven Principles,* they have the "allure of Perfected Men" (*zhenren xingzhuang* 真人形狀), garbed in ceremonial dress and bearing jade tablets in their hands.[93] It should be stressed that, as early as the second century C.E., anthropomorphic representations of the Great Dipper already existed. The well-known bas-relief of the funeral chamber of the Wu Liang shrine 武梁祠 in

---

dating from the Song, for another Zhengyi version of the same register (4/4b–7b). See Schipper and Verellen (2004), vol. 1: 475–476, and vol. 2: 971–972.

92. Dz 336. 8/7a–b.
93. Dz 1265. 2a.

FIG. 4.10. The
nine stars and
their palaces
(Dz 1392).

Shandong, which dates to that period, shows a divinity of the Great Dipper in the form of a functionary sitting upon a chariot composed of the seven stars.[94]

In Taoist literature, the nine stellar lords are often escorted by their nine imperial concubines of the Great Yin (Taiyin jiufei 太陰九妃). The *Guide of the Golden Lock and the Moving Pearls* (*Jinsuo liuzhu yin*), which was mentioned in the preceding chapters and includes important passages on the practice of pacing the Dipper, specifies that complete harems are charged with attending to the pleasures of the seven stellar deities. Each one of the lords possesses one titular empress (*zhenghou* 正后), three imperial concubines (*fei* 妃), two wives of the second rank (*furen* 夫人), and three beauties (*jiaonü* 嬌女).[95] Iconographic details concerning primarily the style and color of their garments as well as their coiffures are sometimes also furnished by Taoist authors, so that one may easily visualize them during meditation.[96]

The Earliest Antecedents

Taken together, these data demonstrate that the Tang Buddhist and Taoist cult of the Great Dipper, together with its maps and iconography, finds its basis in the Taoism of the Six Dynasties, and notably in the Shangqing movement. That said, the cult of the Beidou is already very well attested in the *Baopuzi neipian,* as we have seen in its instructions for meditation on the constellation. Ge Hong also elaborates a ritual for fabricating "forty-nine true and secret talismans of the matrix of the Yellow Court of Lord Lao" (*Laojun huangting zhong tai sishijiu zhenmi fu* 老君黃庭中胎四十九真祕符), which should be inscribed during a nocturnal rite addressed to the Beidou:

---

94. See Chavannes (1913): 212–213. On the Wu Liang shrine, see Wu (1989).
95. Dz 1015. 16/5b.
96. See, for example, *Yunji qiqian* 31/10a–11b.

Before betaking oneself to the mountains and forests, one chooses a *jiayin* day in order to write the talismans in red on raw silk. At night, one places them on a table and, facing the Beidou, one presents to each one offerings of wine and meat. One states one's identity and prostrates twice. Inserted in the collar of one's garment, these talismans assure [the voyager] protection from all demons, miasmas, tigers and wolves, insects, and poisons from the mountains and rivers.[97]

It is unfortunate that the alchemist gives us no further information on these "true talismans," which are also listed in his bibliography.[98] The ritual procedure, specifically dedicated as it is to the circumstances surrounding perilous journeys, is distinct from the horoscopic practice of the Method of Ge Xuan. As for the stark contrast between the food offerings presented to the stars in the former case—namely, wine and meat—and the cereals of Ge Xuan's method, this might be explained by the absolute proscription of blood sacrifice mandated by the early Taoist theologians, whereby the carnal offerings once given to the stars were replaced by a vegetarian treat.[99] That said, the number of *fu* mentioned by Ge Hong—that is, forty-nine—as well as their consecration before the Great Dipper, leaves us with no doubt at all regarding their connection to the constellation.

97. *Baopuzi neipian,* chap. 17, Wang Ming, ed.: 308. See the same rite as described in the *Wushang biyao* (Dz 1138. 97/7a–12b), which quotes the *Dongzhen taishang zidu yanguang shenyuan bian jing* 洞真太上紫度炎光神元變經 (Dz 1332. 9a–10a, 13a–16b). There, too, it is intended for a traveler who is about to take a dangerous trip. In possession of talismans, he visualizes the seven stars of the Dipper above his head, etc. See Lagerwey (1981): 208–210.

98. *Baopuzi neipian,* chap. 19, Wang Ming, ed.: 335.

99. Note, too, that Shangqing Taoism prohibited its adepts from consuming the flesh of the animal corresponding to one's "personal destiny," as well as the animals associated with the "personal destinies" of one's father and mother, given among the ten interdictions of the *Taiwei lingshu ziwen xianji zhenji shangjing* 太微靈書紫文仙忌真記上經 (Dz 179. 1b–3a), which belongs to the early Shangqing canon.

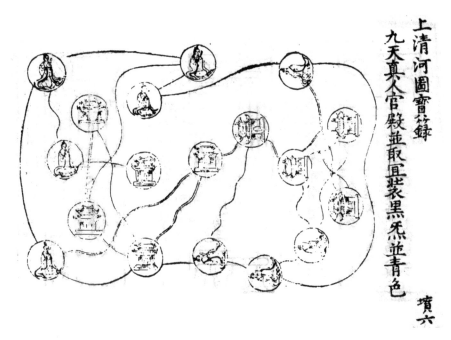

FIG. 4.11. The nine stars and their palaces (Dz 1396).

Material evidence furnished by archeological discoveries allows us to reach even further back in time for the sources of the talismanic tradition of the Beidou. Two *fu* dating to the end of the Han may be cited as examples. One, which figures on an earthen jar exhumed in 1957 from a tomb in the region of Chang'an (Xi'an), presents a diagram of the seven stars of the Beidou with the characters *beidou jun* 北斗君 (lord of the Beidou), beneath which names of demons of the dead are inscribed (fig. 4.13, right).[100] Another talisman of a rarer genre, as it is inscribed on wood, was brought to light that same year in the province of Jiangsu. Written in red on a board twenty by three to four centimeters in size, it bears a diagram of the constellation, followed by an apotropaic formula of invocation (fig. 4.13, left). An infectious demon called "heavenly light" (*tianguang* 天光), also emanating from a dead person, is there summoned by the divine superintendence to "obey the law in all haste," under the threat of being devoured should he resist.[101] Although the ambition of these Han demonifuge *fu* of the Great Dipper is clearly restricted to a funeral context, they nonetheless demon-

---

100. See Wang Yucheng (1991, 1996).

101. "Jiangsu Gaoyou Shaojiagou Handai yizhi de qingli" 江蘇高郵邵家溝漢代的遺址的清理, *Kaogu* 考古 (October 1960): 20–21.

Fig. 4.12. The nine stars of the Dipper in a fifteenth-century painting at the Baoning temple, Shanxi. After Wu Lianching, ed., *Baoning si Mingdai shuilu hua* (1988), plate 74.

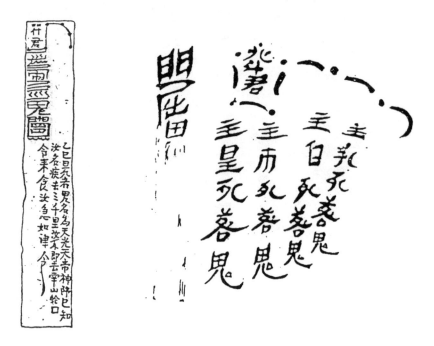

FIG. 4.13. Two Beidou talismans of the late Han period.

strate that the roots of the Chinese talismanic cult of the Great Dipper are deep indeed and are lost in early antiquity.

IN LIGHT OF the materials we have surveyed, we may conclude that the talismanic tradition of the seven stars of the Great Dipper originated in early medieval Taoism, which itself drew upon elements reaching back at least to the Eastern Han. By the eighth century, when the famed esoteric Buddhist masters settled in China, the worship of the Great Dipper that they integrated into their rites for longevity and protection, of both individual and state, therefore already had a long history. It had been maturing for several centuries in Taoist praxis, and had been profusely expounded, above all by the Shangqing movement. The religious rivalry that was then unfolding in court circles certainly prompted the Buddhist masters to appropriate this highly popular and firmly rooted Chinese cult in their liturgy and to promote it in the interests of the state ideology. Although none of the canonical texts preserved from that time can be directly linked to the Yuan-dynasty Buddhist *Beidou jing,* it is nevertheless plausible that a prototype of the apocryphal sūtra was already in circulation during the later half of the Tang. The basic horoscopic, iconographic, and ritual components of the talismanic worship of the Beidou advocated by the Yuan apocryphon are already in evidence in medieval sources from Dunhuang and are set forth in the Method of Sir Immortal Ge for Honoring the Great Dipper. In all events, we are certainly entitled to regard the late medieval Taoist Beidou scriptures and the Yuan Buddhist apocryphal sūtra as the products of the effort to give canonical form to what had long been an established ritual tradition.

In the final stage in the varied legacy of the Chinese Great Dipper tradition, an interesting turn in its pan-Asian distribution emerges through its importation in Korea. Henrik Sørensen has shown how Buddhist worship of the constellation's seven stars played a prominent role in the legitimation of the Koryŏ 高麗 dynasty (918–1392), from the middle of the thirteenth century on. Court-sponsored Buddhist rituals for the protection of the state and dedicated to the Great Dipper were performed in a special building consecrated to the seven stars. In this context, the Chinese *Sūtra of the Great Dipper* had, in all likelihood, become a central text for Korean state Buddhism.[102] Subsequently, during the Chosŏn dynasty (1392–1910), the cult of the constellation spread among the Korean people as a highly regarded practice for the prosperity of individuals and their households. The irony of history was that, by the end of the seventeenth century, while the Buddhist version of the apocryphon continued to be used by Korean Buddhist communities, it so happened that it was the standard Taoist *Supreme Scripture of the Great Dipper of Mysterious Power [Guiding] Destiny and Prolonging Life* that was elected for publication by the Buddhist Songwang (Ch. Songguang) monastery 松廣寺 and incorporated into its liturgy. This mid-Chosŏn recension, Sørensen writes, "is basically a Taoist text to which has been added a Buddhist 'facing.'" Indeed, this Sino-Korean edition faithfully renders the standard Taoist *Beidou jing* and retains the iconographic features of its stellar deities—young dignitaries holding court tablets. The talismans of the seven stars reproduced in this publication are perfectly identical to those given in the *Sūtra of the Great Dipper* in the *Taishō daizōkyō*. The only distinctively Buddhist elements evident within it are the images of the Seven Buddhas.[103] Imitating their Chinese Buddhist predecessors, the seventeenth-century Korean editors thus extracted their materials from both Taoist and Buddhist sources to create a "neo-apocryphon" of the *Beidou jing*. Through this remarkable Buddho-Taoist synthesis, they concluded the cycle of accommodation and reinscription whereby the Great Dipper tradition traversed a millennial path in East and Central Asia.

---

102. Sørensen (1995): 79–84.
103. Ibid., 88 and 102, fig. 3.

CHAPTER 5

Guanyin in a Taoist Guise

He is the most saintly,
the most venerable,
the most precious,
the most efficient.

The bodhisattva Avalokiteśvara decisively entered China at the end of the third century with the translation of the most widely revered Buddhist scripture in East Asia, the *Sūtra of the Lotus Flower of the Wonderful Law* (*Saddharmapuṇḍarīkasūtra, Miaofa lianhua jing* 妙法連華經), or *Lotus Sūtra*.[1] Its twenty-fifth chapter, the "Universal Gateway of Guanshiyin" (Guanshiyin pumen pin 観世音普門品), which is entirely dedicated to the bodhisattva, would have a particularly remarkable legacy,[2] for in Avalokiteśvara (Guan[shi]yin), the *Pumen pin* introduced a new type of deity to Chinese religious life. The compassionate Guanyin was glorified not only as a universal savior but also as a readily accessible miracle worker rescuing persons in need from impending dangers or critical circumstances. The text's narration of the fearsome perils from which the bodhisattva could instantaneously and unfailingly deliver a victim who invokes his name would do much to motivate the tremendous expansion of his worship in China. Elaborately described, these seven (or twelve) hazards—including fire, water, shipwreck in the sea of the *rākṣasa*-demons, (falling from Mount Sumeru,) knives and staves, demons, pillory and shackles, (poison and sorcery,) brigands, (wild beasts,) (snakes,) (thunder and

---

Epigraph: *Taiyi jiuku hushen miaojing* 太一救苦護身妙經 (Dz 351. 5b).

1. The earliest extant translation of the *Lotus Sūtra* in Chinese is attributed to Dharmarakṣa (286 C.E.) and entitled *Sūtra of the Lotus of the True Law* (*Zheng fahua jing* 正法華經; 10 fascicles, 27 chapters, T. 263, vol. 9). The most popular is Kumārajīva's translation (406 C.E.), the *Sūtra of the Lotus Flower of the Wonderful Law* (*Miaofa lianhua jing* 妙法蓮華經; 7 fascicles, 27 chapters, T. 262, vol. 9). A third translation was done in 601 C.E. by Jñānagupta and Dharmagupta, under the title *Sūtra of the Lotus Flower of the Wonderful Law with an Additional Chapter* (*Tianpin miaofa lianhua jing* 添品妙法蓮華經; 7 fascicles, 28 chapters, T. 264, vol. 9). See Shioiri (1989): 23–31.

2. About five thousand copies of the sūtra were found at Dunhuang. On the *Pumen pin,* see Murase (1971); and Yü (2001): 75–77.

storm)—had an enduring impact on the Chinese imagination and were, time and again, pictured in art and literature.[3] Besides this, Guanyin's promise to the faithful—that by means of the same easy expedient of calling his name, one might realize one's wishes for wealth or for the birth of a male or female child—also assuredly contributed to his unparalleled success. The *Pumen pin* probably began to circulate as an independent text soon after Kumārajīva's new translation of the *Lotus Sūtra* in 406 and, in this form, was popularized as the *Guanyin Sūtra* (*Guanyin jing* 觀音經).[4] The text also quickly became the subject of visual depiction, as attested by the earliest surviving illustration of the *Pumen pin* in the relief carving of a fragmented stele recovered from the Wanfo si 萬佛寺 in Chengdu (Sichuan), dated 424 C.E.[5] The popularity of the foreign bodhisattva continued to grow in medieval times, when Guanyin became the protagonist of an expanding corpus of indigenous sūtras, miracle stories,[6] and visual works.

During the sixth century C.E., while Indian artists were carving mural sculptures of Avalokiteśvara as savior from perils in the Western Indian religious sites of Ajantā, Kanherī, Ellorā, and Aurangābad, Chinese painters started to manufacture representations of the Guanyin chapter. In Dunhuang, among the 492 documented grottoes, no less than 28 mural paintings, ranging from the early seventh to the eleventh century, depict different themes from the *Pumen pin*.[7] Illustrated handwritten copies of the *Guanyin jing* started to circulate at the end of the Tang dynasty. The didactic illustrated booklets of the sūtra, dating from the tenth century, that were discovered in the Dunhuang library cave were mentioned in chapter 2.[8]

Later on, the *Pumen pin* also became a subject for large-scale sculptures. The famous twelfth-century Water-Moon Guanyin (Shuiyue Guanyin 水月觀音) in cave 19 at the Pilu 毘盧 monastery site in Anyue 安岳 (Sichuan Province) is an example that can still be admired (fig. 5.1). Sitting in the Potalaka paradise, Guanyin is here surrounded by vignettes of the various perils enumerated in the text.[9]

Considering both the impressive artistic production devoted to the *Pumen pin* and its phenomenal diffusion, it is not surprising to discover that its charis-

3. The number of the perils differs in the prose and *gāthā* sections of the sūtra.

4. Yü (2001): 113–114.

5. See E. Y. Wang (2005): 219–220.

6. Campany (1996).

7. Murase (1971); Shi (1992); Yü (2001): 76.

8. Drège (1999): 124–137.

9. According to Howard (1990): 57, the scenes of the perils were probably restored during the seventeenth century.

FIG. 5.1. The Water-Moon Guanyin at Pilu monastery, Anyue (Sichuan), twelfth century. Photograph by Matthew T. Kapstein, 2001.

matic hero, Avalokiteśvara, became the prototype of a number of "new" Chinese divinities over the centuries. The Princess Miaoshan 妙善, the Queen of Heaven (Mazu 媽祖), the Princess of Azure Clouds (Bixia Yuanjun 碧霞元君), as well as deities associated with Buddhist sectarian movements such as the Unborn Mother (Wusheng laomu 無生老母), are among the popular feminine divinities (niangniang 娘娘) modelled on the great bodhisattva, who are providers of fertility and protectors of children. All of them flourished following Guanyin's initial feminization—that is, from the time of the Five Dynasties or the Song dynasty on—and they became particularly prominent during the Ming dynasty, by which time the bodhisattva was a completely sinicized goddess.[10] His sexual transformation is a topic that has long fascinated scholars of Chinese religions.

Significantly, it is less well known that Avalokiteśvara, in his "orthodox," male aspect, had much earlier also served as a model for Taoism. Yü Chün-fang explains that Guanyin, "like all great bodhisattvas in Mahāyāna Buddhism, cannot be said to possess any gender characteristics," but the deity is nevertheless usually conceived as a handsome and princely young man.[11] It is this masculine image of the bodhisattva that, during the Sui dynasty (581–618), motivated the creation of one of the most prestigious deities of the Taoist pantheon, the Heavenly Venerable Savior from Suffering, the Jiuku tianzun 救苦天尊.

The time and place at which the cult of this prominent Taoist deity first emerged cannot be determined with exactitude, but it is certain that, by the late sixth century or the beginning of the seventh, it was already well rooted, as is attested by the aforementioned *Lingbao Scripture of the Most High Concerning Karmic Retribution,* which dates roughly to that period. This extensive Taoist treatise elaborates the mortuary liturgy to be performed under the deity's patronage by Taoist male and female clerics (*daoshi nüguan* 道士女冠), whether at home or in temples (*lingguan xuantan* 靈觀玄壇).[12] Jiuku tianzun is depicted here as acting efficiently for the release and welfare of those who inhabit the dark spheres of the universe. Funerary ceremonies and rituals of contrition were to remain the predominant trends of the liturgy attached to Jiuku tianzun during the Tang and the Five Dynasties, and the deity's portentous power as a savior of the deceased would persist down to the present throughout the Chinese world.

However, the mission of the Heavenly Venerable Savior from Suffering was not confined to the postmortem world, and mourning and mortuary rituals were not the only periods during which he was worshipped. In a section entitled

---

10. Stein (1986); Yü (2001), chaps. 8 and 10.

11. According to the *Lotus Sūtra,* among the thirty-three forms in which Guanyin can appear to save different types of people, only seven are feminine: nun, laywoman, girl, and the wives of a rich man, a Brahman, a householder, and an official. Cf. Yü (2001): 46.

12. Dz 336. 6/3b–5a.

"Saving from Suffering" (Jiuku 救苦), the *Lingbao Scripture of Karmic Retribution* shows the Taoist deity to have been also revered as an everyday protector.[13] Jiuku tianzun's duly initiated adepts engaged themselves, morally and spiritually, to worship the deity at home, on a regular basis, through a cult called the Method for Salvation and Protection (Jiuhu zhi fa 救護之法). Performed three times per month—on the first, fifteenth, and last days—after a purification by abstaining from meat and alcohol, the rite consisted of burning incense, performing prostrations, invoking the deity in the Ten Directions, and reciting confessional formulae. The adepts were thereby assured a purgation from sins and contagions, and a protection against all adversities, misfortunes, and such particular dangers as bandits, natural calamities, plagues, wild beasts, difficult childbirth, demons, ghosts, and shipwrecks.[14]

The substantial information provided by the *Lingbao Scripture of Karmic Retribution* concerning Jiuku tianzun's domestic and mortuary rituals leaves no doubt that the cult was solidly established by the Sui period. The inclusion of this new deity in the well-constituted Taoist pantheon, inhabited as it was by powerful entities working for the protection and salvation of the faithful, seems understandable in the light of Buddhist influence. Mahāyāna notions of compassion, universal salvation, redemption, and the transfer of merit had already been thoroughly integrated into early Taoism, in particular in the Lingbao (Numinous Treasure) tradition, but the need to compete with prominent and widely venerated bodhisattvas was certainly still strongly felt. Jiuku tianzun's elevation to the very summit of the cosmic order, acting with immense mercy as savior from all pains, can therefore be understood as a Taoist attempt to enhance the pantheon in response to the presence of highly charismatic Buddhist figures. The Heavenly Venerable Savior from Suffering was thus endowed with the attributes of the popular Buddhist saints, such as the arhat Mulian 目蓮 (Maudgalyāyana), who descended to hell to save his mother, or, even more, the bodhisattva Dizang 地藏 (Kṣitigarbha), who ensured the liberation of the dead imprisoned in subterranean jails (*diyu* 地獄, Skt. *naraka*) and the rescue of the living through his capacity to manifest innumerable "bodies of transformation" (*huashen* 化身, Skt. *nirmāṇakāya*).[15] Nevertheless, it was assuredly to the bodhi-

---

13. Dz 336. 6/section 15. See Yusa (1989). Another version of this work has been found among the Pelliot Collection of Dunhuang manuscripts (P. 2387). See Ōfuchi (1978): 159–163.

14. Dz 336. 6/4b–6b.

15. See the fifth-century *Great Extended Sūtra of the Ten Wheels* (*Da fangguang shilun jing* 大方廣十輪經, T. 410, vol. 13: 1/684–685), where forty-four manifestations (including animals) of Dizang are enumerated. By means of them, he can, like Guanyin, save people who "concentrate on him and call his name" from sickness, misery, and various dangers and adversities. On Dizang, see Wang-Toutain (1998). The proximity of Jiuku tianzun and Kṣitigarbha in

sattva Guanyin that the Heavenly Venerable Savior from Suffering owed the most salient features of his personality. His names, titles, and personal qualities as recapitulated in the *Lingbao Scripture of Karmic Retribution* leave no doubt that Jiuku tianzun was, from the beginning of his career, already conceived on the model of Guanyin.[16] His most characteristic appellation, "Savior from Suffering," announcing his universal religious vocation both in this world and the next, is borrowed directly from the Buddhist bodhisattva's most common epithets, and his other titles, such as "Great Benevolent" (Daci 大慈), are also qualifications of Guanyin. Like Avalokiteśvara, Jiuku tianzun engages in prolific salvific activity and demonstrates a capacity to intervene in the "ten directions" (*shifang* 十方) of the universe.[17] Ignoring boundaries, he travels freely from the realm of the gods to the human world and from the terrestrial domain of the living to the underground abode of the dead. Jiuku tianzun was hence first and foremost the "Taoist Avalokiteśvara."

Although prolix in their account of Jiuku tianzun's bodhisattvic activities, the relevant passages given by the *Lingbao Scripture of Karmic Retribution* convey a sense of uncertainty about the deity's actual identity.[18] To gain a more detailed impression of his personal features, we must turn to later Taoist literature, composed from the Tang dynasty on, which provides precise descriptions of the deity. By that time, given the continuous influence of Guanyin, Jiuku tianzun's personality had become clearly defined and his specific iconography established. Still, in spite of the profusion of liturgical texts relating to him and demonstrating his considerable importance, so far as I know, only one extant scripture supplies a hagiographical account of the deity. This Tang work, entitled the *Marvelous Scripture of the Great Unity, the Savior from Suffering and Protector of Life* (*Taiyi jiuku hushen miaojing* 太一救苦護身妙經, Dz 351; hereinafter referred to as the *Scripture of the Savior from Suffering*), is entirely dedicated to Jiuku tianzun and emphasizes his charismatic and iconographic proximity to Guanyin. Besides its descriptive value in regard to the Taoist saint's features and functions, it

---

modern Taoist ritual for the salvation of the souls is mentioned by Schipper and Verellen (2004), vol. 2: 637.

16. Yusa (1989); Verellen (1992): 234–235.

17. Dz 336. 6/4a–4b. The "decamorphic" Heavenly Venerable of the Ten Directions [who appears as] the Saviors from Suffering (Shifang jiuku tianzun 十方救苦天尊), or the Supreme Heavenly Venerable of the Ten Directions [who appears as] Great Compassionate Saviors from Suffering (Shifang jiuku wushang daci tianzun 十方救苦無上大慈天尊), serves as a purger of sins. His assistance is guaranteed to those who worship him, confess their faults, and perform acts of contrition.

18. One has to deal with his decamorphic manifestation while in other cases, it is the intervention of Jiuku tianzun's homologue, the Perfected Savior from Distress (Qiku zhenren 濟苦真人), who works miracles (Dz 336. 6/8b–9a).

appears also, in my view, to be a Taoist adaptation of the *Pumen pin*. Other Tao-ist classics—such as the prominent fifth-century *Most Excellent and Marvelous Lingbao Scripture of Limitless Salvation* (*Lingbao wuliang duren shangpin miaojing* 靈寶 無量度人上品妙經, Dz 1), or *Scripture of Salvation*—have similarly borrowed el-ements from the *Lotus Sūtra*,[19] but in the case of the *Scripture of the Savior from Suffering,* this influence goes beyond conceptual and terminological admix-tures. Overall, the text can be seen as a Taoist transposition of the *Lotus Sūtra*'s *Pumen pin,* created to promote Jiuku tianzun to the level of Guanyin.

The *Scripture of the Savior from Suffering:*
A Taoist Adaptation of the "Universal Gateway"

The *Scripture of the Savior from Suffering* (*Taiyi jiuku hushen miaojing*), edited in the Taoist Canon (Dz 351), bears no indication of date or authorship, but, as will be seen, iconographic details suggest that its composition cannot precede the Tang period. In spite of its first-rate value for any assessment of Jiuku tianzun's wor-ship in medieval Taoist history, it has received no attention from specialists in Chinese religions to date.[20]

Contrary to other Taoist writings dealing with Jiuku tianzun, the *Scripture of the Savior from Suffering* does not emphasize its central actor in his well-known role as protector of the dead but reveals a hitherto hidden aspect of his personal-ity: Jiuku tianzun as the savior from peril, a vocation directly derived from Guanyin. Though prefigured, as already noted, in the *Lingbao Scripture of Karmic Retribution,* this specific role becomes here the main point of focus. In a manner notably resembling the *Pumen pin*'s promotion of Guanyin, the Taoist scripture introduces the Heavenly Venerable Savior from Suffering to the world, pro-claims his thaumaturgical endowments, displays his phenomenal propensity for mutation, and urges devotees to practice the invocation of his name as an im-mediate, individual means of deliverance from various perils. Before we exam-ine these points in detail, let us consider a paraphrase of the scripture:

> In the Hall of Nine-Colored Jade (Jiuse yutang 九色玉堂) of the [Palace of] Myste-rious Light (Xuanjing 玄景), in the Heaven of Pure Subtlety (Taiwei tian 太微天), the Heavenly Venerable of Primordial Commencement (Yuanshi tianzun 元始天 尊), sitting on his throne of seven jewels, reveals this scripture and preaches the

---

19. Dz 1 (beginning of the fifth century). On the *Lotus Sutra*'s influence on the *nidāna* in-troduction of the text, see E. Y. Wang (2005): 153–154. For a translation, see Bokenkamp (1997): 405–438.

20. Yusa (1989) does not mention it. Verellen (1992) makes an allusion to it in a footnote: 241n116.

Marvelous Law (*miaofa* 妙法) to a divine audience composed of the Venerables of the Ten Directions (Shifang tianzun 十方天尊), the Lord of the Dao (Daojun 道君), Lord Lao (Laojun 老君), the lord-emperors (*dijun* 帝君), the Lords of the Origin (*yuanjun* 元君), together with thousands of saints and immortals, as well as the Brahma-king (*fanwang* 梵王) named Shandishi 善帝釋. The Heavenly Venerable deplores the calamitous state of the universe and its ocean of suffering, but announces that in the east, in the World of Great Happiness (*dongfang zhangle shijie* 東方長樂世界), lives the Great Benevolent (*da ciren zhe* 大慈仁者) Heavenly Venerable of the Great Unity, Savior from Suffering (Taiyi jiuku tianzun 太一救苦天尊). He is capable of "transforming his body in as many ways as there are sands [of the Ganges], in accord with the calls [of those who suffer]" (化身如恆[河]沙數物隨聲應), whether he dwells in his palace, descends to earth, or visits the infernal prisons. He can be an immortal lad or a jade maiden, a lord-emperor or a sage, a Heavenly Venerable or a Perfected One (*zhenren* 真人), a *vajra* king (*jingang shenwang* 金剛神王), a demon king, a Heavenly Master (Tianshi 天師), or a Taoist Master (*daoshi* 道士), a sovereign or Lord Lao, a celestial physician or divine official (*gongzao* 功曹), a boy or a girl, a civil or military official, a great general, a religious preceptor (*jiaoshi* 教師), or a master of meditation (*chanshi* 禪師), or else the God of the Wind (Fengshi 風師) or the God of the Rain (Yushi 雨師). His supernatural powers (*shentong* 神通) are innumerable, and his bounty unlimited. He "saves from suffering according to the calls and responds to events according to vicissitude" (尋聲救苦應物隨機). His metamorphoses are countless.

Jiuku tianzun now appears on the front stage, facing the divine audience. He is a boy (*tongzi* 童子) walking on lotus flowers. His mercy is manifest: presenting himself before the Heavenly Venerable of Primordial Commencement, he sobs until his costume is wet with tears. The Yuanshi tianzun affirms to the youth that, thanks to his exceptional faculty of transformation, he will be able to save human beings.

The divine assembly then sees the young man changing successively into four figures who, one after the other, rise into the sky. Each of them is haloed with a bright light, their feet resting on lotus flowers, and each is accompanied by a pair of nine-headed lions. The first of these apparitions is a Heavenly Venerable who holds a willow branch and a pure water bottle. The second one is a lord-emperor (*dijun*) with a scepter (*ruyi* 如意) who, after ascending into the heavens, makes way for a third figure, a Perfected One carrying a divine light (*shenguang* 神光) capable of penetrating the nine levels of the sky and the nine layers of the earth (*xiatong jiudi shangtong jiutian* 下通九地上通九天). Finally, Jiuku tianzun changes himself into a barefoot woman with loose hair who wears a fire-colored brocade costume and holds a gold sword. The pair of nine-headed lions that escort her are spitting flames.

Jiuku tianzun is a saint (*sheng* 聖). He intervenes in the different spheres of the universe, in each of which he bears an appropriate appellation. In heaven, he is the

Deity of the Happiness of Great Unity (Taiyi fushen 太一福神). On earth, he is the Great Benevolent. In hell (diyu), he is the Lord-Emperor of Solar Brightness (Rizhao dijun 日耀帝君). When he chases away the evil of heretic ways, he is the Rāja-lion (Shizi mingwang 獅子明王). In the infernal Office of Water (shuifu 水府), he is the Lord-Emperor of the Abyss (Dongyuan dijun 洞淵帝君). In his original form, he is the essence of the Nine Yang (jiuyang zhi jing 九陽之精). He is the most holy, the most venerable, the most precious, the most efficient.

After reciting an incantation, the Heavenly Venerable of Primordial Commencement explains how one can assuredly avoid the Eight Hardships (baku 八苦) and get through difficulty or peril by concentrating and invoking the saint's name (cunsi song shenghao 存思誦聖號). When the circumstances permit it, one should also recite this scripture, but, however urgent the danger may be, in order to be rescued from it, one must in all cases invoke Jiuku tianzun's name. Thirteen critical or perilous situations from which any individual can be saved by requesting Jiuku tianzun's intervention are then enumerated.

Those suffering from disease or misfortune will be cured. (In case of illness it is additionally recommended that one burn incense and recite this scripture.)

Officials whose careers have been compromised due to treachery, flattery, or lies will be promoted and obtain high salaries.

Travelers on rivers or at sea, who fear swells or aquatic animals, will safely reach the shore.

Those who are terrorized by thunder, wind, or rain will regain their composure. Their celestial and terrestrial souls (hun and po) will be stabilized.

Those in conflict with their parents, masters, relatives, or brothers will find harmony, paternal benevolence, and filial piety. The respect of brothers, friends, and disciples will be spontaneously restored.

Sovereigns or governors whose dignitaries and ministers are conspirators or rebels, initiating conflagrations and bloodshed that bring about meteorological disturbances and torment the public, should observe a retreat (zhai 齋). Thereby they will fend off inclement weather, unmask and subjugate insubordinate ministers, and cause peace and prosperity to return to the land.

Victims of perverse emanations and brigand-demons (guizei 鬼賊) will be able to eliminate curses instantaneously and get rid of malevolent demons.

Those who, having ventured into the mountains and forests, become prey to parasites, snakes, and wild beasts will chase them away.

Women who endure a difficult delivery will receive help and give birth without pain or injury. The child will be either a boy who has wisdom or a devoted girl. The baby's "six roots" (liugen 六根, the six senses) will be complete; and mother and child will live in perfect harmony.

Men and women, whether lay or religious, who aspire to the Way, seek immortality, and practice methods to nourish life will obtain merits and will rise to heaven in full daylight (i.e., they will become immortal).

Prisoners who suffer unspeakably, who are pilloried or shackled, will be freed.

Those whose ancestors down to the seventh or ninth generation, whose disciples or condisciples, whose husband or wife, are condemned to the cold hells (*hanting* 寒庭) without any hope for rebirth will instantly reach heaven.

Those who are in bondage to an enemy family will be liberated from their servitude.

Each third and ninth day of the month, Jiuku tianzun comes down to the human world. At such times, one must worship him in the household's pure chamber by burning incense, performing prostrations, and presenting offerings, including a willow branch and pure water, as well as flowers, medicinal plants, and fresh sprouts of grain. The longevity of the worshippers will be thereby increased, and they will definitively escape the Eight Difficult Conditions (*banan* 八難).

With this, the Heavenly Venerable of Primordial Commencement ends his sermon. All the members of the audience rejoice. Miracles occur in which even animals speak and become human.

THERE IS, UNFORTUNATELY, no external or internal evidence that would enable us to trace precisely the origin of this *Scripture of the Savior from Suffering*. What is sure is that the text was already known in the Song dynasty. During that time, the popularity of Jiuku tianzun's cult was revived, and the rituals of redemption that were placed under the deity's sponsorship acquired a dominant place in Taoist mortuary liturgy, notably the ceremonies for the "universal salvation" of the souls of the dead, the *pudu* 普度.[21] As part of this *pudu* liturgy, specific services known as rituals of the "lake of blood" (*xuehu* 血湖) were performed for the posthumous redemption of women who, having committed sins of female blood pollution, were believed to have fallen into a fearful lake of blood, one of the several dreadful prisons located in the infernal Mount Fengdu 酆都.[22] The *Scripture of the Savior from Suffering* itself does not make any allusion to the "lake of blood" ceremony or, for that matter, to any other *pudu* liturgy, but signifi-

---

21. Yusa (1989): 36–38.

22. One central text for the "bloody pond" ritual is the *Precious Ritual of Contrition for Deliverance from the Bloody Pond, Revealed by the Heavenly Venerable Savior from Suffering* (*Taiyi jiuku tianzun shuo badu xuehu baochan* 太一救苦天尊說拔度血湖寶懺, Dz 538), which dates from the end of the Song or the beginning of the Yuan dynasty.

cantly, one of its passages has been integrated into a major Song-dynasty scripture dealing with the *xuehu* rituals, the *True Scripture of the Heavenly Venerable of Primordial Commencement for Salvation from the Lake of Blood* (*Yuanshi tianzun jidu xuehu zhenjing* 元始天尊濟度血湖真經). The passage in question, which corresponds to the episode introducing the deity's charismatic functions, is employed here in a particular liturgical context removed from its original purpose.[23]

The terminus post quem for the composition of the *Scripture of the Savior from Suffering* may be inferred, thanks to iconographic details furnished by the text. Like Guanyin, Jiuku tianzun is said to hold a willow branch and a water bottle. Although these objects were already mentioned during the Six Dynasties period among required offerings made to Guanyin when invoking his assistance, they seem to have become well-known attributes of the bodhisattva only after Tantric Buddhism rose in influence during the Tang dynasty.[24] The earliest images of Guanyin standing in a relaxed pose and holding an ambrosia bottle and a willow twig most probably date from the second half of the eighth century.[25] Henceforth, underscoring the bodhisattva's healing mission, these attributes would often supplant the lotus flower traditionally held by Avalokiteśvara.[26] The adoption of the willow branch and the flask by Jiuku tianzun, consequently, cannot have preceded the mid-Tang dynasty. The birth of our scripture should therefore be roughly situated during that period.

Whereas the exact origins of the *Scripture of the Savior from Suffering* remain difficult to determine, our reading of it leaves no doubt that the *Lotus Sūtra's Pumen pin* was its source of inspiration. Stylistic elements common to the two texts immediately attract one's attention. Apart from Jiuku tianzun's epithets and titles, which, as we will see later, were borrowed from Guanyin's, one notices typical Buddhist locutions originally found in the *Pumen pin*. Jiuku tianzun's epiphanies, for example, are described there as being "as numerous as the sands of the Ganges River" (*ru heng[he] sha shu* 如恆[河]沙數),[27] a conventional hyperbole in the Mahāyāna scriptures that is used similarly in the *Pumen pin* to describe Guanyin's transformations.[28] Besides such stylistic ornaments, how-

---

23. Dz 72. 2/1b–3a, which corresponds to Dz 351. 1b–2a and 3b. Mentioned in Verellen (1992): 241n116.

24. See the *Dhāraṇī Sūtra Invoking Avalokiteśvara Bodhisattva to Dissipate Poison and Harm* (*Guangshiyin pusa xiaofu duhai tuoluoni zhou jing* 請觀世音菩薩消伏毒害陀羅尼咒經, T. 1043, vol. 20: 36). This sūtra was translated between 317 and 420. Refer to Yü (2001): 49, 78.

25. The oldest extant Dunhuang painting of Guanyin holding a willow spray dates to 757, and the niche 87 cliff sculpture of the "Savior from Peril" Guanyin at Bazhong (Sichuan) was achieved two years later. See Howard (1990): 49.

26. Yü (2001): 78.

27. Dz 351. 2a.

28. Dz 351. 1b–2a. 如恆沙數. In spite of the omission of the character *he* 河 for Henghe

ever, it is the overall content of the Taoist scripture that brings it closest to the Guanyin chapter of the *Lotus Sūtra,* in terms of both hagiographical conventions and ritual procedure. The *Pumen pin* is composed in the form of a dialogue between the Buddha Śākyamuni and the bodhisattva Inexhaustible Intent (Wujin yi 無盡意, Skt. Akṣayamati). Śākyamuni explains the meaning of Guanshiyin's name, the readiness of the compassionate bodhisattva to help those in pain, and how, in response to their calling upon his name, he straightaway assumes the appropriate divine or human incarnation in order to deliver them from the perils that they confront. Although more succinct than the *Pumen pin,* the *Scripture of the Savior from Suffering* shares these features with it. Its aim is to reveal Jiuku tianzun's bodhisattva-like qualities to all the inhabitants of the universe, from the realm of the glorified divinities of the Taoist pantheon to the mundane world of sentient beings who may find here a saintly and reliable protector, offering deliverance from all their troubles and afflictions. Just as the Buddha introduces Avalokiteśvara in the *Pumen pin,* the Heavenly Venerable Savior from Suffering is elevated in this case by his superior, the Heavenly Venerable of Primordial Commencement, the highest figure of the divine hierarchy. Jiuku tianzun's mission is, exactly like Guanyin's, to save all who are in danger or in dire predicaments. The simple recitation of his name induces his appearance in a suitable guise and his instantaneous rescue of the victim.

A Taoist Bodhisattva

Though adorning Jiuku tianzun with Guanyin's major characteristics, the *Scripture of the Savior from Suffering* nevertheless seeks to distance itself from Buddhism by insisting upon the essentially Taoist identity of its protagonist. Jiuku tianzun is affirmed to be a genuine hypostasis of the supreme principle, the Dao, and acts as a cosmic divinity in the ten regions of the universe. In his original form, he bears the specifically male characteristics of a youth (*tongzi* 童子) who concentrates in himself all the Yang forces. He dwells in the east, in the World of Great Happiness, his number is nine (a Yang number), and he is explicitly called to be "the essence of the Nine Yang" (*jiuyang zhi jing* 九陽之精).[29] Escorted by a pair of nine-headed lions and surrounded by a halo of nine colors,[30] he descends to earth on the third and ninth days of each month.[31] All these elements establish

---

恆河 (the Ganges River), one can recognize the expression *"Henghe sha"* 恆河沙 (sands of the Ganges River), as can be found in the *Pumen pin* (T. 262, 57). The same expression is found in Dz 72. 2/2a without this omission.

29. Dz 351. 2a–3b.
30. Dz 351. 3a.
31. Dz 351. 5b.

his nature as an exalted Taoist figure of heavenly origin and masculine gender, a position that will be maintained in later literature, where Jiuku tianzun is often said to be the "compassionate father" (*cifu* 慈父) or the "great compassionate and merciful father" (*daci dabei fu* 大慈大悲父), possibly to contrast him with the increasingly maternal, feminized Guanyin.[32]

As the *Pumen pin* does for Avalokiteśvara, so our Taoist sūtra announces Jiuku tianzun's conspicuous moral and spiritual achievements. The superlative epithets attributed to him emphasize his exceptional charisma: he is the most "saintly" (*sheng*), the most "venerable" (*zun* 尊), the "noblest" (*gui* 貴), the most "efficacious" (*ling* 靈), and, above all, his reputation is one of bountiful altruism. The text narrates Jiuku tianzun's response to the Heavenly Venerable of Primordial Commencement's request, his engagement to act as a universal savior. His infinite compassion is underscored in the evocation of the outpouring of emotion that overwhelms the divine lad when, hearing his superior lamenting the distress of humanity drowning in an "ocean of suffering," he bursts into a flood of tears and sobs.[33] The Taoist deity's mercy is thus quite on a par with that of his double, Avalokiteśvara.

The motif of Guanyin as the Savior from Peril (fig. 5.2), which is widely represented in Dunhuang from the early seventh century on, continued to be favored during the Five Dynasties and the Northern Song, both in murals and in mobile votive paintings, as well as in the illustrated booklets of the "portable" *Guanyin jing,* mentioned above (see chapter 2). Usually depicted, with some variations, in these works are the eight kinds of danger from which the sūtra promises deliverance: fire, weapons, witchcraft, poison, demons, ferocious animals, venomous insects and snakes, and thunder (fig. 5.3).

During the same period, the Taoists similarly elaborated the Heavenly Venerable's response to human fears and produced stereotyped lists of perils, directly patterned on the *Pumen pin.* The crises from which the Taoist deity is supposed to offer rescue, as detailed in the Song-dynasty *Lingbao Scripture for Overcoming Sufferings Revealed by the Heavenly Venerable* (*Taishang dongxuan lingbao tianzun shuo jiku jing* 太上洞玄靈寶天尊說濟苦經), for instance, are disease, affliction, disruption of the soul, imprisonment and torture, difficult childbirth, demonic emanations, and witchcraft.[34] The list of torments given by the *Scripture of the Savior from Suffering* is somewhat longer—disease, calamity, slavery, shipwreck, thunder, familial conflict, political problems, bandits, wild beasts,

---

32. Dz 72. 2/4a; *Qingxuan jiuku baochan* 青玄救苦寶懺. Dz 539. 1b.

33. Dz 351. 2b.

34. Dz 375. 1a–1b. The text advocates a Method of the Seven Ways (*Qidao zhi fa* 七道之法), mainly consisting of a *zhai* with rites of repentance, which permits one to obtain the assistance of the Xunsheng 尋聲.

FIG. 5.2. Guanyin, Savior from Peril, a tenth-century painting from Dunhuang (MG 17665). Courtesy of the Musée Guimet.

FIG. 5.3. Details of salvation from the perils by Guanyin (MG 17665). Courtesy of the Musée Guimet.

risky childbirth, obstacles to religious practice, imprisonment, condemnation to hell, and corvée labor—and like the *Pumen pin,* it promises fulfillment of the wish to have a male or a female child. Interestingly, however, the *Scripture of the Savior from Suffering* moves to accommodate the social background of those to whom it is addressed, including, in its list of perils, hindrance to the promotion of officials, actions against the political and social order, household disharmony, and salvation of ancestors, none of which, among the main preoccupations of traditional Chinese society, could be reasonably neglected.

As is clearly indicated in the *Lingbao Scripture of Karmic Retribution,* when his cult began, Jiuku tianzun had already been assigned the role of a bodhisattva-savior, removing hardships and bestowing happiness, although his aid was impelled exclusively by rituals of contrition and supervised by a higher authority.[35] With the *Scripture of the Savior from Suffering,* the faithful and their families who worship the deity on a regular basis are blessed with merits, longevity, and protection from the Eight Difficult Conditions and the Eight Hardships, that is to say, the problems, dangers, and pains that all human beings encounter during their existence.[36] However, our Taoist bodhisattva's immense mercy is not confined to his intimate, devoted adepts. Following Guanyin's example, Jiuku tianzun answers instantaneously and directly the solicitations of anyone facing distress or danger, or otherwise in critical circumstances. This characteristic earned him the titles "Heavenly Venerable who responds to the calls [of the world]" (*xunsheng jiuku tianzun* 尋聲救苦天尊 and "Savior from Suffering according to calls, responding to events according to vicissitudes" (*xunsheng jiuku yingwu suiji* 尋聲救苦應物隨機).[37] Likely derived from the very name "Guan(shi)yin," which literally means "Perceiver of the (World's) Sounds" and whose origin and explanation as known in China can be also traced to the *Lotus Sūtra's Pumen pin,* these appellations, no less than "Savior from Suffering" as used also to designate Guanyin, no doubt had deep resonances for the Chinese faithful.[38]

---

35. Dz 336. 6/5b. Likewise, the Perfected Savior from Distress manifests himself only after he has received an injunction from his superior, the Lord of the Dao, who has himself been notified by the ritual recitation of the sacred scripture (Dz 336. 6/8b–9a).

36. Dz 351. 5b and 4a. The Eight Hardships, or Eight Distresses, are considered to be birth, age, sickness, death, parting with what we love, meeting with what we hate, unattained aims, and all the ills inherent to human nature. The Eight Difficult Conditions (Skt. *aṣṭāv akṣaṇāḥ*) are the eight conditions of rebirth, which are obstacles to enlightenment: rebirth as a demon in hell, as an animal, in the heavens of long life, in barbarian countries, as one who is blind, as one who is deaf, or as an adept of heretical religions, or living during an intermediate, Buddha-less aeon. These terms were borrowed from Buddhism but were used in a generic sense in this Taoist context.

37. Dz 351. 2a.

38. See chapter 7 of the *Scripture of Good and Bad Karmic Retribution, Revealed by Laozi*

Jiuku tianzun's help can be brought forth by means of an elementary rite of invocation consisting of a prayer for his immediate aid, accompanied by the repetition, as many times as possible, of his name. Nothing more than this is required by the individual who is threatened. Hence, no special implement or preparation is necessary; the invocation can be pronounced anywhere and at any moment, as dictated only by the devotee's need and will, a practice that was inspired by Buddhism. During the Six Dynasties period, the recitation of the names of buddhas and bodhisattvas, such as Amitābha, Maitreya, Kṣitigarbha, and Avalokiteśvara, became common practice among the Buddhist faithful, especially for the adherents of the Pure Land currents. Like the recitation of sūtras, it permitted them to gain spiritual merits and to progress toward *nirvāṇa*.[39] The invocation of Jiuku tianzun's name was therefore not in this sense unusual, although its performance had a more pragmatic and pressing goal than the acquisition of merit. This unrestricted method, advocated time and again by the Taoist scripture, also finds its impulsion in the *Lotus Sūtra*'s *Pumen pin,* which recommends that those in danger call upon Guanyin's assistance by "reciting his name in a state of mental concentration" (*cunsi niansong shenghao* 存思念誦號). In the same way, Jiuku tianzun's believers are promised the deity's personal and spontaneous assistance by "concentrating and invoking the saint's name."[40] Like the bodhisattva, the Taoist savior from peril is expected to appear at the victim's side to offer help.

Yü Chün-fang has judiciously spoken of the recitation of Guanyin's name as a "democratic way of salvation," providing to all who are faithful—without distinction of gender, status, or social class—the possibility of easily entering into intimate contact with the bodhisattva.[41] Jiuku tianzun's invocation corresponds to the same desire for proximity, accessibility, and facility. As in the case of Guanyin, it offers all who suffer and are distressed the hope of obtaining instant relief, whether or not they have been generally pious practitioners. The plain call to the divinity for aid appears as a readily affordable alternative to

---

(*Laozi shuo zuifu baoying jing* 老子說罪福報應經, P. 2818), dating to the beginning of the Tang dynasty (Ōfuchi [1978]: 194–195 and [1979]: 691–693). The "Bodhisattva Guanshiyin Great Compassionate Savior from Suffering" (Dabei jiuku Guanshiyin pusa 大悲救苦觀世音菩薩), as one of Avalokiteśvara's appellations, is already found in the *Lotus Sūtra;* see Hurvitz (1976): 311.

39. See Kuo (1994a): 144–145.

40. Yü (2001): 164, gives the character *nian* 念 the meaning of "vocal invocation and mental meditation at the same time." A sentence found in the *Pumen pin*—"*nianpei Guanyin li* 念彼觀音力"—has been translated in several different ways. Leon Hurvitz (1976): 316, renders it as "By virtue of constant mindfulness of Sound-Observer," while Burton Watson (1993): 303, proposes, "Think on the power of Guanyin."

41. Yü (2001): 91, 489.

chanting sacred books, specially for those who, for cultural or material reasons, could not have availed themselves of them.[42]

Nonetheless, despite its encomium of the power of the name, the *Scripture of the Savior from Suffering* never denies the efficacy of its own repetition. Reciting it is highly recommended when circumstances permit, that is, whenever time is available and the place favorable. Still, the intonation of the scripture must always be accompanied by "invoking the saint's name," which remains the guarantee of Jiuku tianzun's infallible assistance. In urgent cases—dangerous voyages, storms, attack by demons, bandits or wild beasts, torture, or painful child delivery—there is of course no question of chanting the whole book; the invocation alone, on these occasions, will do.

Jiuku tianzun is further characterized by his extraordinary potential for transformation. This capacity relates first and foremost to his interventions in the various realms of the universe and is emphasized by the *Scripture of the Savior from Suffering*. In each part of the world, the deity is endowed with a different personality and bears a particular name. In heaven, he is the Deity of the Happiness of Great Unity, whereas on earth, he is called the Great Benevolent. In the infernal abode, he is either the Lord-Emperor Solar Brightness, who acts in the infernal prisons; Rāja-lion, who battles heresies; or else the Lord-Emperor of the Abyss, whose sphere is the Office of Water.[43]

What the *Scripture of the Savior from Suffering* underscores, however, is the deity's faculty of "mundane" ubiquity, as well as his ability to arrive spontaneously on the spot to which he has been called. His "bodies of transformation" (*huashen*) demonstrate that he is an omnipotent saint whose epiphanies conform to any exigency.[44] Of course, in the context of Taoism, this polymorphism is not an exclusive prerogative of Jiuku tianzun. Already during the Han dynasty, the god Laozi had been accorded the same attribute. One of his most polished hagiographies, the fifth-century *Scripture of the Esoteric Explanations of the Three Heavens* (*Santian neijie jing* 三天內解經), upheld the belief that the supreme deity undergoes numberless transmutations, perpetually changing his appearance as well as his name:

> Sometimes he transforms himself nine times in a single day; sometimes twenty-four times. Through a thousand changes and ten thousand transformations (*hua* 化), he

---

42. See the *Lingbao Marvelous Scripture for Salvation from Suffering* (*Taishang dongxuan lingbao jiuku miaojing* 太上洞玄靈寶救苦妙經, Dz 374. 3b), dating to the Song dynasty, which advocates the recitation of the Taiyi jiuku tianzun's name as an alternative to the recitation of the scripture.

43. Dz 351. 3b.

44. Dz 351. 2a–2b and 3a.

rises up and sinks out of sight through generations—so many times that they cannot all be recorded.[45]

If the Buddhist influence on the Laozi legend is questionable,[46] still there can be no doubt that Jiuku tianzun's transformations were directly modeled on Guanyin's mythology. The bodhisattva's thirty-three forms (or thirty-two, depending on the version) as enumerated in the *Lotus Sūtra* show that Avalokiteśvara can transgress all distinctions of gender, age, and social or spiritual status in order to incarnate himself according to the needs of the individuals he rescues. He can be the Buddha or Brahma, a Brahman, an elder, a rich man's wife, a sovereign or a simple official, a minister or a monk, a boy or a girl, a divinity, a *yakṣa* or a *nāga,* and so on. In its long and famous litany, the *Lotus Sūtra*'s *Pumen pin* systematically rehearses these alternatives, beginning with the most prestigious:

> Good man, if there are living beings in the land who need someone in the body of a buddha in order to be saved, Bodhisattva Perceiver of the World's Sounds (Guanshiyin) immediately manifests himself in a buddha body and preaches the law to them.[47]

Thus, Guanyin metamorphoses in response to the calls of those who suffer, and his talent in this respect is without peer. As has been underscored, he can even take on the aspect of the most important divinities of the non-Buddhist (Hindu or Vedic) pantheon.[48] In China, the theme of Avalokiteśvara's transformations was abundantly depicted, notably at Dunhuang and in the rock carvings of Sichuan—for instance, at Dazu 大足.

Jiuku tianzun's changeability rivals Guanyin's. Like the latter, Jiuku tianzun can appear under the guise that corresponds best to the exigencies of his mission of rescue, assuming contrasting forms in order to accomplish miracles. The *Scripture of the Savior from Suffering* narrates, for example, how Jiuku tianzun performs an amazing show to demonstrate his chameleon-like faculty to his divine spectators. He first manifests as a young man and then successively assumes the shapes of four different figures: a Heavenly Venerable, a Lord-Emperor carrying a scepter, a Perfected Sage holding a light beam, and finally a shamanlike woman, barefoot, with loose hair, and armed with a golden sword. Moreover,

---

45. Dz 1205. 1/3b. I follow here Bokenkamp's translation (1997): 210. See also Anna Seidel's French translation (1969): 98.
46. See Seidel (1969): 105–110.
47. Watson (1993): 301.
48. Yü (2001): 45, 72–75. On the influence of the Hindu pantheon on Avalokiteśvara's mythology, see Regamey (1971): 417–432.

the text makes it quite clear that Jiuku tianzun's metamorphoses are by no means limited to this quartet. As with Guanyin, his exceptional "supernatural powers" (*shentong* 神通) allow him "to divide his body" (*fenshen* 分身) according to his will and thereby to undergo "infinite transformations" (*wuliang bianhua* 無量變化), altering himself "in as many ways as there are sands of the Ganges."

Imitating the *Pumen pin,* the *Scripture of the Savior from Suffering* provides an inventory of the various morphologies that the Taoist deity can adopt, whether as glorified deity or as ordinary human being. Like Guanyin's, Jiuku tianzun's guises are as eclectic as they are typologically democratic: young or old, man or woman, noble or humble—all aspects are possible. Nevertheless, the deity's religious affiliation is never forgotten. Apart from one or two instances in which he assumes the roles of minor Buddhist divinities, Jiuku tianzun evidently prefers to maintain his Taoist identity. He shows up as Laojun, as an immortal or a jade maiden, as a *zhenren* or a Lord-Emperor, as a Heavenly Master or a *daoshi*. If, in any case, he happens to neglect this principle, at least he remains distinctively Chinese, whether by taking the form of a divinity of the traditional pantheon (for instance, the God of the Wind or the God of the Rain) or by becoming a civil or military official.[49]

Images and Ex-Votos

It seems certain that, by the Sui period, an iconography of the Heavenly Venerable Savior from Suffering already existed. His images were not intended for display but had an exclusively ritual usage: they were manufactured for mortuary ceremonies. The *Lingbao Scripture of Karmic Retribution* explains how, just like copies of the scriptures or donations of lamps and banners, Jiuku tianzun's images were offered by the family of the deceased in order to obtain merits and to purge the damned of their faults so that they might escape from the infernal regions and reach paradise. The production of these funerary icons was not left to the donors' discretion but was subject to precise rules. Their numbers, in particular, had to be strictly proportional to the sequence of the mortuary services, which had to be performed according to the usual Buddhist schedule of the "seven sevens," corresponding to the forty-nine days of the intermediate exis-

---

49. Dz 351. 2a. Twenty-two different manifestations of Jiuku tianzun are listed. It is notable that this number differs from the *Pumen pin* which mentions thirty-three (or thirty-two) forms of Guanyin, but is similar to the number of Avalokiteśvara's forms mentioned in the *Karaṇḍavyūha Sūtra.* The influence of this sūtra on our Taoist scripture is however very unlikely since it was first translated into Chinese under the title *Sūtra of the Mahāyāna, the Precious King of Adornment* (*Dacheng zhuangyan baowang jing* 大乘莊嚴寶王經, T. 1050) from a Tibetan version in the year 1000 C.E.

tence before the deceased is reborn. To ensure his salvation in the world beyond, seven consecutive ceremonies would take place during the seven weeks
following his death. Masses were to be subsequently celebrated on the hundredth day and on each anniversary thereafter. The *Lingbao Scripture of Karmic
Retribution* specifies the requirements: one single image of Jiuku tianzun was to
be offered for the ceremony of the first seven, two for the second, and so on up
to seven for the seventh seven. However, on the occasion of the hundredth-day
service, one hundred images were demanded, and many hundreds for the following anniversaries.[50] The replication of so many icons was undoubtedly
achieved not by the skilled and meticulous brushwork of artists but by means of
more expedient and rudimentary processes such as the use of wooden or clay
seals, which predated the block-printing method in medieval China and were
invented for "impressing buddhas" (*yinfo* 印佛) in different media such as paper,
sand, or clay.[51] The character "body" (*qu* 軀) used by the *Lingbao Scripture of Karmic Retribution* to refer to these mass-produced portraits of the Jiuku tianzun
suggests that the deity was represented full-scale. Though nothing, unfortunately, was recorded during this early period about the way in which he was to
be figured, the possibility that his features were modelled on one or another of
the then current Guanyin representations cannot be excluded.

For the first textual records of Jiuku tianzun's iconography, one has to rely
again on the court Taoist Du Guangting. Thanks to three tales narrated in his
tenth-century *Record of Miracles in Support to Taoism* (*Daojiao lingyan ji*), the deity's aspect is finally unveiled.[52] Each of these stories relates how the compassionate Jiuku tianzun accomplishes wonders through his icons. The most thorough
account is given in the "Miracle of Zhang Renbiao by the Heavenly Venerable
of Great Unity" (Zhang Renbiao Taiyi tianzun yan 張仁表太一天尊驗), where
Zhang, a deceitful Taoist cleric who has died of sickness and been condemned
to hell, implores Jiuku tianzun so pathetically that he succeeds in making the
deity appear to him in full majesty:

> Jiuku tianzun sits on a five-colored lotus throne. His feet are posed on two small five-
> colored lotuses. Below, there is a lion of five colors whose nine heads, respectfully
> turned toward the throne, spit flames forming a mandorla of nine colors all around
> him and up to the crown of his head. From this light, myriad rays are projected in the
> shape of spears and swords, which invert to create a canopy of seven jewels.[53]

50. Dz 336. 8/6b–7a.
51. See Tsien and Qian, *Paper and Printing,* in Needham (1985), vol. 5, part 1: 136–148.
On the *yinfo* practice, see Kuo (1994a): 158–159; and Strickmann (2002): 123–125.
52. These four stories have been examined by Yusa (1989).
53. Dz 590. 5/2a–b, "Zhang Renbiao's Miracle by the Heavenly Venerable of the Great

Further information on the deity's portrait is found in a second supernatural story narrated by Du Guangting, entitled the "Miracle of Yuan Feng 袁逢." It concerns a shipwreck (one of the basic perils associated with Guanyin's saving powers) that ends happily, when the efficacy of calling on Jiuku tianzun's name is beautifully exemplified. This, in brief, is the account:

> Yuan Feng faithfully worshipped Jiuku tianzun in a Taoist monastery. One day, while crossing the Yangzi's gorges on a boat trip up to the Shu country (Sichuan),[54] he was caught in an appalling storm. More than a hundred times Yuan Feng invoked Jiuku tianzun's name, and this had finally the effect of calming the waters. All the passengers could see the formation of an enormous red light above the boat, but only Yuan Feng saw Jiuku tianzun, entirely dressed in blue-green, manifesting himself inside an extraordinary halo.[55]

In a third tale, entitled the "Miracle of Sun Jingzhen 孫靜真," Du Guangting also presents the Taoist deity with attributes resembling those of Guanyin. As will be seen below, in this account Jiuku tianzun carries a willow spray and a vase of consecrated water, two major ritual implements.[56]

These stories confirm that, by Du Guangting's time or perhaps somewhat earlier, during the middle Tang period, the Taoist deity had already acquired all the iconographic characteristics that he retains down to the present day. Unlike Guanyin, who has come to be portrayed in numerous forms,[57] and in spite of his reputation for mimesis, Jiuku tianzun's anthropomorphic aspect is confined to a unique set of stereotypes. He is dressed in blue-green, his head adorned with a crown. Accompanied by a nine-headed lion spitting flames that form a mandorla around the deity's body, he sits on a five-colored lotus throne, his feet resting on small lotus flowers, with a canopy hanging above the throne. Finally, he holds a willow branch and a flask of holy water. These two implements are the most distinctive characteristics of Jiuku tianzun and reveal a close affinity with a popular form of Avalokiteśvara.

In its Buddhist contexts, the "precious flask" or "waterpot" (*kuṇḍaka*) has

---

One" (Zhang Renbiao Taiyi tianzun yan 張仁表太一天尊驗). Also edited in *Yunji qiqian* (Dz 1032. 118/6b), "Zhang Renbiao's Miracle of the Heavenly Venerable of the Great One Savior from Suffering" (Zhang renbiao Taiyi jiuku tianzun yan 長仁表太一救苦天尊驗); Yusa (1989): 19–23; and Verellen (1992): 240–243.

54. Du Guangting's miracle tales about Jiuku tianzun take place in Sichuan and the Jiangnan region.

55. Dz 590. 5/3a–b: "Yuan Feng's Miracle of the Heavenly Venerable of the Great One" (Yuan Feng Taiyi tianzun yan 袁逢太一天尊驗); Yusa (1989): 20–21.

56. Dz 590. 5/6a.

57. See the examples in Soymié (2000): 15–25.

the function, among others, of ensuring a good rebirth for living beings.[58] As for the willow twig, though its origin is uncertain, it came to replace the Indian lotus in the popular Chinese forms of Guanyin (fig. 5.4) and was known from early times for its therapeutic and even exorcistic virtues.[59] During the third century C.E., Buddhist thaumaturgists already used it to sprinkle the sick with water in order to cure them. Later it came to be regularly employed in Tantric Buddhism for ceremonies of consecration, *homa,* and healing rites.[60]

Besides their descriptive value with reference to the iconography of the Heavenly Venerable Savior from Suffering, Du Guangting's stories also evoke the ritual functions of the deity's images. We learn that their funerary use, which was already promoted by the *Lingbao Scripture of Karmic Retribution,* was perpetuated during Du's time, but their manufacture had become more sophisticated. On the basis of Du's testimony, one can assume that in the Tang period the Taoist deity's icons were not only, or no longer, mass-produced but were also commissioned by the deceased's relatives from local painters as temple ex-votos. The "Miracle of Li Shao 李邵," also found in his *Record of Miracles,* tells of a high official in Sichuan who commissioned a votive image of Jiuku tianzun as an offering to a Taoist temple in order to save his dead wife from the infernal tortures she was otherwise condemned to suffer as expiation for her sins.[61] More extraordinarily, the story of Zhang Renbiao, mentioned above, relates that, by the intensity of his penance, the recently deceased Taoist cleric succeeded in obtaining from Jiuku tianzun a reprieve of seven years in exchange for the donation of an image and his promulgation of the deity. The Taoist indeed comes back to life, offers an icon of Jiuku tianzun to the prestigious Suming guan 肅明 觀 temple of Chang'an, and then dies seven years later.[62] The Heavenly Venerable Savior from Suffering's image had, in this case, both funerary and ex-voto functions.

Very likely, these offerings of Taoist mobile images to religious establishments were derived from Buddhist practice. Since the beginning of the Tang, the Buddhist faithful had increasingly adopted the custom of casting statuettes or purchasing sacred images—whether painted, molded, or sculpted—

---

58. Yü (2001): 78–81; Soymié (2000): 22–23.

59. The willow twig seems also to have been used in China for Avalokiteśvara's rites of contrition. See Kuo (1994a): 115.

60. Demiéville (1974a): 244, mentions therapy by the aspersion of pure water with a willow branch in the context of fifth-century Buddhism. Strickmann (1996): 151, 153, alludes to the use of the willow branch in Tantric therapeutic exorcism, where it serves for whipping the patient's face or sprinkling the patient with consecrated water. See also chapter 1.

61. Dz 590. 5/3b–5a, "Li Shao's Miracle of the Heavenly Venerable of Great Unity Savior from Suffering" (Li Shao Taiyi jiuku tianzun yan 李邵太一救苦天尊驗); Yusa (1989): 21.

62. Dz 590. 5/1a–3a; Yusa (1989): 20–21; Verellen (1992): 240–242.

FIG. 5.4. Guanyin with a willow twig and a flask, detail of a tenth-century painting from Dunhuang (EO 1142). Courtesy of the Musée Guimet.

for their personal use. Examples of such devotional icons donated for mortuary purposes have been discovered at Dunhuang, where Guanyin is very often depicted. Ordered by pious donors on behalf of their dead parents, some of these icons, dating to the ninth or tenth centuries, bear portraits of the donors as well as inscriptions with their names and the religious purpose of the donation. One can assume that images of Jiuku tianzun were similarly commissioned from local painters by families of worshippers in order to gain merits for themselves and for the souls of their dead relations.

Reading Du Guangting's stories, one may further suppose that Tang-period Taoist temples were promoting the worship of Jiuku tianzun through the production and exhibition of his images. The public veneration of the images of Taoist deities in religious settings had by that time become a widespread custom. Like Buddhist devotees, the Taoist faithful believed that the donation of an icon or other articles to a sanctuary or monastery was an act of merit by which the donor earned the remission of sins and obtained salvation for himself and his ancestors. Offered by the faithful as ex-votos following cures or other presumed miracles, portraits of Jiuku tianzun were likely displayed to visitors, who were encouraged to pay homage to them by burning incense and dedicating prayers.

Du Guangting specifies that Jiuku tianzun's icons were installed not only in temples and public sanctuaries but that private devotees also owned them and made them the centerpieces of the household's oratory, or pure chamber (*jing-tang* 靜堂), a room usually exclusively reserved for individual meditational and devotional practices. But was this piety toward the personal icon of Jiuku Tianzun current earlier? The *Lingbao Scripture of Karmic Retribution* mentions a domestic cult to the deity performed by families of believers who had received initiation in a temple or monastery, but nothing is said there regarding the presence of an image. By contrast, Du, in a tale entitled the "Miracle of Sun Jingzhen by the Heavenly Venerable Savior from Suffering" (Sun Jingzhen Jiuku tianzun yan 孫靜真救苦天尊驗), does provide information on Jiuku tianzun's familial icons and their devotional function among the Taoist faithful of southern China. In this story, the deity manifests his saving force directly through his image, a type of marvel familiar in Chinese literature, where anecdotes relating the animation of miracle-producing "living icons," whether effigies, statues, or paintings, abound. I give here a summary of the story:

> In the year 870, the severe floods that occurred in the Jiangnan region of southern China were followed by devastating epidemics. Though deaths were countless, Sun Jingzhen and about fifty members of his family—fervent devotees of Jiuku tianzun

who used to worship the deity in the household pure chamber, where his icon was hung—were all spared. Sun, moved by his neighbors' distress, offered incense and prayed to the deity to intervene in favor of all the victims. One night, in a dream, Sun saw Jiuku tianzun leaving the altar and flying away to the west. That very same night, the village chief, alarmed by a strange perfume, some light, and the sound of a bell coming from the courtyard, went out to investigate. He found the courtyard to be lit up as if with lanterns. An altar had been installed with a painting of Jiuku tianzun suspended against the wall, and an incense burner produced a bright glow. At the same time, no less than seventeen families affected by disease received, each in their own home, Jiuku tianzun's visit. Preceded by the fragrance of incense, he appeared holding a willow twig and a water cup, with which he sprinkled those who were ill. Nobody was aware that this happened, thanks to the painted scroll, which miraculously flew away from Sun Jingzhen's pure chamber.[63]

It is worth noting that one finds a close parallel to this account in a sixth-century anthology of *dhāraṇī*-sūtras, the *Dhāraṇī Miscellany* (*Tuoloni zajing* 陀羅尼雜經), which includes the earliest description of a Buddhist fire sacrifice (*homa*). Like Jiuku tianzun, Avalokiteśvara materializes in radiant light, thanks to his adepts' prayers:

Chant continuously with your mind uninterrupted in virtue. Avalokiteśvara will appear from the east, issuing a great brilliance that burns on top of the (*homa*) fire. He will appear in the midst of the flame, exactly like the painted image . . . holding a lotus flower and a waterpot. When you see the bodhisattva, do not fear, but know that you will never be born in hell, among animals or hungry ghosts. You will obtain whatever you wish.[64]

The data provided by the *Scripture of the Savior from Suffering* concerning Jiuku tianzun's domestic cult are consistent with Du Guangting's story. According to the stipulations given there, the place of worship is the household's pure chamber, where an image of the deity is hung above an altar equipped with an incense burner. The modalities of the practice seem to have undergone some reform. The cultic obligations formerly performed thrice monthly according to the *Lingbao Scripture of Karmic Retribution* were by the Tang period apparently reduced to two, and the dates changed to the third and ninth days of each month. Moreover, for the *Scripture of the Savior from Suffering*, there is no longer any question of worshipping the Jiuku tianzun of the Ten

63. Dz 590. 5/4b–6a.
64. T. 1336, vol. 21: 612. See also Yü's translation (2001): 52.

Directions, for the deity is now conceived as a unique anthropomorphic figure with established iconographic features. During his fortnightly worship,
the text prescribes that a willow branch and pure water be placed in front of
his icon with a series of other items that further demonstrate the deity's established role as a healer: flowers (current both in Buddhist and Taoist worship),
medicinal plants, and young shoots of cereals[65]—substances that were also
used in Tantric rituals, above all for the consecration of vases of pure water
for therapeutic processes.[66] Clearly then, Jiuku tianzun was not only supposed
to protect, but also to cure his worshippers, a function that was implicit in the
deity's global mission as rescuer from troubles and pains. Although the first
accounts of his cult testify that his devotees were inviting male or female
daoshi to perform penitential rituals at home in order to get rid of misfortune
and sickness,[67] it seems that it was during the Tang that Jiuku tianzun's medical charisma came to the fore. An excellent reflection of this is found in Sun
Jingzhen's miracle tale, where the Taoist deity, armed with a willow twig,
sprinkles water on villagers afflicted with a devastating epidemic.[68]

The Persistence of an Iconography

Archeological evidence of the iconography of the Heavenly Venerable Savior
from Suffering is rare. As far as I have been able to determine, only two cliff-
side sculptures of the deity have survived. One is located in Tongnan 潼南
(Chongqing shi 重慶市) and likely dates to the Southern Song (fig. 5.5). Another stone statue of Jiuku tianzun is roughly contemporaneous with the
Scripture of the Savior from Suffering. It is found at its original site, the eighth-
century Taoist temple of the Marvelous Mystery (Xuanmiao guan 玄妙觀),
located at the foot of White Goat Mountain (Baiyang shan 白羊山), about
twenty kilometers northwest of the town of Anyue in the southeast of Sichuan
Province.[69] The temple, which was built during the reign of the emperor Xuanzong (r. 712–756), has entirely disappeared, but among the surrounding rocks,
more than 1,200 sculptures of different sizes and dating from the same period
have been partially preserved despite the ravages of time and history.

---

65. Dz 351. 5b.

66. Demiéville (1974b): 267. See also Strickmann (1996): 151; and chapter 1 above, note
93.

67. Dz 336 6/5a.

68. Dz 590 5/6a. The willow branch and the water are also used nowadays in rituals for
the salvation of the deceased. See the *Taishang qingxuan Taiyi jiuku bazui fachan* 太上青玄太乙
救苦拔罪法懺 (Baiyun guan, Beijing).

69. Wang Jiayou (1987): 52–54; Yusa (1989): 25–27; Hu (1994): 9–11, 78–79; Liu Changjiu
(1997): 49–50.

FIG. 5.5. The Jiuku tianzun of Tongnan (Chongqing shi). Southern Song dynasty. Photograph courtesy of Lei Yuhua.

Fig. 5.6. The Buddha and Laojun side by side. Xuanmiao temple, Anyue (Sichuan). Eighth century. Photograph by the author, 2001.

As I found during a visit to the site in October 2001, the main carved circular cliff (with a perimeter of about fifty meters and approximately five meters in height) offers a remarkable archeological record of Tang-period Taoist and Buddho-Taoist sculpture that is characteristic of Sichuan Province. Among some seventy-nine niches,[70] which contain a few large Taoist figures as well as several small identical recesses depicting the bearded Laojun and the Buddha seated side by side (fig. 5.6), stands a sculpture of near human dimensions portraying Jiuku tianzun (fig. 5.7).[71] If it were not for a commemorative stele, which is still standing in situ, art historians would probably never have succeeded in identifying the Taoist deity. According to its title, this stele was "erected on the imperial order of the great Tang in the scenic spot of the Xuanmiao temple on Mount Jisheng" (*qi da Tang yuli shengshan Xuanmiao guan shengjing bei* 啟大唐御立集聖山玄妙觀勝境碑), and the last column of the text indicates that it dates to the seventh year of the Tianbao era (天寶七年) of the Tang, that is, 748. The

---

70. Liu Changjiu (1997): 13, mentions 79 niches with 1,293 sculpted figures. Wang Jiayou (1987): 52, mentions 76 niches with 1,250 sculpted figures.

71. Jiuku tianzun's niche is numbered 62.

FIG. 5.7. Jiuku tianzun and his two guardians. Xuanmiao temple, Anyue (Sichuan). Eighth century. Photograph by the author, 2001.

severely damaged inscription stipulates, too, that it was during the year 730 (*Kaiyuan shiba nian* 開元十八年) that a Taoist master named Li Xianze 李玄則 carved twenty divinities in the rock, among which we find "Jiuku tianzun riding nine dragons" (*Jiuku tianzun sheng jiulong* 救苦天尊乘九龍).[72]

Examining the niche containing the presumed image of Jiuku tianzun, we find an imposing 1.5-meter-tall deity escorted by two armed guardians and standing on a small lotus-flower-shaped terrace, with a nine-headed creature underneath. Does this correspond to the "nine dragons" mentioned in the stele inscription?[73] Can we imagine that it might really be a question of a lion with nine heads, as stipulated in the iconographic conventions mentioned earlier?[74] Regrettably, no other attributes permit a definitive confirmation of the image's identification. Its hands are broken, so that it is impossible to see whether or not the deity carries the willow twig and the cup that are its most distinctive signs.

The best-known pictorial images of Jiuku tianzun are two paintings of late manufacture (probably Qing; fig. 5.8). The degree to which the Tang-dynasty iconographic attributes of the deity have been precisely maintained in these paintings is remarkable. Jiuku tianzun, dressed in a blue-green robe, wears a crown; small lotus flowers support his feet; a canopy is spread above his throne; a mandorla of flames surrounds him; and he is holding a willow twig in his right hand and a cup in his left. The nine-headed lion spitting fire is sitting at his feet or serves as his mount. It is notable that the lion is a *hou* 吼, a type of lion that served also as Guanyin's mount in certain Ming iconographies.[75]

The numerous statues of Jiuku tianzun that have been recreated during the past two decades in restored Taoist temples and monasteries, though often poorly executed, attest nonetheless to the enduring importance of his cult and the persistence of his iconographic forms, as seen in the photographs of Taoist sites scattered throughout China that were published by the research team of the Institute of Oriental Culture at the University of Tokyo during the late 1980s and early

---

72. See the complete transcription of the stele (unfortunately in simplified characters) given in Chen (1988): 142–143 and in Hu (1994): 9. See also the partial transcription by Wang Jiayou (1987): 52–53, and by Yusa (1989): 25.

73. The nine-headed dragon is well attested in early Taoism. See the *Dongshen badi miaojing jing* 洞神八帝妙精經 (Dz 640. 8a), a manual of Taoist meditation whose origin could go back to the fourth century C.E. The manual includes a mention of a nine-headed dragon as one of the human body's divinities. The edition of the text in the Ming *Daozang* (Dz 640. 8a) gives an illustration of it.

74. The great specialist of Sichuanese art history and Taoism, Wang Jiayou, in spite of his partial transcription of the stele mentioning "Jiuku tianzun mounting the nine dragons," also speaks of a "nine-headed bird" (*jiutou niao* 九頭鳥) in reference to the statue of Jiuku tianzun (1987: 53).

75. Yü (2001): 88–89.

Fig. 5.8. Two paintings of Jiuku tianzun. After Chinese Taoist Association, *Daojiao shen-xian huaji* (1995): plates on 34–35.

1990s.[76] Six or seven examples demonstrate that Jiuku tianzun is still regularly depicted as seated on a nine-headed lion and holding a willow twig and a cup. In some instances, when he occupies a position of prestige such that an entire hall is consecrated to him, his statue is installed upon the principal altar, with the Jiuku tianzuns of the Ten Directions (Shifang jiuku tianzun) arranged in rows on either side of the hall before him.[77] The deity is also found accompanied by two atten-

76. Hachiya (1990, 1995). This work provides a systematic survey of the some eighty Taoist monasteries.

77. According to the *Chūgoku dōkyō no genjō,* images of Jiuku tianzun exist in the follow-ing monasteries and temples: in the main hall of the Jade Spring Pavilion (Yuquan yuan 玉泉院), at Mount Huashan 華山 (Shenxi), at Mount Li 驪山 (Shenxi), at the Louguan tai 樓觀台 monastery (Shenxi), at Mount Qingcheng (Sichuan), at the Yinyangyang dian 欽賜仰殿 in Shanghai, in the Taiqing gong 太清宮 (Shandong), in the Mangshan gong 邙山宮 in Luoyang,

FIG. 5.9. A statue of Jiuku tianzun under construction at the Qingyang gong monastery, Chengdu. Note the drawing of the divinity to the rear, holding the characteristic flask and willow twig. Photograph by the author, 2001.

dants or sharing the hall with the bodhisattvas Puxian 普賢 (Samantabhadra), mounted on an elephant, and Wenshu 文殊 (Mañjuśrī), who sits astride a lion. The two bodhisattvas are then arrayed with their respective altars to the right and the left of the Taoist deity. It is obvious that in this configuration Jiuku tian-zun occupies the position of Guanyin in the analogous Buddhist temple arrange-

in the Weiwang miao 魏王廟 at Lengjiang 棱江 (Zhenjiang), in the Shengzong shuju 省宗教局 in Fuzhou 福州, and at the Luofu shan 羅浮山 (Guangdong).

FIG. 5.10. The statue of Jiuku tianzun at the Qingyang gong monastery, Chengdu. Photograph by the author, 2004.

ments.[78] Besides those documented by the Japanese team, many other images of Jiuku tianzun have recently returned to their places in sacred sites, as I was able to confirm at the Black Goat monastery (Qingyang gong 青羊宮) in Chengdu (Sichuan), where his statue, in the midst of reconstruction when I first saw it in October 2001, was completed in 2004 (figs. 5.9 and 5.10).

ALTHOUGH THE LITERATURE and iconography related to Jiuku tianzun may seem modest when compared with the massive production devoted to Guanyin, they provide an additional demonstration of the close interaction between Taoism and Buddhism in medieval times. While the Taoist identity of the Heavenly Venerable Savior from Suffering is by no means questionable, it is evident that his religious and iconographic properties were patterned on Guanyin's. Similarly, the *Scripture of the Savior from Suffering* cannot be labeled,

78. This is, for example, the case at the Louguan tai monastery.

strictly speaking, a Taoist plagiarism; it is better described as a literary trans-position, a Taoist "apocryphon" inspired by the *Lotus Sūtra*'s *Pumen pin*. The Taoist authors' intention is obvious: to appropriate the Buddhist "bestseller" for their own ends and, by so doing, to steal the thunder from the illustrious bodhisattva Avalokiteśvara while promoting their own protagonist. This late Taoist "repackaging" of the *Pumen pin* thus further exemplifies the bilateral nature of the patterns of hybridization and influence linking the two religious traditions, their mutual implication in both scriptural and iconographic production, and the considerable extension of their relations in time.

Conclusion

The examples of Buddho-Taoist exchange introduced in the preceding chapters lead us to a new perspective on the religious situation in medieval China. Erik Zürcher's metaphor, comparing the two great traditions to two pyramids rising from a common base, has been often cited by historians of Chinese religion, whether to confirm or to criticize it. The top of each pyramid represents the elite and sophisticated realm of religious "professionals," while the foundations of the pyramids belong to the devotional activities of lower-class "simple believers." Whereas the summits are clearly separate and distinct from one another, the bases merge into a poorly differentiated lay religion, a blurred and confused mass of popular beliefs and practices.

In this respect, the scriptures investigated in this book, which are prominently characterized by their sharing of identical or closely similar texts and rituals under a double religious ascription, permit us to bring an unusual measure of clarity to bear upon this problem. These works are not, by and large, representative of the highest religious scholasticism. Neither, however, do they emerge from an undistinguished religious background. They show, on the contrary, that their authors were keen to make their religious affiliations explicit and to affirm a strong commitment to their denominational identities. How can we therefore imagine that these scriptures and their teachings were addressed to "simple believers" who were unaware of the specific obedience to which they belonged?

One will readily admit, I think, that the adhesion of individuals to a ritual tradition as transmitted or professed by a given religious community is usually more motivated by sociocultural circumstances than it is by a reflective choice on the part of the person concerned or that of his family. Geographical proximity, cultural environment, and social contact (whether fortuitous or ongoing) with a religious organization, together with the reputation, charisma, and apostolic activism of its members and clerics—these are the factors that explain how

it was that certain devotees were brought to place themselves in the care of Taoist masters, while others were taken under the wing of Buddhist monks. Though
this much seems sure, nonetheless, it by no means suggests that the spiritual engagement of the laity was completely blind or that deliberate decisions on their
part were not involved. For, in China, as historians of religion and ethnologists
know well, the transmission of texts and traditions is always subject to strict
rules of initiation.

Even when they are meant to be venerated at home for private devotion,
religious scriptures such as the ones we have examined often proclaim their supremacy and exclusivity, with precise indications of the respect and honor due
to them. How, for example, can one suppose that a practitioner, uneducated
though he may have been, could have had no sense of an involvement in Buddhism, when he was expressly asked, in order to receive the teaching of the
Sūtra of the Three Kitchens, to "take refuge in the Three Jewels" and to observe
the basic precepts of Buddhist lay initiation? How, likewise, could an adept of
the Taoist *Marvelous Scripture for Prolonging Life and for Increasing the Account* not
have been conscious of the text's religious pedigree and of the nature of the
worship that he owed to it as a disciple (*dizi* 弟子), after undergoing a ritual initiation for receiving the sacred text, whose seriousness was underlined by the
strict interdiction against divulging it heedlessly? In the same vein, the surviving iconography demonstrates that people were not at all likely to have been ignorant of the distinction between the Buddha and Laozi. Whether during the
Six Dynasties at Yaowang shan 藥王山 (Mountain of the King of Medicine), in
Shaanxi Province,[1] or in the eighth-century Taoist Marvelous Mystery temple
(Xuanmiao guan), in Anyue County (Sichuan), Śākyamuni with his Buddhist
robes and Laozi with his beard, sitting next to each other (see fig. 5.6), would
certainly not have been viewed as the same figure.

That being said, our investigation of the diverse scriptural and ritual traditions presented here also reveals the presence of a third party animating the religious marketplace in medieval China. This third class of specialists in recipes,
working on the margins of the Taoist and Buddhist organizations, belonged to
the milieux of astrologers, diviners, medicine men, and other experts in pararel-
gious techniques. Permanent actors on the Chinese cultural stage and often cus-
todians of the ancestral patrimony, they are certainly not to be relegated to the
amorphous category of "popular" religion. In the absence of sources, we are
usually at a loss regarding the decisive role these mantic technicians played in
medieval society. Some of the Dunhuang documents relative to the traditions
that we have dealt with serve, in this respect, as rare and eloquent witnesses, im-

---

1. See Zhang Yan (1996); Bokenkamp (1996–1997); and Abe (1996–1997).

plicated, as they are, in this three-dimensional religious dynamic and rooted in the social life of the region.[2] The reputation and adaptability of these ritual procedures, whether for exorcistic, prophylactic, or therapeutic ends, conferred on them the capacity to traverse the permeable boundaries separating Buddhism and Taoism without losing their original features, while at the same time forging a path among parareligious specialists in order to serve more pragmatic goals.

Thus, we have seen that the Taoist Method of the Heavenly Kitchens (chapter 1), which was recuperated by Tang Buddhist orthopraxis, was also privileged by Dunhuang lay physicians of Buddhist obedience, who included it in a pharmaceutical manual together with materia medica. In this way, it could be used for therapeutic ends while conferring supernatural powers and suppressing hunger. Similarly, two to three hundred years after their adoption by Tang Buddhism, the Taoist talismans of the *Sūtra to Increase the Account* (chapter 3) became the tools of a Dunhuang diviner who reprocessed them with diverse apotropaic and mantic recipes in a ninth-century technical manuscript. Another remarkable instance of the incorporation of a Buddho-Taoist tradition into the bosom of the Dunhuang heritage of divinatory science is the case of the Great Dipper cult (chapter 4). Appropriated for medical purposes by ninth-century astrologer-physicians, who were officially appointed at the prefectoral school, the Great Dipper cult was also advocated to serve the general welfare in a calendar edited by the local administration a few decades later.

Removed from their devotional context and more or less emancipated from their canonical moorings, such Buddho-Taoist traditions became, in Dunhuang, the main constituents of pragmatic procedures, whether astromedical or mantic. Thus somehow "desacralized," they were nonetheless not demoted to the jumbled realm of despised "superstitious" practices. Thanks to the circumstantial details relative to their sociocultural environment, as known through certain Dunhuang manuscripts, we learn that the technicians who authored these mantic methods were not at all anonymous figures belonging to a nebulous shamanic or folkloric realm. On the contrary, they were established functionaries who held official positions in the local administration. These elite experts in astrology, "magical" medicine, and many other divinatory domains, including hemerology, topomancy, and cleromancy, were sometimes teachers in charge of the codification and diffusion of their arts. The traditional scientific practices (*shushu*) that they deployed in their manuals and treatises were therefore recognized and sponsored by the Dunhuang government, which authorized them for inclusion in its educational programs. Performed and instructed by these lay professionals, such methods as the Heavenly Kitchens, the Talismans to Increase the Account,

---

2. See Kalinowski (2003): 20–33.

and those of the Great Dipper were no doubt valued as integral parts of the Chinese religio-scientific inherence of the region. We may suppose that similar conditions obtained in other parts of the empire as well.

LOOKING BACK AT THE exploration in which this study has involved me for many years, I have the sense of having traversed only a small part of the path through the enormous labyrinth that is Buddho-Taoism. The inkling I had that there exist many other textual and ritual traditions, besides those treated in this volume, that similarly enjoyed a double or even triple manifestation in the religious life of China has become in the course of my research a certainty. Thus, some of the scriptures and sūtras that are briefly mentioned in my introduction in fact would merit a fuller place in this book. The fear of repetition, together with, I admit, a bit of reticence, have precluded my pushing the investigation further ahead. Other specialists and students of medieval China, if they have the audacity and curiosity to reach beyond the exclusive confines of Taoist or Buddhist materials, in which they are too often firmly ensconced, may find it worthwhile to join in the treasure hunt for scriptural twins, subjecting their discoveries to philological and historical scrutiny analogous to that which I have undertaken here. I have no doubt that their investigations will contribute to amplifying the new light we are beginning to shed on the social and cultural realities of Chinese religious life, of which our predecessors had only the barest hint.

Bibliography

Primary Sources

Baopuzi neipian 抱朴子内篇 (ca. 320), by Ge Hong 葛洪. See Wang Ming, ed., *Baopuzi neipian jiaoshi* (1980).

Beishi 北史 (659), by Li Yanshou 李延壽. Beijing: Zhonghua shuju,

Gaoseng zhuan 高僧傳 (519), by Huijiao 慧皎. Beijing: Zhonghua shuju, 1997.

Jiu Tang shu 舊唐書 (945), by Liu Yu 劉昫 et al. Beijing: Zhonghua shuju, 1975.

Song gaoseng zhuan 宋高僧傳 (988), by Zanning 贊寧 et al. Beijing: Zhonghua shuju, 1987.

Xin Tang shu 新唐書 (1060), by Ouyang Xiu 歐陽修, Song Qi 宋祁, et al. Beijing: Zhonghua shuju, 1975.

Zhuangzi 莊子. *Zhuangzi jishi* 莊子集釋, by Guo Qingfan 郭慶藩. Beijing: Zhonghua shuju, 1961.

Works in the Sino-Japanese Buddhist Canon,
Taishō shinshū daizōkyō 大正新修大藏經 (T.)
(The Buddhist Canon newly compiled during the Taishō era, 1924–1935, edited by Takakusu Junjirō 高楠順次郎 and Watanabe Kaigyoku 渡边边海旭, 100 vols. [Tokyo: Taishō issaikyō kankōkai])

T. 23, vol. 1: *Dalou tan jing* 大樓炭經, translated by Fali 法立 (265–316) and Faju 法炬 (ca. 290–306).

T. 24, vol. 1: *Qishi yinben jing* 起世因本經, translated by Jñānagupta 闍那崛多 (652–710).

T. 25, vol. 1: *Qishi yinben jing* 起世因本經, translated by Dharmagupta 達摩笈多 (?–619).

T. 196, vol. 4: *Zhongben qijing* 中本起經, translated by Kang Mengxiang 康孟詳 et al. (end of second century–beginning of third century C.E.).

T. 262, vol. 9: *Miaofa lianhua jing* 妙法蓮華經, translated by Kumārajīva 鳩摩羅什 (ca. 401–413).

T. 410, vol. 13: *Da fangguang shilun jing* 大方廣十輪經.

T. 428, vol. 14: *Bayang shenzhou jing* 八陽神咒經.

T. 449, vol. 14: *Yaoshi rulai benyuan jing* 藥師如來本願經.

T. 475, vol. 14: *Weimojie suoshuo jing* 維摩詰所說經, translated by Kumārajīva.

T. 551, vol. 16: *Foshuo Modeng nü jing* 佛說摩鄧女經, translated by An Shigao 安世高 (ca. 148–168).

T. 670, vol. 16: *Lengqie aba duolou baojing* 楞伽阿跋多羅寶經.

T. 685, vol. 16: *Yulan pen jing* 盂蘭盆經. Translation attributed to Dharmarakṣa.

T. 839, vol. 17: *Zhancha shan'e yebao jing* 占察善惡業報經.

T. 901, vol. 18: *Tuoluoni ji jing* 陀羅尼集經 (653–654), translation attributed to Ajikuta 阿地瞿多.

T. 1043, vol. 20: *Guanshiyin pusa xiaofu duhai tuoluoni zhou jing* 請觀世音菩薩消伏毒害陀羅尼咒經.

T. 1044–1045, vol. 20: *Liuzi shenzhou jing* 六字神咒王經.

T. 1050, vol. 20: *Dacheng zhuangyan baowang jing* 大乘莊嚴寶王經.

T. 1060, vol. 20: *Qianshou qianyan Guanshiyin pusa guangda yuanman wu'ai dabeixin tuoluoni jing* 千手千眼觀世音菩薩廣大圓滿無礙大悲心陀羅尼經 (650), translated by Bhagavadharma 伽梵達摩.

T. 1220, vol. 21: *Jingang yaosha zhennuwang xizai daweishen yan niansong yigui* 金剛藥叉瞋怒王息災大威神驗念誦儀軌.

T. 1222, vol. 21: *Shengjiani fennu jinggang tongzi pusa chengjiu yi gui jing* 聖迦柅忿怒金剛童子菩薩成就儀軌經.

T. 1229, vol. 21: *Huiji jingang jin baibian fa jing* 穢跡金剛禁百變法經.

T. 1305, vol. 21: *Beidou qixing niansong yigui* 北斗七星念誦儀軌, attributed to Vajrabodhi 金剛智 (669–741).

T. 1306, vol. 21: *Beidou qixing humo biyao yigui* 北斗七星護摩秘要儀軌.

T. 1307, vol. 21: *Foshuo beidou qixing yanming jing* 佛說北斗七星延命經.

T. 1310, vol. 21: *Beidou qixing humo fa* 北斗七星護摩法, attributed to Yixing 一行 (683–727).

T. 1311, vol. 21: *Fantian huolu jiuyao* 梵天火羅九曜, by Yixing.

T. 1313, vol. 21: *Foshuo jiuba yankou egui tuoluoni jing* 佛說救拔焰口餓鬼陀羅尼經, translation attributed to Amoghavajra 不空 (705–774).

T. 1331, vol. 21: *Guanding jing* 灌頂經.

T. 1332: *Qifo bapusa suoshuo da tuoluoni shenzhou jing* 七佛八菩薩所說大陀羅尼神咒經.

T. 1333, vol. 21: *Xukongzang pusa wen qifo tuoluoni zhou jing* 虛空藏菩薩問七佛陀羅尼咒經.

T. 1336, vol. 21: *Tuoloni zajing* 陀羅尼雜經.

T. 1394, vol. 21: *Foshuo anzhai shenzhou jing* 佛說安宅神咒經.

T. 1484, vol. 24: *Fanwang jing* 梵網經.

T. 2102, vol. 52: *Hongming ji* 弘明集 (ca. 518), compiled by Sengyou 僧祐 (445–518).

T. 2103, vol. 52: *Guang hongming ji* 廣弘明集 (664), compiled by Daoxuan 道宣 (596–667).

T. 2145, vol. 55: *Chu sanzang jiji* 出三藏記集 (ca. 515), by Sengyou 僧祐 (445–518).

T. 2146, vol. 55: *Zhongjing mulu* 眾經目錄 (594), by Fajing 法經 (dates unknown) et al.

T. 2147, vol. 55: *Zhongjing mulu* 眾經目錄 (612), by Yancong 彥琮 (557–610) et al.

T. 2153, vol. 55: *Da Zhou kanding zhongjing mulu* 大周刊定眾經目錄 (695), by Mingquan 明佺 (dates unknown).

T. 2154, vol. 55: *Kaiyuan shijiao lu* 開元釋教錄 (730), by Zhisheng 智昇 (668–740).

T. 2882, vol. 85: *Foshuo zhoumei jing* 佛說咒媚經.

T. 2887, vol. 85: *Fumu enzhong jing* 父母恩重經.

T. 2894, vol. 85: *Foshuo sanchu jing* 佛說三廚經.

T. 2897, vol. 85: *Foshuo bayang shenzhou jing* 佛說八陽神咒經.

T. 2904, vol. 85: *Foshuo yan shouming jing* 佛說延壽命經.

Works in the Taoist Canon *Zhengtong daozang* 正統道藏 (Dz)
(Numbered according to Schipper [1975])

Dz 1: *Lingbao wuliang duren shangpin miaojing* 靈寶無量度人上品妙經.

Dz 33: *Shangqing huangqi yangjing sandao shunxing jing* 上清黃氣陽精三道順行經.

Dz 50: *Taishang shuo liujia zhenfu baotai huming miaojing* 太上說六甲真符保胎護命妙經.

Dz 65: *Taishang zhenyi bao fumu enzhong jing* 太上真一報父母恩重經.

Dz 72: *Yuanshi tianzun jidu xuehu zhenjing* 元始天尊濟度血湖真經.

Dz 86: *Taishang bifa zhenzhai lingfu* 太上祕法鎮宅靈符.

Dz 179: *Taiwei lingshu ziwen xianji zhenji shangjing* 太微靈書紫文仙忌真記上經.

Dz 188: *Xuandu lüwen* 玄都律文.

Dz 296: *Lishi zhenxian tidao tongjian* 歷世真仙體道通鑑, by Zhao Daoyi 趙道一 (fl. 1294–1307).

Dz 304: *Maoshan zhi* 茅山志 (ca. 1330), by Liu Dabin 劉大彬.

Dz 335: *Taishang dongyuan shenzhou jing* 太上洞淵神咒經.

Dz 336: *Taishang dongxuan lingbao yebao yinyuan jing* 太上洞玄靈寶業報因緣經.

Dz 351: *Taiyi jiuku hushen miaojing* 太一救苦護身妙經.

Dz 358: *Taishang shenzhou yanshou miaojing* 太上神咒延壽妙經.

Dz 374: *Taishang dongxuan lingbao jiuku miaojing* 太上洞玄靈寶救苦妙經.

Dz 375: *Taishang dongxuan lingbao tianzun shuo jiku jing* 太上洞玄靈寶天尊說濟苦經.

Dz 377: *Taishang lingbao hongfu miezui xiangming jing* 太上靈寶洪福滅罪像名經.

Dz 382: *Taishang lingbao tianzun shuo yanshou miaojing* 太上靈寶天尊說延壽妙經.

Dz 402: *Huangting neijing yujing zhu* 黃庭內景玉經註, commentary by Bo Lüzhong 白履忠 (fl. 722–729).

Dz 405: *Shangqing zijing jun huangchu ziling daojun dongfang shangjing* 上清紫精君皇初紫靈道君洞房上經.

Dz 442: *Shangqing housheng daojun lieji* 上清後聖道君列紀.

Dz 463: *Yaoxiu keyi jielü chao* 要修科儀戒律鈔, by Zhu Junxu 朱君緒 (d. 720).

Dz 538: *Taiyi jiuku tianzun shuo badu xuehu baochan* 太一救苦天尊說拔度血湖寶懺.

Dz 539: *Qingxuan jiuku baochan* 青玄救苦寶懺.

Dz 590: *Daojiao lingyan ji* 道教靈驗記 (after 905), by Du Guangting 杜光庭.

Dz 615: *Chisongzi zhangli* 赤松子章曆.

Dz 622: *Taishang xuanling beidou benming yansheng zhenjing* 太上玄靈北斗本命延生真經.

Dz 623: *Taishang xuanling beidou benming changsheng miaojing* 太上玄靈北斗本命長生妙經.

Dz 632: *Taishang taiqing tiantong huming miaojing* 太上太清天童護命妙經.

Dz 633: *Taishang taiqing huanglao dijun yunlei tiantong yinfan xianjing* 太上泰清皇老帝君運雷天童隱梵仙經.

Dz 634: *Taishang Laojun shuo anzhai bayang jing* 太上老君說安宅八陽經.

Dz 635: *Taishang Laojun shuo buxie bayang jing* 太上老君說補謝八陽經.

Dz 640: *Dongshen badi miaojing jing* 洞神八帝妙精經.

Dz 641: *Taishang Laojun neiguan jing* 太上老君內觀經.

Dz 650: *Taishang Laojun shuo changsheng yisuan miaojing* 太上老君說長生益算妙經.

Dz 652: *Taishang Laojun shuo jieshi zhouzu jing* 太上老君說解釋咒詛經.

Dz 662: *Taishang Laojun shuo bao fumu enzhong jing* 太上老君說報父母恩重經.

Dz 672: *Taishang Laojun shuo yisuan shenfu miaojing* 太上老君說益算神符妙經.

Dz 673: *Taishang Laojun hunyuan sanbu fu* 太上老君混元三部符.

Dz 750: *Taishang xuanling beidou benming yansheng zhenjing zhu* 太上玄靈北斗本命延生真經註 (1334), by Xu Daoling 徐道齡.

Dz 751: *Taishang xuanling beidou benming yansheng zhenjing zhujie* 太上玄靈北斗本命延生真經註解.

Dz 752: *Taishang xuanling beidou benming yansheng jing zhu* 太上玄靈北斗本命延生經註, commented by Fu Dongzhen 傅洞真 (ca. twelfth–fourteenth centuries).

Dz 753: *Beidou qiyuan jinxuan yuzhang* 北斗七元金玄羽章, commented by Fu Dongzhen.

Dz 763: *Laozi shuo wuchu jingzhu* 老子說五廚經註, commented and prefaced by Yin Yin 尹愔 (d. 741).

Dz 785: *Laojun yinsong jiejing* 老君音誦誡經, by Kou Qianzhi 寇謙之 (365–448).

Dz 790: *Nüqing guilü* 女青鬼律.

Dz 795: *Zhengyi chuguan zhangyi* 正一出官章儀.

Dz 830: *Fuqi jingyi lun* 服氣精義論, attributed to Sima Chengzhen 司馬承禎 (647–735).

Dz 858: *Taishang dongshen xuanmiao baiyuan zhenjing* 太上洞神玄妙白猿真經.

Dz 861: *Taishang liuren mingjian fuyin jing* 太上六壬明鑑符陰經.

Dz 879: *Shangqing jinshu yuzi shangjing* 上清金書玉字上經.

Dz 885: *Huangdi jiuding shendan jingjue* 黃帝九鼎神丹經.

Dz 1015: *Jinsuo liuzhu yin* 金鎖流珠引, falsely attributed to Li Chunfeng 李淳風 (602–670).

Dz 1016: *Zhen'gao* 真誥 (499), compiled and annotated by Tao Hongjing 陶弘景 (456–536).

Dz 1032: *Yunji qiqian* 雲笈七籤, compiled by Zhang Junfang 張君房 (fl. 1008–1025).

Dz 1115: *Taishang dongxuan lingbao benxing yinyuan jing* 太上洞玄靈寶本行因緣經.

Dz 1127: *Lu xiansheng daomen kelüe* 陸先生道門科略, by Lu Xiujing 陸修靜 (406–477).

Dz 1130: *Daodian lun* 道典論.

Dz 1138: *Wushang biyao* 無上祕要.

Dz 1163: *Sun zhenren beiji qianjin yaofang* 孫真人備急千金藥方, by Sun Simo 孫思邈 (581–682).

Dz 1205: *Santian neijie jing* 三天內解經.

Dz 1208: *Taishang sanwu zhengyi mengwei lu* 太上三五正一盟威籙.

Dz 1209: *Taishang zhengyi mengwei falu yibu* 太上正一盟威法籙一部.

Dz 1217: *Taishang zhengyi jie wuyin zhouzu bilu* 太上正一解五音咒詛祕籙.

Dz 1224: *Daomen dingzhi* 道門定制 (1188), compiled by Lü Yuansu 呂元素.

Dz 1265: *Beidi qiyuan ziting yansheng bijue* 北帝七元紫庭延生祕訣.

Dz 1288: *Yuanchen zhangjiao licheng li* 元辰章醮立成曆.

Dz 1289: *Liushi jiazi benming yuanchen li* 六十甲子本命元辰曆.

Dz 1317: *Dongzhen shangqing kaitian santu qixing yidu jing* 洞真上清開天三圖七星移度經.

Dz 1332: *Dongzhen taishang zidu yanguang shenyuan bian jing* 洞真太上紫度炎光神元變經.

Dz 1367: *Shangqing hetu neixuan jing* 上清河圖内玄經.

Dz 1372: *Shangqing gaoshang yuchen fengtai qusu shangjing* 上清高上玉晨鳳臺曲素上經.

Dz 1392: *Shangqing qusu jueci lu* 上清曲素訣辭錄.

Dz 1396: *Shangqing hetu baolu* 上清河圖寶錄.

Dunhuang Manuscripts of the Pelliot (P.), Stein (S.), and Beijing Collections

P. 2007

P. 2010

P. 2055 R°

P. 2171

P. 2387

P. 2447

P. 2558 R°

P. 2637

P. 2675 bis R°

P. 2675 V°

P. 2703 R°

P. 2723

P. 2728

P. 2818

P. 3022 R°

P. 3032

P. 3064 R°

P. 3081 V°

P. 3689

P. 3835 V°

P. 3914

P. 3915

P. 4667 V° (P. tib. 2207)

S. 418

S. 612 R°

S. 2081

S. 2088

S. 2404

S. 2428

S. 2498

S. 2517

S. 2673

S. 2680
S. 2708
S. 3852
S. 4311
S. 4524
S. 6146
S. 6983
Beijing 8265
Beijing 8266
Beijing 8267
Beijing 8268
Beijing 8269

Manuscripts from Turfan

Ch. 2190 R°
Ch/U6944 (T.II Y61)

Secondary Sources

Abe, Stanley K. 1996–1997. "Heterological Visions: Northern Wei Daoist Sculpture from Shaanxi Province." *Cahiers d'Extrême-Asie* 9: 69–83.

———. 2002. *Ordinary Images*. Chicago: University of Chicago Press.

Akahori, Akira. 1989. "Drug Taking and Immortality." In Kohn 1989: 73–98.

Andersen, Poul. 1980. *The Method of Holding the Three Ones*. London: Curzon Press.

Akizuki Kan'ei 秋月觀暎. 1996. "Dōkyō to Bukkyō no fubo enchō kyō" 道教と佛教の父母恩重經. *Shūkyō kenkyū* 宗教研究 39/4: 23–54.

———. 1989–1990. "The Practice of Bugang." *Cahiers d'Extrême-Asie* 5: 15–53.

Arrault, Alain, and Jean-Claude Martzloff. 2003. "Calendriers." In Kalinowski 2003: 84–211.

Baker, Janet, ed. 1998. *The Flowering of Foreign Faith: New Studies in Chinese Buddhist Art*. Mumbai: Marg Publications.

Barrett, Timothy H. 1990. "Towards a Date for the *Chin-so liu-chu yin*." *Bulletin of the School of Oriental and African Studies* 53/2: 292–294.

———. 1996. *Taoism under the T'ang: Religion and Empire during the Golden Age of Chinese History*. London: Wellsweep.

Been, Charles D. 1991. *The Cavern-Mystery Transmission: A Taoist Ordination Rite of A.D. 711*. Asian Studies at Hawai'i, no. 38. Honolulu: University of Hawai'i Press.

Birnbaum, Raoul. 1979. *The Healing Buddha*. Boulder, CO: Shambhala.

Blacker, Carmen. 1975. *The Catalpa Bow: A Study of Shamanistic Practices in Japan*. London: George Allen and Unwin.

Bodde, Derk. 1975. *Festivals in Ancient China: New Year and Other Annual Observances during the Han Dynasty 206 B.C.–A.D. 220*. Princeton: Princeton University Press.

Bokenkamp, Stephen. 1983. "Sources on the Ling-pao Scriptures." In Strickmann 1981–1985, vol. 2: 434–486. Brussels: Institut belge des hautes études chinoises.

———. 1990. "Stages of Transcendence: The *Bhūmi* Concept in Taoist Scripture." In Buswell 1990a: 119–147.

———. 1996–1997. "The Yao Boduo Stele as Evidence for the [Dao-Buddhism] of the Early Lingbao Scriptures." *Cahiers d'Extrême-Asie* 9: 55–68.

———. 1997. *Early Daoist Scriptures*. Berkeley: University of California Press.

Boltz, Judith. 1987. *A Survey of Taoist Literature: Tenth to Seventeenth Centuries*. Berkeley, CA: Institute of East Asian Studies.

———. 1993. "Not by the Seal of Office Alone: New Weapons in Battles with the Supernatural." In *Religion and Society in T'ang and Sung China,* edited by Patricia B. Ebrey and Peter N. Gregory, 241–306. Honolulu: University of Hawai'i Press.

Buswell, Robert E., Jr., ed. 1990a. *Chinese Buddhist Apocrypha*. Honolulu: University of Hawai'i Press.

———. 1990b. "Prolegomenon to the Study of Buddhist Apocryphal Scriptures." In Buswell 1990a: 1–30.

Bynum, Carolyn Walker. 1987. *Holy Fast and Holy Feast: The Religious Significance of Food to Medieval Women*. Berkeley: University of California Press.

Campany, Robert Ford. 1996. "The Earliest Tales of the Bodhisattva Guanyin." In Lopez 1996: 82–96.

———. 2002. *To Live as Long as Heaven and Earth: A Translation and Study of Ge Hong's Traditions of Divine Transcendents*. Berkeley: University of California Press.

———. 2005. "The Meanings of Cuisines of Transcendence in Late Classical and Early Medieval China." *T'oung Pao* 91: 126–182.

Chang, K. C. 1977. *Food in Chinese Culture: Anthropological and Historical Perspectives*. New Haven, CT: Yale University Press.

Chavannes, Edouard. 1913. *Mission archéologique en Chine septentrionale*. Paris: Ernest Leroux.

Chen Guofu 陳國符. 1963 [1949]. *Daozang yuanliu kao* 道藏原流考. Revised ed. Beijing: Zhonghua shuju.

Chen Yuan 陳垣. 1988. *Daojia jinshe lue* 道家金石略. Beijing: Wenwu chuban she.

Chinese Taoist Association (Zhongguo daojiao xiehui 中國道教協會), ed. 1995. *Daojiao shenxian huaji* 道教神仙畫集 (Album of Taoist deities and divine immortals). Beijing: Huaxia chubanshe 華夏出版社.

Cole, Alan. 1998. *Mothers and Sons in Chinese Buddhism*. Stanford, CA: Stanford University Press.

Cong Chunyu 叢春雨 et al. 1994. *Dunhuang zhong yiyao quanshu* 敦煌中醫藥全書. Beijing: Zhongyi guji chuban she.

Davis, Edward L. 2001. *Society and the Supernatural in Song China*. Honolulu: University of Hawai'i Press.

Demiéville, Paul. 1974a. "Byō" 病 (Disease). *Hōbōgirin,* vol. 3: 224–265. (English translation by Mark Tatz, *Buddhism and Healing: Demiéville's Article "Byō" from Hōbōgirin*. Lanham, MD: University Press of America, 1985.)

———. 1974b. "Byō" 瓶 (Vase). *Hōbōgirin,* vol. 3: 265–270.

Demiéville, Paul, Hubert Durt, and Anna Seidel, comps. 1978. *Répertoire du Canon boud-dhique sino-japonais.* 2nd ed. Supplement to the *Hōbōgirin.* Paris and Tokyo.

Demiéville, Paul, Sylvain Lévi, and J. Takakusu, eds. 1929. *Hōbōgirin.* Vol. 1. Tokyo: Maison Franco-Japonaise.

Deng Wenkuan 鄧文寛. 2002. *Dunhuang Tulufan tianwen lifa yanjiu* 敦煌吐魯番天文曆法研究. Lanzhou: Gansu jiaoyu.

Despeux, Catherine. 1989. "Gymnastics: The Ancient Tradition." In Kohn 1989: 225–261.

Douglas, Mary. 1966. *Purity and Danger: An Analysis of the Concepts of Pollution and Taboo.* London: Routledge.

Drège, Jean-Pierre. 1999. "Du texte à l'image." In *Images de Dunhuang: Dessins et peintures sur papier des fonds Pelliot et Stein,* 105–168. Mémoires archéologiques 24. Paris: École française d'Extrême-Orient.

Dudbridge, Glen. 1996–1997. "The General of the Five Paths in Tang and Pre-Tang China." *Cahiers d'extrême-Asie* 9: 85–98.

Dunhuang shiku quanji 敦煌石窟全集. 1999–. 26 vols. to date. Hong Kong: Commercial Press.

Duquenne, Robert. 1983a. "Daigensui" (Āṭavaka). *Hōbōgirin,* vol. 6: 610–640.

———. 1983b. "Daiitoku myōō" (Yamāntaka). *Hōbōgirin,* vol. 6: 652–670.

Engelhardt, Ute. 1989. "*Qi* for Life: Longevity in the Tang." In Kohn 1989: 263–296.

Evans-Pritchard, E. E. 1976 [1937]. *Witchcraft, Oracles, and Magic among the Azande.* New York: Oxford University Press.

Fang Guangchang 方廣錩. 1997. "Dunhuang yishu zhong de *Miaofa lianhua jing* ji you-guan wenxian 敦煌遺書中的妙法連華經及有關文獻" (The *Lotus Sūtra* in Dun-huang books and other documents). *Zhonghua foxue xuebao* 10: 212–231.

Faure, Bernard. 1988. *La volonté d'orthodoxie dans le bouddhisme chinois.* Paris: Centre na-tional de la recherche scientifique.

Feng, H. Y., and J. K. Shryock. 1935. "The Black Magic in China Known as *Ku.*" *Journal of the American Oriental Society* 55: 1–30.

Forte, Antonino. 1976. *Political Propaganda and Ideology in China at the End of the Seventh Century.* Naples: Istituto Universitario Orientale.

———. 1990. "The Relativity of the Concept of Orthodoxy in Chinese Buddhism: Chih-sheng's Indictment of Shih-li and the Proscription of the *Dharma Mirror Sūtra.*" In Buswell 1990a: 239–249.

Forte, Antonino, and Jacques May. 1979. "Chōsai 長齋" (Long fast). *Hōbōgirin,* vol. 5: 392–407.

Franke, Herbert. 1990. "The Taoist Elements in the Buddhist *Great Bear Sūtra (Pei-tou ching)." Asia Major* 3/1: 75–111.

Fujieda Akira 藤枝晃. 1973. "Tonkō rekijitsu 敦煌曆日譜." *Tōhō gakuhō* 東方學報 (Kyoto) 45: 377–441.

Gao Guofan 高國藩. 1993. *Dunhuang minsu ziliao daolun* 敦煌民俗資料導論. Taipei: Xin-wen feng chuban 新文豐出版.

Gernet, Jacques. 1956. *Les aspects économiques du bouddhisme dans la société chinoise du Ve au Xe siècle*. Saigon: École française d'Extrême-Orient. (English translation by Franciscus Verellen, *Buddhism in Chinese Society: An Economic History from the Fifth to the Tenth Centuries*. New York: Columbia University Press, 1995.)

———. 1998. "Moines thaumaturges." In Jacqueline Pigeot and Hartmut O. Rotermund, eds., *Le vase de béryl: Études sur le Japon et la Chine,* 13–25. Paris: Éditions Philippe Picquier.

Gernet, Jacques, and Wu Chi-yu, eds. 1970. *Catalogue des manuscrits chinois de Touen-houang, Fonds Pelliot de la Bibliothèque nationale*. Vol. 1 (nos. 2001–2500). Paris: Bibliothèque nationale.

Giès, Jacques, Michel Soymié, and Jean-Pierre Drège, et al., eds. 1994. *Les arts de l'Asie centrale: La collection Paul Pelliot du Musée national des arts asiatiques Guimet*. 2 vols. Tokyo: Kodansha.

de Groot, J. J. M. 1907. *The Religious System of China*. 6 vols. Leiden: E. J. Brill.

———. 1893. *Le code du Mahāyāna en Chine, son influence sur la vie monacale et sur le monde laïque*. Amsterdam: Johannes Müller.

Hachiya Kunio, ed. 1990. *Chūgoku Dōkyo no genjō: Dōshi, dōkyo, dōkan* 中国道教の現状: 道士・道協・道観. 2 vols. Tokyo: Kyūko Shoin.

———, ed. 1995. *Chūgoku no Dōkyō: Sono katsudō to dōkan no genjō* 中国の道教:その活動と道観の現状. 2 vols. Tokyo: Tōkyō Daigaku Tōyō Bunka Kenkyūjo.

Hansen, Valerie. 1996. "The Law of the Spirits." In Lopez 1996: 284–292.

Harper, Donald. 1996. "Spellbinding." In Lopez 1996: 241–250.

———. 1998. *Early Chinese Medical Literature: The Mawangdui Medical Manuscripts*. London: Kegan Paul International.

———. 2003. "Iatromancie." In Kalinowski 2003: 471–512.

Hiraoka Takeo 平岡武夫. 1960. *T'ang Civilization Reference Series*. Vol. 6. Kyoto: Kyōtō daigaku jimbun kagaku kenkyūsho.

Hou Ching-lang. 1975. *Monnaies d'offrande et la notion de trésorerie dans la religion chinoise*. Paris: Collège de France.

———. 1979. "The Chinese Belief in Baleful Stars." In Welch and Seidel 1979: 193–228.

Howard, Angela F. 1990. "Tang and Post-Tang Images of Guanyin from Sichuan." *Orientations* 21/1: 49–57.

———. 1998. "The Development of Buddhist Sculpture in Sichuan: The Making of Indigenous Art." In Baker 1998: 118–133.

Hu Wenhe 胡文和. 1994. *Sichuan daojiao fojiao shiku yishu* 四川道教佛教石窟藝術. Chengdu: Sichuan renmin chubanshe.

Hurvitz, Leon, trans. 1976. *Scripture of the Lotus Blossom of the Fine Dharma*. New York: Columbia University Press.

Inoue Yutaka 井上豐. 1992. "Rikutei, rikukōshin no henyo: Shoki dōkyō to kyōten o chūshin ni shite 六丁, 六甲神の變容: 初期道教と經典を中心にして." *Tōhō shūkyō* 東方宗教 80: 15–32.

Kalinowski, Marc. 1985. "Le dispositif des Neuf Palais sous des Six Dynasties." In Strickmann 1981–1985, vol. 3: 773–811.

———. 1990. "La littérature divinatoire dans le *Daozang*." *Cahiers d'Extrême-Asie* 5: 85–114.

———, ed. 2003. *Divination et société dans la Chine médiévale: Études des manuscrits de Dunhuang de la Bibliothèque nationale de France et de la British Library.* Paris: Bibliothèque nationale de France.

Kaltenmark, Max. 1979. "The Ideology of the *T'ai-p'ing ching*." In Welch and Seidel 1979: 19–52.

Kamata Shigeo 鎌田茂雄. 1986. *Dōzō nai bukkyō shisō shiryō shūsei* 道藏內佛教思想資料集成. Tokyo: Daizō shuppansha.

Kleeman, Terry F. 2005. "Feasting without Victuals: The Evolution of the Daoist Communal Kitchen." In *Of Tripod and Palate: Food, Politics, and Religion in Traditional China*, edited by Roel Sterckx, 140–162. New York and Hampshire, UK: Palgrave Macmillan.

Kohn, Livia, ed. 1989. *Taoist Meditation and Longevity Techniques.* Ann Arbor: Center for Chinese Studies, University of Michigan:

———. 1995. *Laughing at the Tao: Debates among Buddhists and Taoists in Medieval China.* Princeton: Princeton University Press.

———. 1998. "Counting Good Deeds and Days of Life: The Quantification of Fate in Medieval China." *Asiatische Studien* 52: 833–870.

Kubo Noritada 窪德忠. 1981. *Kōshin shinkō no kenkyū* 庚申信仰の研究. Tokyo: Tōkyō daigaku tōhō bunka kenky ū 東京大學東洋文化研究.

Kuo Liying. 1994a. *Confession et contrition dans le bouddhisme chinois du Ve au Xe siècle.* Paris: École française d'Extrême-Orient.

———. 1994b. "Divination, jeux de hasard et purification dans le bouddhisme chinois: Autour d'un *sûtra* apocryphe chinois, le *Zhancha jing*." In Fukui Fumimasa and Gérard Fussman, eds., *Bouddhisme et cultures locales: Quelques cas de réciproques adaptations,* 145–167. Paris: École française d'Extrême-Orient.

———. 2000. "Sur les apocryphes bouddhiques chinois." *Bulletin de l'École française d'Extrême-Orient, Mélanges du centenaire* 87/2: 677–705.

Lagerwey, John. 1981. *Wu-shang pi-yao: Somme taoïste du VIe siècle.* Paris: École française d'Extrême-Orient.

Lai, Whalen. 1990. "The *Chan-ch'a ching:* Religion and Magic in Medieval China." In Buswell 1990a: 175–206.

Lamotte, Étienne. 1962. *L'Enseignement de Vimalakīrti.* Louvain, Belgium: Université de Louvain.

Lau, D. C., and Roger T. Ames. 1996. *Sun Bin: The Art of Warfare.* New York: Ballantine.

Leidy, Denise Patry. 1998. "Avalokiteshvara in Sixth-Century China." In Baker 1998: 88–103.

Lévi, Jean. 1983. "L'abstinence des céréales chez les taoïstes." *Études chinoises* 1: 3–47.

Li Hui 李卉. 1960. "Shuo gudu yu wushu" 說蠱毒與巫術. *Minzu xue yanjiusuo jikan* 民族學研究所集刊 9.

Lin Baoyao 林保堯, ed. 1991. *Dunhuang yishu tudian* 敦煌藝術圖典. Taipei: Yishu chubanshe.

Liu Changjiu 劉長久. 1997. *Anyue shiku yishu* 安岳石窟藝術 (The grotto art in Anyue). Chengdu: Sichuan renmin chubanshe.

Liu Hongliang 柳洪亮. 1986. "Tulufan asita nagumu qunxin faxian de taoren mupai 吐魯番阿斯塔那古群新發現的挑人木牌." *Kaogu yu wenwu* 考古与文物 7: 24–30.

Loewe, Michael. 1970. "The Case of Witchcraft in 91 B.C." *Asia Major,* 3rd ser., 15: 159–196.

Lopez, Donald S., Jr., ed. 1996. *Religions of China in Practice*. Princeton: Princeton University Press.

Ma Jixing 馬繼興, ed. 1998. *Dunhuang yiyao wenxian jijiao* 敦煌醫藥文獻輯校. Jiangsu: Guji chubanshe.

Makita Tairyō 牧田諦亮. 1976. *Gikyō kenkyū* 疑經研究. Kyoto: Kyoto University, Jinbun Kagaku kenkyūsho.

Makita Tairyō and Ochiai Toshinori 落合俊典, eds. 1994–2000. *Nanatsu-dera kōitsu kyōten kenkyū sōsho* 七寺古逸經典研究叢 (The long-hidden scriptures of Nanatsu-dera, Research Series), vols. 1 (1994), 2 (1996), 3 (1995), 4 (1999), 5 (2000), and 6 (1998). Tokyo: Daitō shuppansha.

de Mallman, Marie-Thérèse. 1948. *Introduction à l'étude d'Avalokiteśvara*. Paris: Annales du Musée Guimet.

Maspero, Henri. 1971 [1950]. *Le taoïsme et les religions chinoises.* [=Mélanges posthumes.] Paris: Gallimard. (English translation by Frank A. Kierman, Jr., *Taoism and Chinese Religion*. Amherst: University of Massachusetts Press, 1981.)

Masuo Shinichiro 増尾伸一郎. 1996. "救護身命經の傳播と厭魅蠱毒." In Makita and Ochiai 1994–2000, vol. 2: 815–852.

Miyai Rika 宮井里佳. 1996. "咒媚經一卷." In Makita and Ochiai 1994–2000, vol. 2: 699–742.

Mochizuki Shinkō 望月信亨. 1936–1963. *Bukkyō daijiten* 佛教大辭典. 10 vols. Tokyo: Seikai seiten kankō kyōkai.

Mollier, Christine. 1990. *Une apocalypse taoïste du début du Ve siècle: Le Livre des Incantations Divines des Grottes Abyssales*. Mémoires de l'Institut des hautes études chinoises, vol. 31. Paris: Collège de France.

———. 1999–2000. "Les Cuisines de Laozi et du Buddha." *Cahiers d'Extrême-Asie* 11: 45–90.

———. 2001. "De l'inconvénient d'être mortel pour les taoïstes de la Haute Pureté." In Brigitte Baptandier, ed., *De la malemort en quelques pays d'Asie,* 79–105. Paris: Karthala.

———. 2003. "Talismans." In Kalinowski 2003: 403–429.

———. 2006. "Visions of Evil: Demonology and Orthodoxy in Early Taoism." In Benjamin Penny, ed., *Daoism in History: Essays in Honour of Liu Ts'un-yan*. London: Routledge.

———. 2007. "Les talismans du Buddha et de Laozi pour 'Accroître le capital-vie.'" In *Études de Dunhuang et Turfan,* edited by Jean-Pierre Drège and Olivier Venture, 155–188. École Pratique des Hautes Études, Hautes Études Orientales 41, Extrême-Orient 6. Geneva: Droz.

Murase, Miyeko. 1971. "Kuan Yin as Savior of Men: Illustrations of the Twenty-fifth Chapter of the *Lotus Sutra*." *Artibus Asiae* 33/1–2: 39–74.

Needham, Joseph, et al. 1959. *Science and Civilisation in China*. Vol. 3: *Astronomy*. Cambridge: Cambridge University Press.

———. 1985. *Science and Civilisation in China*. Vol. 5, part 1: Tsien Tsuen-Hsuin and Qian Cunxun, *Paper and Printing*. Cambridge: Cambridge University Press.

———. 1986. *Science and Civilisation in China*. Vol. 6, part 1 (with Lu Gwei-Djen and Huang Hsing-Tsung): *Biology and Biotechnical Technology 1: Botany*. Cambridge: Cambridge University Press.

Ngô Van Xuyêt. 1976. *Divination, magie et politique dans la Chine ancienne*. Bibliothèque de l'École des hautes études 78. Paris: Presses Universitaires de France.

Nickerson, Peter. 1997. "The Great Petition for Sepulchral Plaints." In Bokenkamp 1997a: 230–274.

Nishiwaki Tsuneki 西脅常記. 1999. "ベルリン.トルファン.コレクション. 道教問書" (On the Taoist fragments in the Berlin Turfan Collection). *Kyōto daigaku sōkai ningengakubu kiyō* 京都大學總合人間學部紀要, 47–66.

Niu Ruji 牛汝极. 1997. *Weiwuer guwenzi yu guwenxian daolun* 維吾尔古文字与古文獻導論. Urumqi: Xinjiang chubanshe.

Obringer, Frédéric. 1997. *L'aconit et l'orpiment: Drogues et poisons en Chine ancienne et médiévale*. Paris: Fayard.

Ochiai Toshinori 落合俊典. 1991. *The Manuscripts of Nanatsu-dera: A Recent Discovered Treasure-House in Downtown Nagoya*. Ed. Silvio Vita. Kyoto: Istituto Italiano di Cultura, Scuola di Studi sull'Asia Orientale.

Ōfuchi Ninji 大淵忍爾. 1978. *Tonkō dōkyō* 敦煌道教, *Mokurokuhen* 目錄編. Tokyo: Fukutake shoten.

———. 1979. *Tonkō dōkyō, Zurokuhen* 圖錄編. Tokyo: Fukutake shoten.

———. 1983. *Chūgokujin no shūkyōgirei, Bukkyō, Dōkyō, minkan shinkō* 中國人の宗教儀禮, 佛教道教民間信仰. Tokyo: Fukutake shoten.

Orzech, Charles D. 1998. *Politics and Transcendent Wisdom: The Scripture for Humane Kings in the Creation of Chinese Buddhism*. Hermeneutics: Studies in the History of Religions. University Park: Pennsylvania State University Press.

Orzech, Charles D., and James H. Sanford. 2000. "Worship of the Ladies of the Dipper." In David G. White, ed., *Tantra in Practice*, 383–395. Princeton: Princeton University Press.

Osabe Kazuo. 長部和雄. 1963. *Ichigyō zenji no kenkyū* 一行禪師の研究. Kobe: Shōka daigaku gakujutsu kenkyūkai.

Padoux, André. 1980. *L'Énergie de la Parole: Cosmogonies de la Parole Tantrique*. Paris: Le soleil noir.

Pelliot, Paul. 1911. "Le rôle des apocryphes bouddhiques an Asia centrale et en Chine." Unpublished lecture held at the Académie des inscriptions et belles-lettres.

Penny, Benjamin. 1990. "A System of Fate Calculation in the *Taiping jing*." *Far Eastern History* 41: 1–8.

Regamey, Constantin. 1971. "Motifs vichnouites et sivaïtes dans le Kāraṇḍavyūha." In *Études tibétaines*, 411–432. Paris: Adrien Maisonneuve.

Reiter, Florian C. 1998. "The Taoist Canon of 749 A.D. at the 'Southern Indian Belvedere' in Jen-shou District, Szechwan Province." *Zeitschrift der Deutschen Morgenländischen Gesellschaft* 146: 111–124.

Robert, Jean-Noël. 1997. *Le Sûtra du Lotus*. Paris: Fayard, 1997.

Robinet, Isabelle. 1979. *Méditation taoïste*. Paris: Albin Michel.

———. 1984. *La révélation du Shangqing dans l'histoire du taoïsme*. 2 vols. Paris: École française d'Extrême-Orient.

Rong Xinjiang. 2000. "The Nature of the Dunhuang Library Cave and the Reasons for Its Sealing." *Cahiers d'Extrême-Asie* 11: 247–275.

———. 2004. "Official Life at Dunhuang in the Tenth Century: The Case of Cao Yuanzhong." In S. Whitfield 2004: 57–62.

Sawada Mizuho 澤田瑞穂. 1992 [1984]. *Chūgoku no juhō* 中國の咒法. Tokyo: Hirakawa shuppansha.

Schafer, Edward H. 1963. *The Golden Peaches of Samarkand: A Study of T'ang Exotics*. Berkeley: University of California Press.

———. 1977. *Pacing the Void: T'ang Approaches to the Stars*. Berkeley: University of California Press.

———. 1980. *Mao Shan in T'ang Times*. Berkeley: University of California, Society for the Study of Chinese Religions.

Schipper, Kristofer. 1965. *L'empereur Wou des Han dans la légende taoïste*. Paris: École française d'Extrême-Orient.

———, ed. 1975. *Concordance du Tao-tsang: Titres d'ouvrages*. Paris: École Française d'Extrême-Orient.

———. 1982. *Le corps taoïste*. Paris: Fayard. (English translation by Karen C. Duval, *The Taoist Body*. Berkeley: University of California Press, 1993.)

———. 1985a. "Chiens de paille et tigres en papier: Une pratique rituelle et ses gloses." *Extrême-Orient, Extrême-Occident* 6: 83–94.

———. 1985b. "Taoist Ordination Ranks in the Tunhuang Manuscripts." In Gert Naundorf et al., eds., *Religion und Philosophie in Ostasien: Festschrift für Hans Steininger*, 127–148. Würzburg: Könighausen und Neumann.

———. 1994. "Purity and Strangers: Shifting Boundaries in Medieval China." *T'oung Pao* 80: 61–81.

Schipper, Kristofer, and Franciscus Verellen, eds. 2004. *The Taoist Canon: A Historical Companion to the Daozang*. 3 vols. Chicago: University of Chicago Press.

Schipper, Kristofer, and Wang Hsiu-huei. 1986. "Progressive and Regressive Time Cycles in Taoist Ritual." In J. T. Fraser et al., eds. *The Study of Time V: Time, Science, and Society in China and the West*, 185–205. Amherst: University of Massachusetts Press.

Schlegel, Gustave. 1875. *Uranographie chinoise*. 2 vols. Leiden: E. J. Brill.

Schmitt, Jean-Claude. 2001. *Le corps, les rites, les rêves, le temps: Essais d'anthropologie médiévale*. Paris: Gallimard.

Seidel, Anna. 1969. *La divinisation de Lao tseu dans le taoïsme des Han*. Paris: École française d'Extrême-Orient.

———. 1970. "The Image of the Perfect Ruler in Early Taoist Messianism: Lao-tzu and Li Hung." *History of Religions* 9: 216–247.

———. 1984. "Le Sûtra merveilleux du Lingbao suprême traitant de Laozi qui convertit les barbares (le manuscrit S. 2081)." In Michel Soymié, ed., *Contributions aux études de Touen-houang*, vol. 3: 305–352. Paris: École française d'Extrême-Orient.

Sen, Satiranjan. 1945. "Two Medical Texts in Chinese Translation." *Visva-Bharati Annals* 1: 70–95.

Sharf, Robert H. 2002. *Coming to Terms with Chinese Buddhism: A Reading of the* Treasure Store Treatise. Honolulu: University of Hawai'i Press.

Shi, Pingting. 1992. "A Brief Description on the *Jingbian* Buddhist Illustrations at Dunhuang." *Orientations* 23/5: 61–64.

Shioiri Ryōdō. 1989. "The Meaning of the Formation and Structure of the *Lotus Sūtra*." In Tanabe and Tanabe (1989): 15–36.

Shirasu Jōshin 白須淨真. 1980. "Zaichi gōzōku, meizoku shakai 在地豪族, 名族社会" (Society of powerful and famous provincial families). In Ikeda On 池田溫, ed., *Tonkō no shakai* 敦煌の社会, 3–49. Tokyo: Daitō shuppansha 大東出版社.

Sivin, Nathan. 1987. *Traditional Medicine in Contemporary China*. Ann Arbor: University of Michigan Press.

Sørensen, Henrik H. 1995. "The Worship of the Great Dipper in Korean Buddhism." In Henrik H. Sørensen, ed., *Religions in Traditional Korea*, 75–105. Copenhagen: Seminar for Buddhist Studies.

Soymié, Michel. 1971–1972. *Annuaire de L'EPHE* (1971–1972): 661–666.

———. 1972–1973. *Annuaire de L'EPHE* (1972–1973): 703–705.

———. 1981. "Un recueil d'inscriptions sur peintures." In *Nouvelles contributions aux études de Touen-houang*. Geneva: Librairie Droz.

———, ed. 1991. *Catalogue des manuscrits chinois de Touen-houang: Fonds Pelliot de la Bibliothèque nationale*. Vol. 4 (nos. 3501–4000). Paris: École française d'Extrême-Orient.

———, ed. 1995. *Catalogue des manuscrits chinois de Touen-houang: Fonds Pelliot de la Bibliothèque nationale*. Vol. 5, in 2 parts (nos. 4001–4500). Paris: École française d'Extrême-Orient.

———. 2000. "Peintures et dessins de Dunhuang: Notes d'iconographies." In Jean-Pierre Drège, ed., *Images de Dunhuang: Dessins et peintures sur papier des fonds Pelliot et Stein,* 13–53. Paris: École française d'Extrême-Orient.

Stein, Rolf A. 1963. "Remarques sur les mouvements du taoïsme politico-religieux au IIe siècle après J.C." *T'oung Pao* 50: 1–78.

———. 1970. "Les cultes populaires dans le taoïsme organisé." *Annuaire du Collège de France*: 437–443.

———. 1971. "Les fêtes de cuisine du taoïsme religieux." *Annuaire du Collège de France*: 431–440.

———. 1972. "Spéculations mystiques et thèmes relatifs aux Cuisines du taoïsme." *Annuaire du Collège de France*: 489–499.

———. 1979. "Religious Taoism and Popular Religion from the Second to the Seventh Century." In Welch and Seidel 1979: 53–81.

———. 1986. "Avalokiteśvara/Kouan-yin, un exemple de transformation d'un dieu en déesse." *Cahiers d'Extrême-Asie* 2: 17–77.

Strickmann, Michel. 1981. *Le taoïsme du Maoshan: Chronique d'une révélation*. Mémoires de l'Institut des hautes études chinoises, vol. 17. Paris: Collège de France.

———, ed. 1981–1985. *Tantric and Taoist Studies in Honour of R. A. Stein*. 3 vols. Brussels: Institut belge des hautes études chinoises.

———. 1982. "India in the Chinese Looking-Glass." In Deborah E. Klimburg-Salter, ed., *The Silk Route and the Diamond Path*, 52–63. Los Angeles: University of California Art Council.

———. 1983. "Homa in East Asia." In Frits Staal, ed., *Agni: The Vedic Ritual of the Fire Altar*, vol. 2: 418–455. Berkeley: Asian Humanities Press.

———. 1990. "The Consecration Sūtra: A Buddhist Book of Spells." In Buswell 1990a: 75–118.

———. 1993. "The Seal of the Law: A Ritual Implement and Origins of Printing." *Asia Major*, 3rd ser., 6/2: 1–83.

———. 1996. *Mantras et mandarins: Le bouddhisme tantrique en Chine*. Paris: Gallimard.

———. 2002. *Chinese Medical Medicine*. Edited by Bernard Faure. Stanford, CA: Stanford University Press.

Sun Xiushen 孫修身. 1987. "Dunhuang bihua zhong de *Fahua jing Guanyin Pumen pin* tantao 敦煌壁畫中的法華經普門品探討" (Research on the Dunhuang frescoes relating to the *Guanyin Pumen pin* chapter of the *Lotus Sūtra*). Silu lun tan 1: 61–69.

Swann, Nancy Lee. 1950. *Food and Money in Ancient China: The Earliest Economic History of China to A.D. 25, Han Shu 24*. Princeton: Princeton University Press.

Tanabe, George J., Jr., and Willa Jane Tanabe, eds. 1989. *The Lotus Sutra in Japanese Culture*. Honolulu: University of Hawai'i Press.

Teiser, Stephen F. 1988. *The Ghost Festival in Medieval China*. Princeton: Princeton University Press.

———. 1994. *The Scripture on the Ten Kings and the Making of Purgatory in Medieval Chinese Buddhism*. Kuroda Institute Series. Honolulu: University of Hawai'i Press.

Tokuno, Kyoko. 1990. "The Evaluation of Indigenous Scriptures in Chinese Buddhist Bibliographical Catalogues." In Buswell 1990a: 31–74.

Twitchett, Denis, and Michael Loewe, eds. 1986. *The Cambridge History of China*. Vol. 1, *The Ch'in and Han Dynasties, 221 B.C.–A.D. 220*. Cambridge: Cambridge University Press.

Unschuld, Paul U. 1985. *Medicine in China: A History of Ideas*. Berkeley: University of California Press.

Verellen, Franciscus. 1989. *Du Guangting (850–933), taoïste de cour à la fin de la Chine médiévale*. Institut des hautes études chinoises, vol. 30. Paris: Collège de France.

———. 1992. "Evidential Miracles in Support of Taoism: The Inversion of Buddhist Apologetic Tradition in Late Tang China." *T'oung Pao* 78/4–5: 217–263.

———. 2004. "The Heavenly Master Liturgical Agenda According to Chisong zi's Petition Almanac." *Cahiers d'Extrême-Asie* 14: 291–343.

Wagner, Rudolf. 1973. "Lebensstil und Drogen im Chinesischen Mittelalter." *T'oung Pao* 49: 79–178.

Wang, Eugene Y. 2005. *Shaping the Lotus Sutra: Buddhist Visual Culture in Medieval China.* Seattle: University of Washington Press.

Wang Jiayou 王家祐. 1987. *Daojiao lungao* 道教論稿. Chengdu: Bashu chubanshe.

Wang Ming 王明, ed. 1960. *Taiping jing hejiao* 太平經合校. Beijing: Zhonghua shuju.

———, ed. 1980. *Baopuzi neipian jiaoshi* 抱朴子內篇校釋. Beijing: Zhonghua shuju.

Wang Yucheng 王育成. 1991. "Donghan daofu shilie 東漢道符釋例." *Kaogu xuebao* 考古學報 1: 45–55.

———. 1996. "Wenwu suojian zhongguo gudai daofu shulun 文物所見中國古代道符述論." *Daojia wenhua yanjiu* 道家問化研究 9: 267–301.

Wang-Toutain, Françoise. 1994. "Le bol du Buddha: Propagation du bouddhisme et légitimation politique." *Bulletin de l'École française d'Extrême-Orient* 81: 59–82.

———. 1998. *Le Bodhisattva Kṣitigarbha en Chine du Ve au XIIIe siècle.* Paris: École française d'Extrême-Orient.

———, ed. 2001. *Catalogue des manuscrits chinois de Touen-houang: Fragments chinois du fonds Pelliot tibétain de la Bibliothèque nationale de France.* Paris: École française d'Extrême-Orient.

Watson, Burton, trans. 1964. *Chuang Tzu: Basic Writings.* New York: Columbia University Press.

———, trans. 1993. *The Lotus Sūtra.* New York: Columbia University Press.

Weinstein, Stanley. 1987. *Buddhism under the T'ang.* Cambridge: Cambridge University Press.

Welch, Holmes H., and Anna Seidel, eds. 1979. *Facets of Taoism: Essays on Chinese Religion.* New Haven, CT: Yale University Press.

Will, Pierre-Étienne. 1980. *Bureaucratie et famine en Chine au 18e siècle.* Paris: Mouton et École des hautes études en sciences sociales. (Translated in English by Elborg Foster as *Bureaucracy and Famine in Eighteenth Century China.* Stanford, CA: Stanford University Press, 1990.)

Whitfield, Roderick, ed. 1982–1985. *The Art of Central Asia: The Stein Collection in the British Museum.* 3 vols. Tokyo: Kodansha International.

Whitfield, Roderick, and Anne Farrer. 1990. *Caves of the Thousand Buddhas: Chinese Art from the Silk Road.* London: British Museum Publications.

Whitfield, Susan. 1998. "Under the Censor's Eye: Printed Almanacs and Censorship in Ninth-Century China." *British Library Journal* 24/1: 4–22.

———, ed. 2004. *The Silk Road: Trade, Travel, War, and Faith.* Chicago: Serindia.

Wu Hung. 1989. *The Wu Liang Shrine: The Ideology of Early Chinese Pictorial Art.* Stanford, CA: Stanford University Press.

Wu Liancheng 吳連城, ed. 1988. *Baoning si Mingdai shuilu hua* 寶寧寺明代水陸畫. Beijing: Wenwu chubanshe.

Xiao Dengfu 蕭登福. 1993. *Daojiao xingdou fuyin yu fojiao mizong* 道教星斗符印與佛教密宗. Taipei: Xinwen feng chuban she.

———. 1994. *Daojiao shuyi yu mijiao dianji* 道教術儀与密教典籍. Taipei: Xinwen feng chuban she.

Yabuki Keiki 矢吹慶輝. 1930–1933. *Meisha yoin kaisetsu* 鳴沙餘韻解說. Tokyo: Iwanami shoten, 3 vols.

Yoritomo Motohiro 賴富本宏. 1997. "Mikkyō no juyō shita gozō setsu 密教 の 受容 した 五藏說" (The System of the Five Organs in Tantric Buddhism). *Tōhō shūkyō* 90: 66–89.

Yoshioka Yoshitoyo 吉岡義豐. 1959. *Dōkyō to bukkyō* 道教と佛教. Vol. 1. Tokyo: Kokusho kankōkai.

———. 1964. "Rikuchō dōkyō no shumin shisō 六朝道教の種民 思想." *Nippon chūgoku gakkai hō* 日本中國學會報 16: 90–107.

———. 1970. *Dōkyō to bukkyō*, vol. 2. Tokyo: Toshima Shobō.

———. 1976. *Dōkyō to bukkyō*, vol. 3. Tokyo: Kokusho kankōkai.

Yü, Chün-fang. 2001. *Kuan-yin: The Chinese Transformation of Avalokiteśvara*. New York: Columbia University Press.

Yusa Noboru 遊左昇. 1989. "Tōdai ni mirareru Kyūku tenson shinkō ni tsuite 唐代に 見られる救苦天尊信仰について," *Tōhō shūkyō* 東方宗教 73: 43–94.

Zhang Guangda 張廣達 and Rong Xinjiang 榮新江. 1993. *Yutian shi congkao* 于闐史叢考, *Shanghai shuju*: 291–292.

Zhang Yan 張燕. 1996. *Beichao fodao zao xiangbei jingxuan* 北朝佛道造像碑精選. Tianjin, Guji chuban she.

Zürcher, Erik. 1959. *The Buddhist Conquest of China: The Spread and Adaptation of Buddhism in Early Medieval China*. 2 vols. Leiden: E. J. Brill.

———. 1980. "Buddhist Influence on Early Taoism: A Survey of Scriptural Evidence." *T'oung Pao* 66: 84–147.

———. 1982. "Prince Moonlight: Messianism and Eschatology in Early Medieval Chinese Buddhism." *T'oung Pao* 68: 1–75.

———. 1990. *Bouddhisme, Christianisme et société chinoise*. Conférences essais et leçons du Collège de France. Paris: Julliard.

Index

Ming Wenzhang (divinity). *See* Generals of the Six *jia*

Mingquan, 107, 108

miracle stories, 175; of Li Shao, 196; of Sun Jingzhen, 195, 198; of Xingduan, 25–26; of Yuan Feng, 195; of Zhang Renbiao, 194

Mobile or Traveling Kitchens. *See* Kitchens

mofa (decline of the Dharma), 17, 27, 50, 58, 67. *See also* eschatology

monastic libraries, 4, 16. *See also* Mount Kōya; Nanatsu-dera; Songwang

monkey, 150

moshi (end of the world), 57. *See also* eschatology

Mount Fengdu, 183

Mount Kōya (Japan), 11, 25, 27, 28, 29, 32, 33, 34, 45, 50, 51, 143

Mount Longhu (Jianxi). *See* Heavenly Masters

Mount Sumeru, 43, 75, 174

Mount Tai, 157, 158

mudrās, 51, 145

mustard seeds, 97

Nanatsu-dera (monastery and manuscripts, Japan), 5, 9, 16, 18, 56, 68, 70

natal star, 140, 143, 155, 156, 162. See also *benming*

Needham, Joseph, 53

nidāna (introductory scenario), 27, 180

nine stars (of the Beidou), 135, 163, 164, 166. *See also* Beidou; Bixing; Funxing; seven stars

nine transformations, 135

nine-headed lion. *See* lion

nine-headed dragons, 204

nirvāṇa, 28, 29, 42, 75, 190

Nongzheng quanshu, 53

Nüqing guilü, 49, 104

Ochiai Toshinori, 5, 9

offerings: of medicinal plants, 41, 183, 200; of rice of destiny, 102; of sprouts of grain, 183, 200; vegetarian, 169; of willow branch and pure water, 183,

200; of wine and meat, 169. *See also* cereals and grains

Office of Water, 182, 191. *See also* hells

Original Spirit of Personal Destiny, 142, 149–151, 153–154, 155, 161, 169

Original pneuma (*yiqi*), 38

Padoux, André, 91

paintings: of the Beidou divinities, 167, 171; of Guanyin, 186, 192, 196, 197, 198; and illustrations of the *Pumen pin* in Dunhuang, 60–62, 65, 175, 186–188; of Jiuku tianzun, 199, 204–205; of Laozi's conversion of the barbarians, 9; ritual, 139, 167

Pāla trees, 15

paper camels, 154

pathology, 33, 47, 56; demonic pathologies, 55, 62, 65, 88, 96–97, 127; demonic possession, 57; evil illness, 65, 96; leprosy and epilepsy, 97; mutism, 97

peach: man (*taoren*), 86; wood, 98. *See also* effigies

Pelliot, Paul, 4, 5, 6, 7–8

perfumes and aromas, 31, 50

perils, 61, 62, 169, 174–175, 178, 180, 182, 185–189, 195. *See also* Guanyin; Jiuku tianzun; *Pumen pin*

perverse energies, 89

Petition Almanac of Master Red Pine. See *Chisongzi zhangli*

petitions (Zhengyi), 66–67, 88, 116, 117–119. See also *Petition Almanac of Master Red Pine*

Pilu monastery (Anyue), 62, 175

Pimo monastery (Khotan), 77

Piśāca. *See* demons

pledge, 108

poluomen (Brahman or Indian), 28, 34, 137

popular religion, 211

Potalaka, 175

pratyekabuddha, 29

prenatal life, 135

primordial pneuma (*yuanqi*), 23, 38, 46

Pumen pin (Universal Gateway of Guanshiyin), 17, 19, 59, 61, 174–175, 180,

Production notes for Mollier / *Buddhism and Taoism Face to Face*

Jacket design by Julie Chun.

Text design by Paul Herr with text in Bembo and display in Champers

Composition by inari information services

Printing and binding by The Maple-Vail Book Manufacturing Group

Printed on 55 lb. Glatfelter Offset B18, 360 ppi

About the Author

Christine Mollier is a research scholar specializing in the history of medieval Taoism at the French National Center for Scientific Research (CNRS). She is the author of *Une apocalypse taoïste du début du Ve siècle: Le Livre des Incantations Divines des Grottes Abyssales* and a contributor to leading publications in the fields of Chinese religions and Dunhuang studies.